Disclaimer: The Publisher and the Author make no representation or warranties concerning the accuracy or completeness of the contents of this work and specifically disclaim all warranties for a particular purpose. No warranty may be created or extended through sales or promotional materials. The advice and strategies contained herein may not be suitable for every situation. This work is sold with the understanding that the Author and Publisher are not engaged in rendering legal, technological, or other professional services. If professional assistance is required, the services of a competent professional should be sought. Neither the Publisher nor the Author shall be liable for damages arising therefrom.

The fact that an organization or website is referred to in this work as a citation and/or potential source of further information does not mean that the Author or the Publisher endorses the information, the organization, or website it may provide or recommendations it may make. Further, readers should be aware that websites listed in this work may have changed or disappeared between when this work was written and when it is read. Disclaimer: The cases and stories in this book have had details changed to preserve privacy.

The following pages provide consumers a simulation of actual documents on record or public court cases gathered from internet research. Readers must be allowed to construct their own opinion based on the information provided. The motive is to also introduce pertinent information that escapes the general public at large.

ISBN: Paperback 978-1-64873-165-5
ISNB: EBOOK 978-1-64873-166-2

Printed in the United States of America
Published by: Writer's Publishing House
Prescott, Az 86301

Cover and Interior Design by Creative Artistic Excellence Marketing
Project Management and Book Launch by Creative Artistic Excellence Marketing
https://lizzymcnett.com

HUDCO Scam Series

Book Four

Andrews Ganj Land Scam Continuing

By Alborz Azar

Acknowledgment

I acknowledge the co-operation of Mr. Pavan Sachdeva who had earlier declined to disclose much of the facts. However, after collecting all the materials through my friends, and advocates he understood my efforts were honest. By getting copies of the documents for this book, Mr. Pavan Sachdeva granted forty-five minutes of his time, which allowed me to conclude this book and continue further with the Andrews Ganj land Scam.

Table of Contents

Chapter: One

HUDCO Place Scam Continues

Let the story of HUDCO place go on–Andrews Ganj land– Government of India during the Congress Government and the present Government, the scam continues without any corrections till date. HUDCO without the title, without the sanctions of the building plans of Guest House Blocks, without the land-use of the hotel, and the approval of the revised layout plans forfeited the amount of Rs. 68.68 Crores (US Dollar 21.89 million) paid by MS Shoes in 1994- early 1995. HUDCO continued to earn interest @ 16 to 18% with monthly compounded by lending the monies received from MS Shoes, which till now comes to about Rs. 4000 Crores (US Dollar 1275.10 million) and for that reason, HUDCO's balance sheet is rich in figures.

To date of forfeiture by HUDCO of the amounts received from MS Shoes, HUDCO never disclosed the legitimate facts, and discriminatory treatment was granted by granting interest-free extensions to Ansals who were allotted Shopping Arcade under the same tender conditions. HUDCO continued to enjoy the possession of the property and gained undue riches by getting the appreciation of the properties, as the value of the properties had appreciated tremendously.

Similarly, there was a scam by HUDCO as by Harshad Mehta, the name that received its by-product as "the big bull" smashed to silicon after a mountainous property devised entirely out of a scam considered the biggest and most magnificent stock market scam of all time. Who was Harshad Mehta? How did he become a name? How much mayhem did he cause in the stock market and trading? How skillfully did he dupe the entire system? How was he exposed? The parallel scene! Dramatic personae: Government of India - Indian Economy. These two characters were working hand in hand. They developed a strong bond.

Let's rewind to the 50s when the entire plot of Andrews Ganj was leased for Rs. 25000/- to Pinjrapole Society, who held the possession of the property until 1985, when the Supreme Court came to the rescue of the property by directing Pinjrapole Society to vacate. Thereafter, the Congress Government allotted the same land to the societies of the Member of Parliaments, which was rescued by the Supreme Court of India by directing the societies to vacate the property in 1989. Thereafter, HUDCO came into the picture by taking possession of land in 1989.

HUDCO constructed the whole complex without any approval of the building plans, layout plans, Fire Department, local bodies, Delhi Urban Art Commission, as the Government of India was hand in hand in doing the same. HUDCO could not initially sell the properties at the Community Center for three years, but later decided to conceal the facts to realize the amounts from the bidders of which MS Shoes was made scapegoat, and the entire investments made by MS Shoes in the properties were forfeited illegally, and HUDCO committed the fraud and the Government at the relevant time.

Initially, the Government had entrusted the land to HUDCO for development, but later the allotment was issued and the lease was required to be executed by Government with HUDCO, which was never executed until the time the entire amount was paid by MS Shoes was forfeited. HUDCO could not even take the permission under the Income Tax Act and Urban Land Ceiling Act, since they had no title in their favor. The Government factually could not have allotted the land to HUDCO in violation of the General Finance Rules 282(3). The only way was to regularize the allotment to HUDCO by placing it before the Cabinet. Various times it was decided to get approval from the Cabinet, but since the Government policy did not permit so. The plan of regularization of allotment by the Cabinet was dropped.

This was a year that boomed Harshad Mehta's career, had he not dipped his leg into the sea of corruption. In a single financial year (1990-1991), Harshad was entitled "The Big Bull". Magazines like Business Today got his photo published on the cover page. He almost became an overnight sensation in the world of finance in India. Harshad Mehta from a mediocre Gujarati man working as a junior clerk became a symbol of a cozy lifestyle. But how could he hoard such gigantic property and money? Was he industrious in his work? Yes, he was. Was he a genius at stock market trading? Oh, come on, he was, indeed!

Let us dig deeper about HUDCO's genius scam strategy. It was discussed with the Government at the relevant time, the facts of title, the illegal buildings, the non-approval of revised layout plans, be not disclosed in the brochure to realize the market value of the properties. Who could doubt the Government and HUDCO, a government-owned company, involved in such fraudulent acts? Like Harshad Mehta got issued fake bank receipts having no backing of bank securities, the same way HUDCO faked the offer of the properties by specifically stating in the brochure that the Urban Design of the complex is approved by the Government. I feel this was a bigger scam than the Harshad Mehta scam since the scam was by the Government and HUDCO.

HUDCO after taking permission from the Government to sell the properties without disclosing the truth in the brochure. HUDCO mastered it, grabbed the whole deal in hand, like Harshad Mehta, who had gone for a ride with the whole banking system. Similarly, HUDCO grabbed the amounts received from MS Shoes, and on the other side continued to extend the interest-free installments of Ansals until the building plans were regularized. It is to be noted how Ministers, Government Officers and HUDCO's Officers with their Architects went handling the auction of properties, concealing various facts required to be disclosed. It is similarly the same as how was Mehta handling his trade mechanism? Let us elucidate how HUDCO's sale of the properties led to the scam of Andrews Ganj land.

HUDCO was charging 17% p.a. interest to the Government on the investments made in the constructions, and the Government was unwilling to bear the burden. Both the parties, Government and HUDCO in the closed rooms, decided to defraud the bidders by not disclosing the truth. The Government and HUDCO discussed that in any case, the building plans will be sanctioned in the due course, but in fact, it turned out to be the opposite.

After obtaining large amounts by HUDCO from MS Shoes, HUDCO had excess funds in their hand which was invested/loaned to the private lenders to earn interest @ 16 to 18% monthly compounded, as admitted by HUDCO in the documents on record. The burden of 17% interest charged by HUDCO on the investments made by them was neutralized, rather the additional earnings started. The real game player was Mr. V. Suresh, the director of Corporate Planning, who finally was promoted as Chairman of HUDCO. In fact, Mr. V. Suresh demanded the amounts from MS Shoes through Mr. G.K. Iyer, the Executive Director of MS Shoes. But MS Shoes declined to get involved in any bribery of any nature.

Chapter: Two

Modi's Government Neglecting HUDCO's Scam Continuing

HUDCO's scam is the same as the case of Harshad Mehta, who had excess funds in his hand, and started transmitting them towards purchasing stocks from the stock market. FEW!!! You have just created a maze without letting anyone realize they were merely being out-jockeyed. Harshad had a coterie of brokers who had a very smooth skin in the game. He did not just stop issuing fake Bank receipts for the bank, but he rather started producing fake Bank receipts for himself. This made him a man of excellence as if he was a sorcerer's stone. Whatever he would touch would turn into gold. ACC, Videocon, and name what may where he had his eye on got their value quadrupled overnight. He was turning from rugged to rich. He was the king of Worli.

Similarly, HUDCO's Corporate Planning Director, Mr. V. Suresh, created a maze by concealing the material facts and built a false brochure claiming false facts, thereby leading to cheating the bidders. But here, in this case, there was nobody to expose HUDCO. But Harshad Mehta was exposed!!!! Because the villain of his film was watching the entire story from the other side of the lens. Sucheta Dalal ripped off Mehta's dubious activity by exposing him in an article in The Times of India on April 23rd, 1992. In the present case of HUDCO, the

Government of India was involved. There could not have been any villains, rather the enemies of MS Shoes were still bent upon pulling him down.

On December 31, 2001, Mehta passed away in a Mumbai jail. Had the man been as honest as he was a genius, a much-celebrated life story could have been written. However, the story could never be averted or ignored by the B-Town. 2006, Bollywood Drama almost did justice to the incredible and dark-shaded journey of Mehta. A new Bollywood venture is also being talked about to be loosely based on Harshad Mehta's life: "The Big Bull" starring Abhishek Bachchan.

In the case of MS Shoes, Pavan Sachdeva's case was closed in 1998, and the Court accepted the closure report, but he continued to struggle for his rights against HUDCO.

If we talk about the gist, the Indian economy has been and still is being shattered by a humongous amount of monetary scams. The RBI report says only the financial year 2019 has witnessed bank frauds worth ₹71,500 crores. If someone points out that effective measures are not being taken, then this is completely a superficial statement. When the entire system falls within a complex law mechanism, a reliable outcome takes time to be brought forth into the light under a long-term solution.

In addition, with hundreds of charges of a civil and criminal nature leveled against Mehta, which was perhaps the most high-profile case of the 1990s, spiced up with rumors about the involvement of senior politicians. But HUDCO and the Government at the relevant time have gone scot-free, and even the present Government is not bothered to expose the Andrews Ganj land scam by the Congress Government.

The present Government is busy promoting various schemes for the public at large. The Modi Government has promoted many schemes, of which some of them are:

PM-KISAN (Pradhan Mantri Kisan Samman Nidhi) Scheme

Main purpose: This scheme promises to pay all poor farmers (small and marginal farmers having lands up to 2 hectares) Rs 6,000 each yearly in 3 installments through Direct Bank Transfer. It would reportedly benefit around 14.5 crore farmers all over India.

Pradhan Mantri Kisan Pension Yojana:

Main purpose: To address the problems of farm sector distress, the Modi 2.0 Cabinet has approved a proposal to provide small and marginal farmers with a minimum Rs 3,000 per month fixed pension, costing Rs 10,774.5 crore per annum to the exchequer.

The eligible farmers in the 18-40-year-old age group can participate in this voluntary and contributory pension scheme.

Once the beneficiary of the pension dies, the spouse will be entitled to receive 50% of the original beneficiary's pension amount.

Mega Pension Scheme

Main purpose: A Mega Pension Scheme has been approved for the traders, shopkeepers, and self-employed persons (whose GST turnover is less than Rs 1.5 crore).

The scheme guarantees a minimum assured pension of Rs 3,000 per month for around 3 crores lesser traders, self-employed persons, and shopkeepers, once they attain 60 years of age.

New Jal Shakti Ministry

Main purpose: It aims at providing piped water connection to every Indian household by the year 2024. Reports say the ministry will now formulate plans to address water management.

Jan Dhan Yojana

Main purpose: Pradhan Mantri Jan Dhan Yojana is a National Mission on Financial Inclusion, which has an integrated approach to bring about comprehensive financial inclusion and provide banking services to all households in the country. The scheme ensures access to various financial services, like availability of a basic savings bank account, access to need-based credit, remittances facility, insurance, and pension.

Skill India Mission

Main purpose: They have developed The Mission to create convergence across sectors and States in terms of skill training activities. Further, to achieve the vision of 'Skilled India', the National Skill Development Mission would not only consolidate and coordinate skill efforts but also expedite decision-making across sectors to achieve skill at scale with speed and standards.

Make in India

Main purpose: PM Narendra Modi launched the 'Make in India' campaign to facilitate investment, foster innovation, enhance skill development, protect intellectual property & build best-in-class manufacturing infrastructure.

'Make in India' has identified 25 sectors in manufacturing, infrastructure, and service activities, and detailed information is being shared through interactive web-portal and professionally developed brochures. FDI has been opened up in Defence Production, Construction, and Railway infrastructure in an important way.

Swachh Bharat Mission

Main purpose: On 2nd October 2014, the Swachh Bharat Mission was launched throughout the length and breadth of the country as a national movement. The campaign aims to achieve the vision of a 'Clean India' by 2nd October 2019.

The Swachh Bharat Abhiyan is the most significant cleanliness campaign by the Government of India.

Sansad Adarsh Gram Yojana

Main purpose: It is a rural development program broadly focusing upon the development in the villages, which includes social development, cultural development, and spread motivation among the people on social mobilization of the village community.

Pradhan Mantri Shram Yogi Maan-Dhan (PM-SYM)

Main purpose: It is a voluntary and contributory pension scheme, under which the subscriber would receive the following benefits:

(i) Minimum Assured Pension: Each subscriber under the PM-SYM shall receive a minimum assured pension of Rs 3000/- per month after attaining the age of 60 years.

(ii) Family Pension: During the receipt of a pension, if the subscriber dies, the spouse of the beneficiary shall be entitled to receive 50% of the pension received by the beneficiary as a family pension. Family pension applies only to spouses.

(iii) If a beneficiary has given regular contribution and died due to any cause (before age of 60 years), his/her spouse will be entitled to join and continue the scheme

subsequently by payment of regular contribution or exit the scheme as per provisions of exit and withdrawal.

Beti Bachao Beti Padhao

Main purpose: The goal of this scheme is to give girls socially and financially self-reliant through education.

Hridaya Plan

Main purpose: To take care of world heritage sites and to build these sites economically viable.

PM Mudra Yojna

Main purpose: Pradhan Mantri MUDRA Yojana (PMMY) is a scheme launched by the Honorable Prime Minister on April 8, 2015, for providing loans up to 10 lakhs to non-corporate, non-farm mini/micro-enterprises.

To create an inclusive, sustainable, and value-based entrepreneurial culture, in collaboration with our partner institutions in achieving economic success and financial security.

Ujala Yojna

Main purpose: State-run Energy Efficiency Services Ltd (EESL) has distributed over 30 crores light-emitting diode (LED) bulbs across the country under the zero-subsidy Unnat Jyoti by the Affordable LEDs for All (UJALA) scheme.

Atal Pension Yojana

Main purpose: Atal Pension Yojana is a pension scheme mainly aimed at the unorganized sector, like maids, gardeners, delivery boys, etc. This scheme replaced the previous Swavalamban Yojana, which wasn't accepted well by the people.

Prime Minister Jeevan Jyoti Bima Yojana

Main purpose: Pradhan Mantri Jeevan Jyoti Bima Yojana is a government-backed Life Insurance Scheme in India. Pradhan Mantri Jeevan Jyoti Bima Yojana is available to people between 18 and 50 years of age with bank accounts.

Pradhan Mantri Suraksha Bima Yojana

Main purpose: Pradhan Mantri Suraksha Bima Yojana is a government-backed accident insurance scheme in India. As of May 2016, only 20% of India's population has any type of insurance. This scheme aims to increase the number.

AMRUT Plan

Main purpose: Providing basic services (e.g., water supply, sewerage, urban transport) to households and building amenities in cities which will improve the quality of life for all, especially the poor and the disadvantaged, is a national priority.

The purpose of Atal Mission for Rejuvenation and Urban Transformation (AMRUT) is to:

Ensure every household has access to a tap with the assured supply of water and a sewerage connection.

Increase the amenity value of cities by developing greenery and well-maintained open spaces (e.g., parks) and

Reduce pollution by switching to public transport or constructing facilities for non-motorized transport (e.g., walking and cycling). All these outcomes are valued by citizens, particularly women, and indicators and standards have been prescribed by the Ministry of Housing and Urban Affairs in Service Level Benchmarks (SLBs).

Digital India Mission

Main purpose: The Digital India program is a flagship program of the Government of India with a vision to transform India into a digitally empowered society and knowledge economy.

Gold Monetization Scheme

Main purpose: Gold Monetization Scheme was launched by the Government of India in 2015. Under this scheme, one can deposit their gold in any form in a GMS account to earn interest as the price of the gold metal goes up.

UDAY

Main purpose: Ministry of Power, GoI launched Ujwal DISCOM Assurance Yojana (UDAY), which was approved by the Union Cabinet on 5th November 2015.

The scheme envisages: Financial Turnaround, Operational Improvement, Reduction of cost of generation of power, Development of Renewable Energy, Energy efficiency & conservation

Start-up India

Main purpose: Startup India is a flagship initiative of the Government of India, intended to catalyze startup culture and build a strong and inclusive ecosystem for innovation and entrepreneurship in India.

Setu Bhartam Yojana

Main purpose: This yojana aims to reach all national highways free of railway crossings by 2019.

Stand Up India

Main purpose: Stand-Up India Scheme Facilitates bank loans between 10 lakhs and 1 crore to at least one Scheduled Caste (SC) or Scheduled Tribe (ST) borrower and at least one-woman borrower per bank branch for setting up a greenfield enterprise.

Prime Minister Ujjwala Plan

Main purpose: Pradhan Mantri Ujjwala Yojana (PMUY) was launched by Prime Minister of India Narendra Modi on May 1, 2016, to distribute 50 million LPG connections to women of BPL families.

Namami Gange Yojana

Main purpose: The Government launched an integrated Ganga conservation mission called 'Namami Gange' to arrest the pollution of the Ganga River and revive the river.

PM CARES Fund

Prime Minister's Citizen Assistance and Relief in Emergency Situation Fund: This is a public charitable trust initiated by Prime Minister Narendra Modi. This national trust is created to meet the distressed and dreadful situation like COVID-19 in times ahead. PM CARES was initiated on March 28, 2020, under the chairmanship of the Indian Prime Minister with the Ministry of Home Affairs, Defence Minister, and Finance Minister as the ex officio Trustee.

Ayushman Bharat *Launched in 2018 by Prime Minister Narendra Modi, Ayushman Bharat is a health scheme. It is the largest government-funded healthcare program in the world, with over 50 crore beneficiaries. The Ayushman Bharath program has two submissions : PM-JAY & HWCs.*

***Pradhan Mantri Jan Arogya Yojana (PM-JAY)**, earlier known as the National Health Protection Scheme (NHPS), will cover the financial protection for availing healthcare services at the secondary and tertiary levels.*

***Health and Wellness Centers (HWCs)** aimed at improving access to cheap and quality healthcare services at the primary level. Read about Ayushman Bharat in detail in the link provided above.*

UMANG

*Unified Mobile Application for New-Age Governance is a mobile application launched by PM Narendra Modi to provide secured access to the citizens to multiple government services at one platform. UMANG is a key component of the Digital India initiative of the government that intends to appoint all traditional offline government services available 24 *7 online through a single unified app.*

PRASAD Scheme

Pilgrimage Rejuvenation and Spirituality Augmentation Drive. The Scheme was launched under the Ministry of Tourism in the year 2015. The aim of the PRASAD Scheme is the integrated development of pilgrimage destinations in a prioritized, planned, and sustainable manner for providing a complete religious tourism experience. The focus of Pilgrimage Rejuvenation and Spirituality Augmentation Drive - PRASAD is on the development and beautification of the identified pilgrimage destinations. Further, details on the PRASAD scheme are given in the related page link given above in the article.

Through these schemes, the Narendra Modi government has brought a positive change in the society by uplifting the poor, empowering the last man standing in the queue. But the present Government is neglecting the Andrews Ganj land Scam of the period when the Congress Government was in power.

Chapter: Three

Electricity Grid Not Yet Established to Energize Guest House Blocks

Chief (Disposal) HUDCO, Mr. P.K. Garg on 28 May 1996 to B.R. Dhiman Officer on Special Duty (Land) Ministry of Urban Affairs & Employment Department of Urban Development (land Division) New Delhi. Regarding: - Use of land as a resource for supplementing General Pool Accommodation _ Utilization of surplus on account of development and disposal of Community Center Complex at Andrews Ganj.

Please refer to your No. J-13014/6/90-LD dated 20 March 1996 on the above-captioned subject. In this regard, please find enclosed the latest status note on Andrews Ganj Project, along with the summarized cash flow statement for the reference of the Empowered Committee meeting. Financial implication on account of extension given to Ansals:

A	2nd installment originally due	9 March 1996
	Amount	Rs.50,64,27,960/- (US Dollar 14.29 million)

	Extension granted Up to	8 September 1996
	Interest/Penal interest @ 16.48 per annum for 6 months, which would have become due in absence of non-extension	Rs.4,17,29,664 (US Dollar 1.17 million)
B	3rd installment originally due	9 September 1996
	Amount	Rs. 33,76,18,640/- (US Dollar 9.52 million)
	Extension granted Up to	8 March 1997
	Interest/Penal interest @ 16.48 per annum for 6 months which would have become due in absence of non-extension	2,78,19,775/- (US Dollar 0.78 million)

C	Monthly interest/penal interest due on Ian installment if no further extension is granted	69,54,944/- (US Dollar 0.19 million)
D	Monthly interest/penal interest due on third installment if no further extension is granted	45,36,630/- (US Dollar 0.12 million)
E	Amount of interest which could have been claimed by M/s Ansals for delayed handing over of site from 1 July 1995 to 10 November on the first installment of Rs 84,40,46,600/- (US Dollar 23.82 million) @ 6 per annum (132 days)	Rs 1,83,14,655/- (US Dollar 0.51 million)

HUDCO in its board meeting at Item No. 31.2.1.–decided regarding power connection to HUDCO Place Project, Andrews Ganj from Delhi Electricity Supply Undertaking 33KV Grid Substation.

For setting up of a Grid substation in the HUDCO place complex at Andrews Ganj, an estimate of Rs. 600 Lakhs

(US Dollar 1.85 million) has been provided for as per the approval given by COD in the meeting held on 2 March 1995 vide Item no. 28:2:1. This estimate is for the indication given by Delhi Electricity Supply Undertaking as a probable estimate to establish a Grid substation, including civil works at an estimated cost of Rs. 45 Lakhs (US Dollar 0.13 million).

HUDCO has already demarcated an area measuring 75 m x 45 m and constructed an appropriate dividing wall structure and metering room building in the said area, as per the requirement of Delhi Electricity Supply Undertaking.

In a meeting held on 16 November 1995 between HUDCO and Delhi Electricity Supply Undertaking, the company requested that to keep the aesthetic in the neighborhood architecture, the building of the grid be constructed by HUDCO as per the detailed design to be provided by Delhi Electricity Supply Undertaking, and the cost of establishing the grid substation shall be borne by Delhi Electricity Supply Undertaking.

The facts given above would indicate the various actions taken by HUDCO and Delhi Electricity Supply Undertaking concerning the power connection to the

Andrews Ganj project and concerning the construction of the Grid substation for providing an electricity supply to the complex and the adjoining area. The proposal is put up to the COD for approval of the following: -

a) Allotment of land measuring 45 m x 75 m for the grid substation at a nominal rate of Rs.1/- per annum.
b) Construction of the building of Grid substation at HUDCO cost, since this must be structured to suit our aesthetic requirements following the Urban Design. A provision of Rs.45 lacs (US Dollar 0.13 million) already exists in the estimate for this purpose.

COD may kindly consider.

It is to be noted that until the date of cancellation and forfeiture of the amount paid by MS Shoes, there was no electricity connection to the guest house blocks. How a Government Company can expect an allottee to pay another Rs.40 crores (US Dollar 11.01 million) *in addition to Rs.40 Crores* (US Dollar 11.01 million) *already paid. Till this date, even land for establishing a grid by Delhi*

Electric Supply Undertaking had not been allotted. Is it not a scam by HUDCO?

Chapter: Four

HUDCO Floated Another Brochure for Guest House Blocks Disclosing the Material Facts

At the end of May 1996, HUDCO called for another bid on 17 June 1996 of Guest House Blocks, disclosing that the building plans have already been sanctioned by the Municipal Corporation of Delhi and Delhi Urban Art Commission. However, the regular electric connection from Delhi Electricity Supply Undertaking and Occupancy certificate from Municipal Corporation of Delhi is awaited. Such material disclosures were not made at the time the bids were called on 15.07.1994 from MS Shoes. This itself is evident that HUDCO did not have building plans sanctioned and electricity connection until the date the amounts received from MS Shoes were forfeited.

HUDCO also stated that timely payment will be the essence of allotment, which was not stipulated in the allotment of MS Shoes.

HUDCO also disclosed in the present brochure that the Government has given the land to HUDCO on 99 years lease in July 1990. This was never disclosed in the brochure of 15.07.1994, under which amounts were received from MS Shoes. These terms could have not been disclosed at the relevant time until forfeiture. HUDCO never had an allotment in its favor for 99 years' lease but allotted the properties to MS Shoes on perpetual lease or 99 years' lease.

Due to such disclosures, no offers came from any of the parties, as now they knew the truth of the properties allotted by HUDCO to MS Shoes, and the public at large came to know that HUDCO has cheated MS Shoes.

- **HUDCO PLACE**
- **A Unique Urban Experience**
- **HUDCO Bhawan, Lodhi Road, New Delhi**
- **HUDCO Place**

A Unique Urban Experience*: INTEGRATED URBAN DESIGN* - The HUDCO Place, an integrated urban design complex with design control, graphic design, landscape, parking, and other common services, is being developed by Housing and Urban Development Corporation Ltd. (A Government of India Undertaking) under direction from the Ministry of Urban Affairs & Employment. It is a perfect blend of traditional ambiance and up-to-date modern facilities. A spacious Central Plaza has been designed to create an environment of social interaction. A Five-Star Hotel, two clusters of centrally air-conditioned Guesthouses, each with six blocks, a Shopping Arcade, a

Cultural Center, and a swimming pool are the highlights of this integrated urban complex. The two Guest House clusters on either side of the Central Plaza are designed as self-contained units with facilities comparable to Star Hotel.

LOCATION - Located in the heart of South Delhi, HUDCO Place is spread over 17.6 acres of land in the Andrews Ganj area, flanked by Khelgaon Marg and Josef Broz Tito Marg. HUDCO Place lies midway between Ring Road and Outer Ring Road to the South, making it eminently accessible and suitable for the location of a Commercial Center.

LANDSCAPE - An 18 acre stretch of land demarcated as a Green Zone with parks. Jogging paths and water bodies, including musical fountains, lie in the vicinity of HUDCO Place, offering an added attraction.

HUDCO offers the following properties for sale on a leasehold basis: -

GUEST HOUSES (9 Blocks) - These are built with high standards of construction. Each four-storied block consists of an average of 40 rooms on three floors, with the ground floor comprising restaurants, kitchen, entrance, lobby, shops, and service area.

- The cluster approach to urban design has been a deliberate choice following the dictates of urban form and the need to achieve a high density notwithstanding the low-rise structure.
- The Guest House rooms are placed around an internal courtyard.

SPECIFICATIONS - The Guest Houses are finished in permanent materials, using a machine-built brick tile, with blue glass mosaic on the roof. The glazed doors and windows are in anodized aluminum. The internal doors have teakwood frames with block board shutters. The rooms are finished in ceramic tile, mosaic tile, Kota stone, marble from various interior designs. The toilets have ceramic tiles on the floor and wall, while the flooring of the lobby and other areas is marble.

FACILITY - With due regard for the economy in capital expenditure, energy, and maintenance costs, the services provided at the complex will be centralized, thereby ensuring greater efficiency in the systems. These services include:

- Air-conditioning plant
- Boilers
- Electric substation
- Standby diesel generator sets
- Water storage and pumping
- Telephone Exchange

FACILITIES AT GUEST HOUSES - All the rooms at the Guest House are centrally air-conditioned, with attached bathrooms, running hot and cold water, and are equipped with a telephone connection.

INTERIORS - Each Guest House block interior has been designed with a distinct and individual finish. Care has been taken to maintain a high aesthetic quality in the design, reflecting a sense of creativity and artistic conception. The rooms are on the first, second and third floor. The ground floors have lobbies and service areas, etc.

- **One Bay room** - This room is from about 15 sqm to 22 sqm. Carpet area, with an additional area for bathroom vestibule area and cupboard.
- **One and Half Bay Suite** - This is a larger room, between 22 Sqm. To 33 Sqm. Providing separate

space for beds and sitting areas. The bathroom and vestibule are in general like the standard room.

- **Two Bay Suites** - These are suites (more than 33 Sqm.) Having a regular standard guest room, a bathroom, a vestibule area, and an additional sitting room.

AREA DETAILS AND RESERVE PRICE

The total built-up area includes built-up area floor-wise, proportionate area of common facilities/services At Ground Floor, i.e., Entrance Lobby, Reception, Lobby Toilets, lift (s), staircases, AHU Lobby and Plant Room, etc. The details are as under:

FLOORWISE DETAILS OF GUEST HOUSE (ANDREWS GANJ)

Name of Block	Floor	No. of Rooms			TOTAL	Total Built up-Area Floorwise (In Sqm.) (approx.)
		1 Bay	1.5 Bay	2.0 Bay		
A1	First Floor	16	2	1	19	925
A1	Second Floor	13	3	1	17	870
A1	Third Floor	13	1	1	15	710

	TOTAL A1	42	6	3	51	2505

Name of Block	Floor	No. of Rooms			TOTAL	Total Built up-Area Floor wise (In Sqm.) (approx.)
		1 Bay	1.5 Bay	2.0 Bay		
A3	First Floor	11	1	-	12	556
A3	Second Floor	11	2	-	13	561

A3	Third Floor	5	4	-	9	444
	TOTAL A3	27	7	0	34	1561

Name Of Block	Floor	No. of Rooms			TOTAL	Total Built up-Area Floor wise (In Sqm.) (approx.)
		1 Bay	1.5 Bay	2.0 Bay		
A4	First Floor	16	-	1	17	771

A4	Second Floor	14	2	1	17	737
A4	Third Floor	6	2	3	11	605
	TOTAL A4	36	4	5	45	2113

Name Of Block	Floor	No. of Rooms			TOTAL	Total Built up-Area Floor wise (In Sqm.) (approx.)
		1 Bay	1.5 Bay	2.0 Bay		
B1	First Floor	14	1	-	15	663
B1	Second Floor	12	2	1	15	656
B1	Third Floor	10	2	-	12	528
	TOTAL B1	36	5	1	42	1847

Name Of Block	Floor	No. of Rooms			TOTAL	Total Built up-Area Floor wise (In Sqm.) (approx.)
		1 Bay	1.5 Bay	2.0 Bay		
B2	First Floor	13	1	-	14	636
B2	Second Floor	11	3	-	14	613
B2	Third Floor	10	2	-	12	498
	TOTAL B2	34	6	0	40	1747

Name Of Block	Floor	No. of Rooms			TOTAL	Total Built up-Area Floor wise (In Sqm.) (approx.)
		1 Bay	1.5 Bay	2.0 Bay		
B3	First Floor	12	2	-	14	628
B3	Second Floor	12	3	-	15	650
B3	Third Floor	1	4	3	8	518

	TOTAL B3	25	9	3	37	1796

Name Of Block	Floor	No. of Rooms			TOTAL	Total Built up-Area Floor wise (In Sqm.) (approx.)
		1 Bay	1.5 Bay	2.0 Bay		
B4	First Floor	13	1	-	14	629
B4	Second Floor	12	2	-	14	648

B4	Third Floor	11	1	-	12	518
	TOTAL B4	36	4	0	40	1795

Name Of Block	Floor	No. of Rooms			TOTAL	Total Built up-Area Floor wise (In Sqm.) (approx.)
		1 Bay	1.5 Bay	2.0 Bay		

B5	First Floor	12	2	-	14	629
B5	Second Floor	12	3	-	14	648
B5	Third Floor	1	3	4	9	518
	TOTAL B5	25	8	4	37	1795

Name Of Block	Floor	No. of Rooms	TOTAL	Total Built up-Area Floor wise (In

						Sqm.) (approx.)
		1 Bay	1.5 Bay	2.0 Bay		
B6	First Floor	11	-	1	14	678
B6	Second Floor	11	-	3	14	680
B6	Third Floor	4	1	4	9	542
	TOTAL B6	28	1	8	37	1900

The Guest House will be sold on a minimum of one full floor basis.

1. Reserve Price: Rs. 75,000/- per sqm. (Built-up space)
2. Earnest Money: Rs. 50.00 lacs (US Dollar 0.14 million) per block or Rs. 20.00 lakhs (US Dollar 0.05 million) per floor
3. Payment Schedule
    a) Within one month of the date of allotment - 40%
    b) Within four months of the date of allotment - 40%
    c) At the time of handing over possession- 20%

RESTAURANT/KITCHEN IN GUEST HOUSES (8): The ground floor of each of the Guest Houses is having a restaurant/coffee. Apart from the Kitchen and Restaurant, the ground floor consists of a Party Room, Toilets, Garage Room, Store Room, AHU Restaurant, Central Courtyard, Corridors, etc., which will go along with the kitchen and restaurant. For a buyer taking the whole block of Guest

House, the restaurant/Kitchen of the floor could also be offered to him. The built-up area of the Restaurant/Kitchen also includes a proportionate area of common facilities/services on the Ground Floor, i.e., Lobby, Toilet(s), Reception, Plant Room, AHU for Lobby, etc.

The details of the area in each block are as follows:

Block No.	Area (In Sqm.) Ground Floor
A-1	606
A-3	203
A-4	320
B-1	410
B-2	283

B-4	323
B-5	328
B-6	323

There are also a few shops on the ground floor which are being offered separately.

- Reserve Price - Rs. 85000 per sq. mt. (Built-up space)
- Earnest Money - Rs. 8.00 lacs (US Dollar 0.22 million) per blocks of restaurant/kitchen

PAYMENT SCHEDULE

i. Within one month of the date of allotment - 40%
ii. Within four months of the date of allotment - 40%
iii. At the time of handing over possession- 20%

SHOPS: Each block (ground floor) of Guest Houses has some shopping space. These are designed for exclusive and select shopping facilities. These could be given to the party who buys that block of Guest House or sold separately. The final decision in this regard will rest with HUDCO.

The Built-Up area of the Shop includes the area of the Shop, the attached toilet, and a proportionate built-up area under common services and corridor in front of the Shop. The details are as under:

Block No.	**No. of Shops**	**Total Area (In Sqm.)**			
		1	**2**	**3**	**4**
A-1	2	62	55	15	-
A-3	3	64	89	76	-
A-4	4	70	39	94	99

B-1	3	22	56	63	-
B-2	-	-	-	-	-
B-3	1	86	-	-	-
B-4	3	33	68	65	-
B-5	2	72	90	-	-
B-6	3	65	68	61	-

- Reserve Price - Rs. 90, 000/- per sq. mt. (built-up Shop)
- Earnest Money - Rs. 1.50 lacs per Shop

PAYMENT SCHEDULE

- Within one month of the date of allotment - 40%

- Within four months of the date of allotment - 40%
- At the time of handing over possession - 20%

STATUS OF STATUTORY APPROVALS - The building plans have already been sanctioned by the Municipal Corporation of Delhi and the Delhi Urban Art Commission. However, the regular electric connection from Delhi Electricity Supply Undertaking and Occupancy certificate from Municipal Corporation of Delhi is awaited.

DISPOSAL TERMS –

A. No extension of time will be allowed for the payment of the first installment. The Earnest Money paid will be adjusted in the first installment. In case of default, the allotment without any further reference to the allottee shall stand automatically canceled, and in such case. Earnest Money paid shall be forfeited.
B. After the payment of the first installment, the allottee, with the help of HUDCO, shall initiate action to take all required approvals under the Income Tax Act and Urban Land (Ceiling & Regulation) Act so that there is no delay in handing over the possession of the properties as soon as the

entire payment of the price has been fixed by the allotted to HUDCO.

C. The second installment will have to be paid on or before the date specified in the allotment letter. In the event of the allottee's inability to pay the second installment on the specified date, the allottee will have the option to pay this installment within three months of the date specified for the payment of this installment with interest calculated @ 18% p.a. for three months on the amount of the installment due. If the payment is delayed beyond three months, the allotment shall stand automatically canceled without any further reference to the allottee, and in such a case 50% of the amount paid up to that date shall be forfeited, and the balance 50% of the amount will be refunded to the allottee without interest.

D. If the third installment, i.e. 20% of the premium, is not paid by the allottee within one month from the date of issue of the letter offering the allottee to take over the possession, then the allotment letter stands automatically canceled without any further reference to the allottee, and thereafter 50% of the amount paid up to that date shall be forfeited, and the balance 50% of the amount will be refunded to be allotted without interest, and thereupon HUDCO will be free to re-auction the properties allotted

E. . It is noted the time for payment of the premium as per the allotment letter shall be the essence of the contract.

F. The possession of the properties is likely to be handed over within six months from the date of allotment letter, subject to full payment of the allotted property by the allottee and compliance of paragraph "B" above. In case of any delay in handing over possession due to the fault of HUDCO for more than six months from the date of allotment. HUDCO will pay 6% simple interest on the amount paid by the allottee for the delayed period only, i.e., beyond six months from the date of allotment letter or from the date specified for payment of the third installment, whichever is later, and no further damages will be payable by HUDCO to the allottee for the delayed possession.

G. All built-up areas will be given on a long-term lease basis. The government has given the land to HUDCO on 99 years lease in July 1990. The built space will in turn be leased to buyers on a long-term lease co-terminus, with the 99 years' lease period given to HUDCO. The buyer will also have to pay Annual Ground Rent, as may be fixed by the Government (Presently Annual Ground Rent is payable @ 2.5% of the proportionate cost of land in respect of built spaces). The allottee will also be liable to pay property tax as per the prevailing rates fixed by the Competent Board/Authority. (Delhi Municipal Corporation) from the date of possession of the properties allotted.

H. In case any allottee desires to use Guest Houses allotted to them as hotel/office, necessary approval for the same will have to be obtained by the allottee from the concerned local authorities.

I. HUDCO shall have the right to consider the offers from those buyers opting for purchase full Block (i.e., Restaurant/Kitchen & shops at Ground Floor and Guest House in the Upper Floors) in preference to offering the individual floor.

MAINTENANCE - Habitat Service Center (HSC), a Society registered under the Societies Registration Act, 1860, or any other agency identified by HUDCO will be the maintenance agency for the common area/services of the complex until maintenance arrangements are handed over to the Maintenance Society, proposed to be informed by all the allottees following the provisions of the Apartment Ownership Act or any other agency established as per terms and conditions of the Perpetual Sub-Lease documents. The allottee shall be deemed to have agreed to become a member of the Maintenance Society and abide by its bye-laws.

The buyer shall deposit maintenance charges with HUDCO, including depreciation (if any) for the common services of the complex with HUDCO in advance quarterly. The tentative expenses are estimated to be around Rs. 1200/- per sq. mt. per annum of the built-up space. An initial interest-free deposit equivalent to two quarters will have to be deposited at the time of payment of the second installment to be used as a Corpus Fund for maintenance purposes by the society.

EARNEST MONEY- Offers, as mentioned above. The earnest money would be refunded within a maximum of Mr. M.T. Meshram's 30 days from the date of opening of the bid, without any interest to the unsuccessful bidders. The earnest money should be in Demand Draft drawn towards "Housing and Urban Development Corporation Ltd." payable at Delhi. If for any reason the EMP is not refunded within 30 days from the date of opening of the tender, simple interest @ 6% would be payable beyond 30 days.

Interested parties may send offers for one or more of the above properties. The offer should be on a sealed cover in three separate envelopes put together in a fourth sealed envelope.

Bids should be sent in separate envelopes for each property.

- **ENVELOP I:** Earnest Money
- **ENVELOP II:** Technical information about the party Containing viz:
    1. Name of the offeror and address
    2. Present Business
    3. Brief History of the offeror with particular reference to financial parameters (enclose copies of Annual Report, Audited Balance Sheet/Profit and Loss Account of the last three years).
    4. Details of collaboration proposed if any
    5. Experience in managing the business
    6. Any other relevant detail
- **ENVELOP III:** Price Offered for each property

- **ENVELOP IV:** will be opened only to those parties who have paid the requisite earnest money.
- **ENVELOP V:** will be opened only after Envelop II is found to be in order.

Offer should be submitted to:

- Chief (Disposal)
- Housing and Urban Development Corporation
- "HUDCO Bhawan,
- India Habitat Center
- Lodhi Road
- New Delhi-110003

Telephone–091-11-464 9610, Fax–091-11-469 7378/462 5308

The last date for submission of offer is 2.30 PM on 17 June 1996. The bids will be opened the same day at 3.00 PM.

Any further details can be obtained from the above address.

HUDCO reserves the right to reject any or all offers without assigning any reason. Any conditional offer will automatically stand rejected.

HUDCO, in the brochure of 17 June 1996 for calling bids of Guest House blocks, doubled the reserve price of the properties allotted to MS Shoes, against which HUDCO had obtained more than Rs. 40 Crores (US Dollar 11.01 million), *being 40% of the total bid amount. HUDCO forfeited the amount in being greedy, and also the game played by Mr. V. Suresh, the Corporate Planning Director, who has handled the subject properties.*

Chapter: Five

To Date, Guest Houses Were Not Energized Electricity

A Member of Parliament, Ms. Vasundhara Raje Scindia is an Indian politician and former Chief *Minister of Rajasthan. She is a member of the Bharatiya Janata Party. She is also the head of the Dholpur royal family and is the acting queen of Dholpur.*

In 1984, Raje entered the Indian political system. Initially, she was elected a Member of the National Executive of the newly formed Bharatiya Janata Party (BJP). She was elected as a member of the 8th Rajasthan Assembly from Dholpur. The same year, she was appointed Vice President of the Yuva Morcha, Rajasthan BJP.

She was Member of Parliament in the year 1989-91: Member, 9th Lok Sabha, from Jhalawar, 1991-96: Member, 10th Lok Sabha, 1996-98: Member, 11th Lok Sabha, 1998-99: Member, 12th Lok Sabha, 1999-03: Member, 13th Lok Sabha.

He wrote a letter to the Minister of Urban Affairs to stop the re-tender of the Guest House blocks at Andrews Ganj, as the public money of the banks are involved and is in litigation with MS Shoes.

Mr. M. Arunachalam was the Minister of Urban Affairs & Employment from 1 June 1996 to 29 June 1996. He was an Indian politician and former Member of Parliament elected from Tamil Nadu. He was elected to the Lok Sabha from Tenkasi constituency as an Indian National Congress candidate in 1977, 1980, 1984, 1989, and 1991 elections, and as a Tamil Maanila Congress (Moopanar) candidate in 1996 elections.

After he got his law degree, his ambition of becoming a lawyer was fulfilled. He started his career as a junior advocate under T.S. Ramanathan Iyer – a straightforward, upright person with Gandhian principles who was called 'Tiger of the Bar' in Tenkasi.

By sheer hard work and perseverance, he had a roaring practice. Soon he established an office for himself and expanded it with four colleagues and two juniors. He was selected for the post of Munsif for Pondicherry Sessions court, which he did not want to join. He was always ready to subordinate his advancement for the cause of the country and for the cause of depressed classes, for whom he was the only hope.

Despite several acknowledgments of Arunachalam, the handicaps, and limitations, Arunachalam rose from humble beginnings, entering politics at an early age, and was quickly enticed to national politics at his young age. As a mere party volunteer, he was Youth Congress Secretary in Tirunelveli (District Congress Committee). In 1977, the first contested won, and became the Member of Parliament from Tenkasi (Reserved constituency). That was the period when The Janata Party formed its government in the center for the first time. Since power did not matter to Arunachalam, he was ready to be in the opposition. As a man of Gandhian Principles, he did not hesitate to stand by the democratic values of his party.

Throughout his long political career, he was steadfast in his loyalty to the Congress and the Gandhian moral and political ideology, and he never considered himself persuaded by the rationalist, atheistic, religious, iconoclastic, communal, and secessionist ideologies of his time.

Drawn by an irresistible inner spirit of nationalism, he reached the possible highest rank in the country (Union Cabinet Minister), also achieved a high reputation for his record of performance as a competent and efficient

Member of Parliament during his six consecutive terms of his office to the Lok Sabha, giving up two decades and an outstanding national leader. He provided an unprecedented style of leadership with simple, astute, and pragmatic principles.

The Financial Institutions and the banks who had given a bridge loan to MS Shoes by paying the amounts directly to HUDCO jointly wrote a letter dated 13 June 1996 to the Government not to re-tender the properties and keep them in abeyance as the amounts of the banks and institutions are involved.

On the receipt of the letter of Member of Parliament of Ms. Vasundhara Raje Scindia, and the letter of the banks and financial institutions, Mr. M. Arunachalam, Minister of Urban Affairs and Employment, issued directions to HUDCO on 14 June 1996, which were delivered to HUDCO on the afternoon of 14 June 1996 when the tenders had already been received. The directions issued were as follows:

Ms. Vasundhara Raje, honorable Member of Parliament, has in her letter expressed concern about the huge public funds of various institutions/Banks involved in the two projects at Andrews Ganj, New Delhi, and it would be in the interest of public money to reschedule the payment towards these projects.

On perusal of the files of HUDCO, it is noticed the guest house blocks/restaurants/shops at Andrews Ganj, New Delhi are being re-tendered on 17 June 1996, and re-tendering of a five-star hotel site is under process, and that all these properties are under litigation and the matter is pending with the Delhi High Court. This is also mentioned in the tender brochure. The public notice issued for the tender also stipulates the property proposed is under dispute, and the outcome would hinge on the decision of the court.

In a situation where the re-tendering is being done with the stipulation of the property being under litigation, it may not be possible to fetch the correct price, which could further lead to loss of public funds. In the public interest, it would be appropriate to stop the tenders of all the concerned properties until further directions. A public notice for cancellation of tender is issued in leading newspapers immediately.

Senior Vice President, Ansal Properties & Industries Ltd., Mr. Pradeep Seth, on 24 July 1996 to Shri PK. Garg, Chief (Disposal), HUDCO regarding Shopping Arcade at HUDCO Place Andrews Ganj, New Delhi rescheduling of payment of installments.

You were kind enough to give us an extension of time for the second installment for six months on our representation, dated 21 February 1996. This extension was accorded for the reason that the Municipal Corporation of Delhi did not sanction the plans for the Shopping arcade at HUDCO Place through many regularities in the construction of basements and other structures which were constructed by HUDCO. These irregularities were pointed out by the Municipal Corporation of Delhi from time to time, and they had refused to consider the plans for the shopping arcade and had also refused to de-link the shopping arcade plans from the rest of the complex.

In our letter dated 21 February 1996, we had mentioned the period of delay until the end of February 1996 works out of approximately eight months, and therefore the extension was granted without interest until November 1996. However, in case there is a further delay in obtaining all the sanctions and commencement of construction, or for other reasons beyond our control, the further extension would be granted to us by HUDCO.

However, HUDCO only gave us an extension of time until 9 September 1996, vide their letter dated 7 March 1996. Vide letter dated 20 March 1996. HUDCO threatened to withdraw the extension of six months already granted, in case we do not send out acceptance of the same. Since we did not want to precipitate the issue. We have no option but to accept the extension.

Even after February 1996, the plans for the shopping arcade were not considered/sanctioned by the Municipal Corporation of Delhi because the basement under the shopping arcade for the car park constructed by HUDCO had not been approved by them. Notwithstanding our persistent efforts with the Municipal Corporation of Delhi, the building plans of the shopping arcade could not be approved by them, as they had decided to consider the whole issue in its entirety.

On 13 March 1996, vide their letter dated 13 March 1996, Municipal Corporation of Delhi asked HUDCO to deposit an amount of Rs. 7,84,160 and comply with other requirements before the plans for a shopping arcade could be considered. After HUDCO deposited the said amount, another letter was issued by the Municipal Corporation of Delhi on 8 April 1996, urging HUDCO to comply with the requirements intimated earlier and to deposit a further compounding fee of Rs. 3,25,040 to regularize the unauthorized constructions.

Subsequently, on 24 April 1996, Municipal Corporation of Delhi vide its letter dated 24 April 1996, urging HUDCO that the sanction of the shopping arcade plans will not be granted unless full compliance with the observations mentioned in a previous invalid notice dated 10 February 1996 is done.

Thus, you will observe that despite our regular and day-to-day follow-up with the Municipal Corporation of Delhi, they wanted the regularization of the constructed portions before the sanction of the shopping arcade plans. It was only after HUDCO complied with all the requirements of the Municipal Corporation of Delhi that we, with great difficulty, were able to get the plans finally sanctioned on 11 July 1996 vide their letter dated 11 July 1996.

It is not only the delay in sanctioning of the plans but even handing over the site for execution of the shopping arcade was delayed by several months through non-completion of the construction work by the earlier contractor. As per terms of the brochure issued based on which tenders were invited, the possession of the site was to be handed over to us on 1 June 1995, whereas it was handed over to us only on 10 November 1995. However, even this delayed possession was of hardly any use, as construction activity could not be started for the sake of regularization of the constructions carried out by HUDCO, and the time they forage in getting the same regularized after paying a compounding fee. The delay in handing over the site and sanction of plans has affected the project adversely and jeopardized the basic contractual obligation, and adversely affected fund mobilization in the following manner.

It will be appreciated that the aforementioned delays have adversely affected the credibility of our Group. Our technical inputs and marketing strategies have been set back considerably, and any project of this prestige and magnitude cannot attract investment in these circumstances. The philosophy behind giving a schedule for payments was to enable the sub-lease to start construction at the site, and thus enable the sub-lease to raise funds. However, abnormal delay in sanctioning of plans for no fault of the sub-lessee completely jeopardized the scheme of raising funds from the prospective allottees or other financial institutions.

As per the revised schedule, we are expected to require payment of second and third installments on or before 9 September 1996. However, the revised schedule stipulating the second and third installment on the same date is not fair and equitable, and this is unacceptable to us. Contractually. A gap of six months is envisaged between these two installments to facilitate easy payment terms. A reduction in the time gap of six months between the two installments is against the spirit of the contract. Further, the installments are linked with the progress of construction. A time gap of six months between second and third installments will provide time for construction to progress at the site, thus ensuring further mobilization of funds. Extension of the second installment without rescheduling the entire payment schedule, especially when the project has not taken off from the ground, is inequitable and needs to be reviewed as follows: -

1. Due to non-sanctioning of the plans, for no fault of ours, the entire project has been delayed, and therefore the extension of time dated 21 February 1996, we were justifiably entitled to an extension of

time for nine months. After that later, there have been further reasons for the delay, as mentioned above, and we are entitled to another four months of extension. Thus, in all, we are entitled to thirteen months of extension of time. Against our total entitlement of extension of time of thirteen months, we have already been granted an extension of time of six months up to 9 September 1996 for payment of the second installment. A further extension of time from 9 September 1996 for a period of seven, i.e., up to 9 April 1997, may kindly be granted for payment of the second installment and the third installment to be automatically extended.

2. Contractually, there is a gap of six months between the second and this installment, therefore, the third installment should become payable on 9 October 1997.

Since the delay is not due to any default on our side, all extensions should be without payment of any interest. The earlier extension of time was granted without any payment of interest.

Merely granting of an extension of time will not offset the financial losses that we have suffered on account of

HUDCO not disclosing the fact at the time of tender that the construction of the basement under the shopping arcade and other structures forming part of the entire HUDCO complex has not been approved by Municipal Corporation of Delhi and other concerned authorities. On the contrary, the impression given to us throughout was that the project under construction stands approved. We retain our right to claim for various financial losses and compensation that we might be entitled to for the delay in sanctioning of the plans and starting of construction work at the site.

Keeping in view the above facts, we would request you to kindly grant us an extension of time free of interest in payment of the second and third installment i.e., 2nd Installment to be paid on 9 January 1997 and 3rd installment for six months thereafter, i.e., 8 October 1997.

Ansals were granted six months extensions already without interest in the first installment and the second installment, while the allotment of the MS Shoes was canceled and the amounts forfeited. HUDCO has refused to accept the payments in court through an appreciation of the value of the properties. Ansals further sought another interest-free extension of 2nd and 3rd installments since the entire building was constructed, including Guest Houses and Car

Park, constructed without any sanctions of building plans. Ansal's plea was that the impression was given throughout that the project under construction stands approved. Ansals further threatened to claim damages from HUDCO.

Chapter: Six

HUDCO Appraised Government, the Prices Have Doubled of The Properties Allotted to MS Shoes

Until July 1996, Electric Supply was not energized, rather even the land was not allotted to Delhi Electric Supply Undertaking to build the Grid for energizing the Andrews Ganj complex. The amounts obtained by HUDCO from MS Shoes were forfeited without all such facilities committed by HUDCO in the brochure, leading to cheating MS Shoes of Rs. 68.68 Crores (US Dollar 21.89 million) received deceptively.

HUDCO, Mr. K. K. Bhatnagar on 24 July 1996 to Shri M.S. Srinivasan, Joint Secretary, Ministry of Urban Affairs & Employment regarding allotment of land to Delhi Electricity Supply Undertaking for establishing 33 KV Grid Substations and power connection to HUDCO Place project at Andrews Ganj

Establishing a grid substation to cater to the need of power to the HUDCO Place at Andrews Ganj was a requirement by Delhi Electricity Supply Undertaking, and accordingly, an area measuring 75 m x 45 m was earmarked and reserved at the above project site for this purpose. The modalities to be followed for handing over the said area to Delhi Electricity Supply Undertaking were discussed in various meetings with the Ministry. The Under Secretary informed HUDCO, MOUA&E vide letter dated 16

February 1994 (copy enclosed) that the land should be allotted to Delhi Electricity Supply Undertaking at a nominal rate of Re.1/- per annum in case the cost of land earmarked for the substation has been loaded on to the other components in the Community Center which are being disposed of at predetermined rates, otherwise, it should be charged at Rs. 20 lacs (US Dollar 0.05 million) per acre as premium plus 2.5% thereof as ground rent per annum.

Accordingly, during the 31st meeting of the Committee of Directors of HUDCO held on 8 July 1996, it was decided to allot the said land to Delhi Electricity Supply Undertaking @ Rs.1/- per annum and to undertake the construction of the building of a grid substation (civil works) by HUDCO, as agreed during a meeting held on 16 November 1995 between HUDCO & Delhi Electricity Supply Undertaking. This cost will be included in the project cost of development of HUDCO of the 31st Committee of Directors meeting. This is also enclosed for your information.

HUDCO submitted a note to the Ministry on the note served on HUDCO on 14 June 1996 to stop the tenders, and from the comments hereinbelow, it shows HUDCO was being greedy due to the valuation of the properties appreciated more than twice, in which the Government of India was the part of it. The earlier minister, Mr. M. Arunachalam, the charge was taken over by Mr. Deve Gowda, who was elected Prime Minister of India. He held the charge of the Ministry of Urban Affairs from 29 June 1996 to 21 April 1997.

Chairman & Managing Director, HUDCO, Mr. H.K. Bhatnagar on 25 July 1996 to Mr. K.S. Sharma Secretary (UPA) regarding Disposal of Guest House and hotel Plot in Andrews Ganj:

Note sheet page 1/N of Secretary (UD) and Secretary (UEPA) on the above subject may please be noted. A copy of the note of the hon'ble minister was sent directly to the Director (Finance of HUDCO, who was looking after the duties of Chairman & Managing Director since the Chairman & Managing Director and DCP were both out of the country at that time. There were also persistent telephone calls from the office of the Minister to comply with the instructions contained in the note. Director (Finance) HUDCO attempted to seek instructions from the Ministry, but since both the Secretaries were also out of town, he could not get any other instructions. After discussions with the Private Secretary to Minister, he complied with instructions contained in the note by putting up a notice in the office intimating about the cancellation of the tender on 15 June 1996. In any case, there was no time for any other action since the 15th & 16th were holidays, and 17 only two bidders came with bids for shops, and they were informed of HUDCO's decision on the subject. The matter was put up to the HUDCO Board for their consideration in its 22nd meeting, and they decided as follows: CMD HUDCO placed before the Board, detailed facts of the case, as indicated in the agenda note. This note dated 17 June 1996 of the Secretary (UEPA) was placed before the Board. It was brought to the notice of the Board that 95% of the work of Guest Houses was completed, and if these were not allotted, the property will deteriorate. JS also informed the Board (UEPA) that there were no directions from the Government on the subject. After deliberations, the Board decided that action should be initiated for re-auction under intimation to the Ministry. Action is accordingly being taken for re-auction of the Guest Houses and the Hotel plot by issuing advertisements in newspapers. Please note for information. This may also be brought to the kind notice of the Hon'ble Minister of Urban Affairs since the original instruction had flowed from his office. A concise note on the subject is also enclosed, which may be used for briefing the Minister.

Concise note for information conduct of M/s MS Shoes (East) Ltd in effecting payments:

STATUS		GUEST HOUSES RESTAURANT/KITCHEN, SHOPS		HOTEL SITE INCLUDING CAR PARKING
Total Amount to be paid		99.01		78.10
Date of Payment of 1st installm	28.11.94	39.604	28.11.94	27.4

ent & amount				
Date on which 1st installment paid & amount (with interest)	28.2.95	39.604	28.2.95	27.4
Date on 2nd installment becomes due and amount	31.1.95	39.604 (Without Interest)	31.10.95	24.83

	30.4.95	(With Interest @ 16.48%)	(31.1.96)	
Time is given by High Court for payment	31.12.95		(8.4.96) (11.4.96) (25.4.96)	
Present position		No payment has been made yet and the High Court vacated the order of maintenance of status-quo and permitted re-auction		

Total interest @ 16.48% with quarterly rest for Guest House and Hotel Site: 2.03 crores, this was permissible as part of the bid conditions.

RISE IN VALUE OF PROPERTY:

In February 1995, we had auctioned a commercial site at the same location, which fetched an extreme value of Rs. 1, 06,800/- per sqm. Accordingly, the board revised the reserve price for the guest houses and the hotel plot in the following manner:

	Guest House	Restaurant/Kitchen	shops	Hotel site
	Rate per sqm.			
Original Reserve Price	38,000	40,000	45,000	50.00cr
Revised Reserve Price	75,000	85,000	90,000	96.15cr

It is obvious that MS Shoes can never pay based on the revised reserve price, since they have not been able to pay the earlier price as well, and there is no reason why HUDCO and the Government should suffer any loss.

ISSUES RAISED BY FINANCING INSTITUTIONS:

There is no legal transaction between HUDCO and the financing institution. They must have appraised the projects submitted to them by MS Shoes and decided as per their procedures. HUDCO was nowhere involved in that. Even now, the entire amount sanctioned by them to MS Shoes has not come to HUDCO, and in no way can they ask for any accommodation from HUDCO in this regard. In case they suffer certain losses and may have omitted certain points while making a decision, it is for them and the ministry of finance to look into the matter. We have taken legal opinion which states there is no way in which HUDCO can give any relief to the financing institutions in these transactions. If at all, it will only strengthen the case of MS Shoes in the High Court, which we have been contesting and have obtained orders from the Division Bench in our favor for the reaction of the property. As a matter of fact, if this decision is made known or in any way indicated to the court, we may be left with no defense at all.

RETURNS FROM THE TRANSACTIONS:

HUDCO is developing the Andrewsganj properties for the benefit of the government since the entire returns are earmarked for the construction of office and residential accommodation for central government employees. There is no reason why we should not raise the maximum possible resources from the development for this purpose.

PENDENCY OF CASES IN THE HIGH COURT:

It is a fact that the suits filed by MS Shoes are still pending in the High Court, and attending to the general situation of disposal of cases, it may take years before these are disposed of MS Shoes will be willing to continue them indefinitely since the properties will remain in limbo and his rights will not be extinguished. It is possible that this fact may also adversely affect the disposal to some extent, but that we have to recognize and hear to take appropriate decisions at the appropriate time. In any case, once another party comes in, third-party rights will be created, and the maximum relief to MS Shoes could be relating to amounts which they had deposited and forfeited by HUDCO following the contract between the two parties. The disposal of the property is unlikely to be affected.

LIKELY DETERIORATION IN PROPERTIES:

Guest Houses constructed at a total cost of Rs. 61.31 crores (US Dollar 16.88 million) (including services) are almost fully complete. Three of them are sold to state governments and PSUs are likely to be handed over shortly as soon as we get the power connection. In case the disposal of the remaining blocks is delayed, the services and properties may deteriorate considerably, requiring additional expenditure from HUDCO. Maintenance expenditure in any case will have to be incurred for this interim period.

There is no construction, of course, on the hotel site, but once again encroachment is always a serious problem in Delhi, and presently when the property values are at appropriate levels, this should also be disposed of. The board also found an advantage in disposing of these properties together to enable extensive operators to bid for both the properties for setting up a huge hotel in this prime area of Delhi.

HUDCO submitted the report, which was false, as the High Court never permitted HUDCO to re-tendered the properties.

Chapter: Seven

MCD Demanded Ownership Documents/Lease Documents for Sanctioning Building Plans, HUDCO Failed to Supply

The Architects who had submitted the building plans for approval of the buildings already constructed without any sanctions. Municipal Corporation of Delhi demanded the title deeds towards HUDCO, which HUDCO could not provide until the end of July 1996, while the properties allotted to MS Shoes were canceled on 1 January 1996.

Jasbir Sawhney & Associates, Architects, Mr. Dinesh Sareen on 2 August 1996 to Mr. M. N. Joglekar, Executive Director (DD) regarding HUDCO Place- Municipal Corporation of Delhi Submission:

This has reference to our telephonic conversation regarding the submission of drawings to the Municipal Corporation of Delhi.

We had approached Municipal Corporation of Delhi, Building Section twice earlier, but the concerned Jr. Engineer was not available. Today we had again gone to Municipal Corporation of Delhi, wherein they refused to accept our drawings on account of the following documents which were 'Doc; available with us.

Ownership documents/lease documents, No due certificate from the Land and Development Office, Property tax receipt from the Municipal Corporation of Delhi.

Kindly send these documents to us immediately, to satisfy the requirement of the Municipal Corporation of Delhi.

The building plans were sanctioned for Guest House Blocks in August 1996, but subject to various conditions which HUDCO could not comply with since the buildings were already constructed, it was requested to compound the buildings? The compounding fee was fixed by the PSUs Municipal Corporation of Delhi, which HUDCO had to pay to get the building plans sanctioned.

The Commissioner, Municipal Corporation of Delhi on 9 August 1996 to Mr. M.N. Joglekar, Executive Director, HUDCO regarding Sanction U/s 336 of the Municipal Corporation of Delhi Act:

Construction of Guest House at HUDCO Place, Pinjrapole, Andrews Ganj, New Delhi.

Regarding your letter dated 6 November 1995 regarding the construction of the Guest House at HUDCO Place, Pinjrapole, Andrews Ganj, New Delhi, you are informed that sanction is granted by Municipal Corporation of Delhi, subject to the following terms & modifications made in the map.

1. These maps are to be submitted by 8 August 1998.
2. Construction work will be done as per the sanctioned map, and without sanction under Bye-laws, no change will be permissible. Any changed construction against Bye-laws can be demolished, and the license of the architect appointed as the observer can be canceled.
3. There will be no compromise in case of violation by Building bylaws.
4. This will be a duty of the house owner, and the architecture it is ensured that sanctioned maps are as per applicable building bye-laws. If any violation of bye-laws is unnoticed, if noticed, later on, the Municipal Corporation of Delhi will have the power to change the maps, and in this matter, no compensation will be made by the Municipal Corporation of Delhi.
5. Municipal Corporation of Delhi will be informed before starting building construction as per bye-laws. Accordingly, the Municipal Corporation of Delhi will be informed on reaching the construction work at the plinth level.
6. Unless the Officer does not issue an occupation certificate, the party will not occupy the building or

will not permit occupying the building or will not permit occupying the building or the building or any part of it which is constructed, will not use and will not permit us.

7. Consequent upon sanctioning the building maps by Municipal Corporation of Delhi, may claim all expenses/losses/claims or is liable to claim, will be free from any loss or compensation before any court proceedings and other authorities.
8. Doors & windows may be fixed in such a way they do not open into a street.
9. Building construction will not be done within the minimum distance from voltage lines specified in Indian Electricity Rules.
10. Vacant land will be part of the public street as per Set Back Rules.
11. If the above-said terms are not complied with, the sanction will be treated as illegal from the beginning.

All the conditions of the Chief Fire Office communicated vide their letter No. F6/DFS/HS/MP/96/GH/642 dated 14 May 1996 shall be adhered to.

Chief (disposal), HUDCO, Mr. P.K Garg to Ansal Properties & Industries Limited on 20 August 1996 regarding shopping Arcade at HUDCO Complex. Please refer to your letter dated 24 July 1996 requesting for the further extension of the payment of the 2nd installment, which falls due on 9 September 1996 to 8 April 1997, and extension of the 3rd installment by six months thereafter, i.e., on 8 October 1997.

As you are aware, the grounds on which you have sought a further extension for the payment of the 2nd installment have already been considered by HUDCO, and we regret it is impossible to grant any further extension of time for the payment of the 2nd installment, which falls due on 9 September 1996. You are therefore advised to please make arrangements for the payment of a 2nd installment on or before 9 September 1996 without interest and thereafter with interest, as per the provision of sanction letter No. HUDCO/AG/SA/95 dated 10 March 1995.

Your request for an extension of the date for the payment of the third installment is being placed before HUDCO's competent authority, and its decision will be intimated to you in due course of time.

HUDCO on one side rejected the further extension of two installments to be paid by Ansals, but on the other side agreed to place it before a board for consideration. Ansals reiterated the buildings are yet to be regularized and interest-free extensions are granted.

Senior Vice President, Ansal Properties & Industries Ltd., Mr. Pradeep Seth on 27 August 1996 to Mr. P. K. Garg, Chief Disposal, HUDCO regarding Shopping Arcade at HUDCO Complex, Andrews Ganj, New Delhi– Rescheduling of payment of installment.

We are surprised to receive your letter dated 20 August 1996 rejecting our request for an extension of time for payment of the second installment from 9 September 1996 to 6 April 1997, while for the extension of time for payment of the third installment, you have put our request, before the HUOCO's Competent Authority for their decision. Perhaps you have not appreciated the circumstances and. Compelling reasons under which the extension has been sought. We would, therefore, once again, request you to consider our request for an extension of time on the merits of the case, as enumerated below:

1. The first extension of time given to us on September 9 September 1996 was on certain grounds, as mentioned in our letter dated 22 February 1996. The same grounds have continued to exist beyond February 1996. The unauthorized constructions carried out by HUDCO in the basement of the shopping arcade remained unregularized by the Municipal Corporation of Delhi. The compounding fee for regularizing the unauthorized constructions was first demanded by the Municipal Corporation of Delhi on 13 March 1996 for Rs.7,84,160, and later on an additional compounding fee of Rs.3,25,040 on 8 April 1996. Further, on 24 April 1996, Municipal Corporation of Delhi vide its invalid Note dated 24 April 1996, informed HUDCO that sanction of the shopping arcade plans will not be granted unless full compliance was done of the objections raised in their previous invalid Notice dated 10 December 1995. However, it was only after a prolonged tussle, vide their letter dated 28 May 1996 that the unauthorized constructions of HUDCO were regularized, and thereafter, the Municipal Corporation of Delhi sanctioned the building plans for the superstructure on 11 July 1996.

2. Thus, you will find that the same reasons continued to exist based on which you had given us the first extension of time, and therefore, there is no reason or justification for ignoring those facts for the second extension of time.
3. Further, we have been zealous in pursuing the matter of sanction vigorously and untiringly, both verbally and in writing, from the date of acceptance of our bid vide HUDCO's letter dated 10 March 1996, evidenced from the following:
   a) Even before the receipt of the letter of allotment accepting our bid, we engaged the services of M/s. Jasbir Sawhney and Associates, as our architects, confirmed their appointment on 24 February 1995, and payment against their first bill dated we paid 1 March on 2 March 1995, before the date of receipt of the letter of allotment on 10 March 1996.
   b) We also appointed M/s. Ahluwalia Contracts India Pvt. Ltd., who was engaged by HUDCO for construction of the basement and other development works at the project site for construction of the shopping arcade. We continued with the services of the same

contractor, as they were already fully mobilized at the site, thereby seeking to avoid the possible delay in commencement of construction from our side.

c) Our correspondence will reveal we had initiated all steps and had asked for the layout plans and building plans from HUDCO so that our plans could be prepared from the already sanctioned/built plans.

d) We also asked for (d) a Draft agreement on 26 June 1995 but sent to us on 19 July 1995, which was different from the terms of the tender. On our representation, the same was modified to be in tune with the terms of the tender, and thereafter immediately executed on 1 August 1995.

e) On learning that the Municipal Corporation of Delhi is not entertaining building plans for the shopping arcade until the Delhi Urban Art Commission clearance for the revised layout plans was obtained, and the Municipal Corporation of Delhi regularized the unauthorized constrictions, we wrote our letter to HUDCO on 6 April 1995, and thereafter many other letters followed it which are on record.

Thus, you will find that there is no slackness or insufficient follow-up on our part to delay the sanctioning of the plan. After having paid over Rs.84 crores (US Dollar 23.70 million), how can any organization not pursue with full earnestness the requisite sanctions and other obligations on their part to ensure commencement of construction?

4. As per terms of the tender, we were to commence the work from June 1995, but since the earlier contractors of HUDCO did not complete the basement work, and as the site was not clear, the site could not be handed over to us. It was finally handed over to us on 10 November 1995, after a delay of almost five months.
5. In normal circumstances, if there were valid sanctions for work already executed by HUDCO, our plans could have been easily sanctioned much before the handing over of the site, and we could have started construction on the next day of handing over the site to us. Unfortunately, as events will reveal, this did not happen.

After receiving the sanction of the shopping arcade plans on 11 July 1996, we started construction the following day, and now the construction work is in full swing.

6. The delay in sanctioning of the plans and the consequential delay in commencement of construction has completely upset the confidence of the investors in the project, and booking of commercial spaces in the project has been adversely affected. Further, the prospective buyers who had booked spaces with us were expected to pay further installments linked with the progress of construction. Since the construction did not proceed, we could not call further installments, which adversely affected the collection of funds. Few prospective parties had booked spaces have recalled their booking amounts, as there was no progress of construction at the site. Incidence of Interest on borrowed funds increased, and delay in the project has resulted in financial losses, for which HUOCO is responsible.
7. Under normal circumstances, we would have started construction during June 1995 by when we would have got our plans approved. Unfortunately, due to reasons stated in our two letters dated 21 February 1998 and 24

July 1996 requesting for an extension of time, the total delay in commencement of work has been 13 months. We were granted an extension of six months vide your letter dated 7 March 1996, which we had hesitatingly accepted because HUDCO vide their letter dated 20 March 1996 had threatened to withdraw the extension if we did not send our acceptance. We did not want to precipitate the issue and had no option but to accept the extension at that time. Further, in all fairness, after deducting six months, the balance extension for seven months should be granted to us, as requested in our letter dated 24 July 1996. Thus, the extension of time for payment of the second Installment should be given to us until 8 April 1997. Since contractually there is a time gap of six months between the second and third installment, the third Installment automatically should become payable on 8 October 1997.

8. Thus, you will find that the above extension of time requested by us is on merits, and it is requested that the same should be granted to us, and we are not compelled to seek redress through other alternative sources.
9. We would appreciate it if our request is considered before 9 September 1996, the due date for payment of the second Installment.

10. Chief (Disposal), HUDCO, Mr. PK Garg on 7 September 1996 to Mr. Pradeep Seth Senior Vice-President M/s. Ansal Properties and Industries Limited New Delhi regarding Shopping Arcade at HUDCO Complex Andrews Ganj New Delhi–rescheduling of payment of installments:

We are writing with further reference to your letters of 24 July 1996 and 27 August 1996 requesting for a re-extension for payment of the second installment due on 9 September 1996, and an extension for the payment of the third installment due.

You are well aware that the payments of the second installment and the third installment were unrelated to any stage of development or construction, but were to be fixed-time payments. However, having regard to that the project was still at its inception stage and your communication that you were facing various difficulties, we have already extended the time for payment of the second installment by you to 9 September 1996, without interest and thereafter with interest as per the provision of the letter of allotment dated 10 March 1995. We do not accept your contention that we had granted the said extension of time for the reasons stated in your said letter. We repeat the said extension for the second installment was granted by us at your request, only for the consideration stated above. We further repeat that there cannot be any linkage between the installments to be paid at the times fixed and stipulated, and any delays alleged by you constitute reasons for seeking an extension of time. We do not agree with your contention that the said you paid installments have been delayed due to the non-completion of the construction work by the earlier contractor. We also do not agree there was any delay in handing possession of the site to you, as alleged by you. You had delayed in accepting the possession of the site on various grounds. The various reasons given and contentions raised by you in your letters are neither tenable nor justified in any way. We have deliberately avoided joining issues with you on these matters, as the same in view does not affect the contract or the contractual stipulations and understandings, nor would in the interest of the project; it is singularly unfair that the accommodation granted by us to you has not been properly acknowledged.

Please note we cannot grant you any further extension of time for payment of the second installment as sought by you and would request you to pay the same following your letter of 7 March 1996, and confirmed by us in a letter dated 20 August 1996.

We wish to make it clear that there cannot be any linkage between the payment of the second installment and the payment of the third installment. However, purely because of the difficulties expressed by you, we agree to grant you a final extension of time for payment of the third installment up to 8 March 1997.

On one side, HUDCO stated to Ansals that the extensions as requested cannot be granted, but purely given the difficulties expressed, the extension of time of the third installment is further extended up to 8 March 1997. These difficulties of MS Shoes were not considered by HUDCO, but they granted various favors to Ansals through the corruption involved by Ansals with HUDCO officers, while MS Shoes never wanted to indulge in such unscrupulous practice.

Chapter: Eight

Discriminatory Treatment MS Shoes Viz-a-Viz Ansals

The building plans of the car park, allotted along with 5-star hotel land and guest house blocks, were compounded by the Municipal Corporation of Delhi, subject to approval from the Chief Fire Officer. The building plans were compounded at the insistence of the Ministry of Urban Development. The part of the same car park had been allotted to Ansals, but the building plans of Shopping Arcade allotted to Ansals, of which possession had also been given to Ansals, could not be sanctioned due to the illegal car park and guest house blocks, as it was one layout plan of 17.6 acres of Community Center at Andrews Ganj.

Zonal Engineer (Building)/Central Zone Municipal Corporation of Delhi – Regarding Completion Certificate in respect of Car Parking Basement, Guest Houses & Type VI Housing of HUDCO, Andrews Ganj. Vide Reference No. H/DD/AGP/96 on 19 September 1996.

As per telephonic message received from C.E. (Central) regarding issuance of completion certificate in respect of the above-mentioned subject, on scrutiny of files, it was noted the building plans of the said project have been regularized by paying the necessary compounding fee at Building, Headquarter. The detail of compounding has not been intimated to the Zone. It may therefore be clarified since the drawings have been regularized at Building, Head Quarter, and the compounding fee has also been paid at Building, Head Quarter, it is requested that the detail of the area be regularized and compounding may be intimated to this office.

HUDCO sought legal opinion from Barrister & Senior Advocate, Mr. Dipankar P. Gupta, to consider extensions of installments for a further period, as asked for by Ansals. The legal opinion was obtained to help Ansals to extend the matter, and the opinion of the board was that in commercial prudence, the extensions be granted. In the case of MS Shoes, no such legal opinion was obtained, nor was the commercial prudence applied by HUDCO. In fact, legal opinion was obtained at the behest of Ansals and from the Senior Advocate known to them.

Barrister & Senior Advocate, Supreme Court of India, Mr. Dipankar P. Gupta to HUDCO on 22 September 1996 regarding shopping Arcade at Pinjrapole Andrewsganj New Delhi.

OPINION

An area of 17.6 acres approximately of Land at Pinjrapole Andrewsganj New Delhi was allotted to the cuarist HUDCO by the president of India for the development of a community center. HUDCO constructed a double storied basement at the site as part of the Center. The president of India also allowed HUDCO to dispose of 4800 sqm of the land on a sub-lease basis for the construction of a shopping arcade. Tenders were invited for the construction of the shopping arcade, and Ansals was accepted for a total sum of Rs. 168.80 crores. An allotment letter dated 10 March 1995 was issued towards Ansals, or an arrangement was stipulated as under: -

- 50%, i.e., Rs 34.4 acres on or before 6 April 1995.
- 30%, i.e., Rs 50.64 acres on or before 9 March 1996 and
- 20%, i.e., Rs 32.76 acres on or before 9 September 1996.

Ansals paid the first installment before 6 April 1995. After an agreement or sublease was executed on 1 August 1995, wherein the payment schedule for the second and third installment was incorporated. The agreement to sublease, specially provided HUDCO shall have the right to rescind and revoke the agreement, and the demised premises, including superstructures, shall revert to HUDCO (or the president) if Ansals fail to pay any amount including installments if any due and payable under the agreement. The sublease agreement also contains an arbitration clause.

Possession of the site which was to be given around June 1995 was handed over by HUDCO to Ansals on 10 November 1995.

It appears HUDCO had constructed a double storied basement at the site where the shopping arcade was to come up, without having obtained a sanctioned building plan from the Municipal Corporation of Delhi. The regularization compounding process in respect of the basement construction took some time. Ansals had the responsibility of obtaining the sanction for the building plans of the superstructure of the shopping arcade, but the Municipal Corporation of Delhi was not prepared to consider that plan for sanction until the basement portion was regularized. By the time these problems could be sorted out, some delay took place.

By letters dated 22 November 1996 and 22 February 1996, Ansals complained of these delays and alleged they were suffering a heavy loss of interest and overheads due to the project not taking off in time, for which they claimed HUDCO to be responsible. They also requested for extension of time for payment of the second and third installment by 8 months and contended that further extension of time would be required in case there was further delay.

The request of Ansals was considered at the Board of HUDCO in their 218th meeting held on 1 March 1996. The agenda notes state there has been a delay, which can be attributed to both parties. Having considered the facts and circumstances, the Board decided an extension for 6 months, i.e., up to 9 September 1996, for payment of the second installment without interest, be granted. Accordingly, the time for payment of the second installment was extended up to 9 September 1996. Nothing has mentioned the installments.

By a letter dated 24 July 1996 (followed by a letter dated 27 August 1996), Ansals have now claimed a further extension of 7 months for the payment of the 2nd installment, i.e., till 8 April 1997, and a time gap or 6 months thereafter for the payment of the 3rd installment, i.e., till 8 September 1997. Ansals allege that delays in handing over the site and in obtaining sanctioned plans (for which they hold HUDCO responsible) have affected the project adversely and jeopardized the basic contractual obligations, and adversely affected the fund mobilization by Ansals. Ansals sought to retain their right to claim compensation against HUDCO.

The request and the contentions or Ansals were considered by the board of HUDCO at their 223rd meeting, and it was decided no extension of time for the payment of the 2nd installment was called for, but that an extension of 6 months from 9 September 1996 for payment of the 3rd installment be granted by a letter dated 7 September 1996. HUDCO declined to extend the time for the 2nd installment but agreed to grant a final extension of time for payment of the 2nd installment up to 8 March 1997. HUDCO also denied any liability for any alleged delay on their part.

Ansals has been sought on the following questions: -

a) What actions Ansals possibly brought HUDCO for non-acceptance of its requests exactly on the lines contained in its letter dated 24 July 1996?

b) . In its letter dated 24 July 1996, Ansals have also indicated that the delay in handing over the site and sanction of the plan has affected the project adversely and jeopardized the basic contractual obligation and adversely affected the fund mobilization by Ansals and that Ansals retained its right to claim the compensation it might be entitled to the delays on the part of HUDCO are the remedies available to Ansals and will HUDCO be liable to any damages on these grounds.

c) The central issue is whether having altered the originally stipulated payment schedule on Ansals request, once HUDCO could consider the second request of 24 July 1996 for further extension of 2nd installment and will it again have a consequential effect of further stretching the recently extended third installment.

d) The sublease agreement contains Clause XXI (at page 223) under which any question dispute of affirmance arising under these presents or in connection therewith will or require to be referred to the arbitration of a person appointed by HUDCO. In view of this clause, will it be open for the Ansals to approach the Court for seeking any relief or remedy against or it of it will necessarily to have to asked for the arbitration for it disputes distributes with HUDCO? Is the answer to this is yes, what course or of action will HUDCO advise be advice to adopt adapt to avoid any litigation by Ansals? Is a remedy in writing available to Ansals for seeking direction against HUDCO regarding the extension of time?

e) . HUDCO is taking steps to file a caveat. Will HUDCO be advised to take any other steps in case Ansals decides to file any action against HUDCO?

Possible legal proceedings which Ansals may commence in the present case include arbitration proceedings, a suit, or writ proceedings. Since the alleged cause of action of Ansals is for damages and compensation, together with the return, and since factual disputes will be involved, a writ is unlikely to succeed. If a suit is filed. HUDCO will be entitled to pray for a stay of the suit on the ground of the arbitration agreement. If the prayer for stay is sustained, Ansals will then be compelled to commence arbitration proceedings. Generally, it is extremely difficult to anticipate what type of legal action an opponent is likely to take, and in a case like these where various factual questions will be involved, it is practically impossible to assess and predict the results of any litigation which may be commenced. I would therefore confine myself to formulate the following general comments.

The stand taken by Ansals in the correspondence is they were unaware of the fact that the basement portion had been constructed without a normal sanction. This may not be wholly correct. There was a common architect who was aware of all the facts relating to the grand of sanction. It is nightly improbable that such an enormous sum of money would have been paid without being aware of the position and prospects of the sanction. In any event, by 17 May 1995, i.e., before the signing of the agreement for sublease, Ansals had become aware of the absence of a valid and complete building sanction. They knew also that the basement construction would first have to be regularized/compounded by the Municipal Corporation of Delhi, and only after that will Ansal's building plans for the arcade be taken up by the Municipal Corporation of Delhi for scrutiny necessary action. This is clear from a letter dated 17 May 1995 written by Ansals. These are the arguments that may be open to HUDCO to resist Ansals claims.

It cannot be said there has been a delay on the part of HUDCO in handing over possession of the site. Moreover, Ansals have been prevented from commencing the project because the construction of the basement did not have a valid sanction and had to be regularized compounded. This is implicitly recognized by the fact that extensions without payment of interest have been granted by HUDCO. It is therefore extremely difficult to anticipate the result of any opinion litigation involving these issues, nor am I in this opinion attempting to assess the merits of the respective contentions or the relative strength thereof.

Should HUDCO wish to take steps on the ground of default of Ansals to obtain payment of the installment of the position is as follows, although the agreement for sublease entitles HUDCO to rescind and revoke the same in case of default in payment of installments (Clause xxi) at the same time, it also provides for payments of interest in three months, cancellation of allotment, and forfeiture for delays beyond three months clause III. It will not, in my opinion, be advisable for HUDCO to cancel the agreement without waiting for 3 months. In addition, if HUDCO desires to cancel the agreement, it would not be advisable to do so without serving a notice clearly expressing the intention to terminate unless payments are received within the 3 months.

Whether HUDCO should accede to the request for an extension of time delivered by Ansals is a commercial decision that HUDCO will have to take. I would however like to make the following comments.

If litigation results at this stage either by the cancellation of the agreement or claim for damages, or otherwise, the project which is in the public interest will suffer. Simultaneously, if HUDCO gives an extension as asked for by Ansals, the claim for damages already performed by them will remain an outstanding issue and may be revised later. Thus, this is a case which, in my view, ought to be negotiated and settled at this stage itself. Now is the opportunity where the prayer for and the period of the extension may be considered by negotiation, on the condition that Ansals would drop all their claims for damages or otherwise on account of alleged delays on the part of HUDCO which may have occurred to date. If this is done, then the parties will commence the project on a clean slate without any outstanding dispute, having the potential of erupting in subsequent stages and leading to disastrous litigation.

The legal opinion stated that the project is in the public interest and it may be negotiated with Ansals accepting their extensions and asking them to withdraw the notice of claim of damages due to the delays by HUDCO to avoid disastrous litigation. In the case of MS Shoes, nothing of this sort was considered, because the valuation of the properties had doubled, and the greed of the Government, as well as HUDCO with their deceptive intentions, kept the monies of MS Shoes.

Chapter: Nine

Building Electricity Grid Land Allotted in September 1996
When MS Shoes Allotment Already Cancelled

Chief (Disposal), HUDCO on 24 September 1996 to The General Manager, Delhi Electric Supply Undertaking regarding allotment of land to Delhi Electricity Supply Undertaking for establishing 33 KV Grid Sub-station and Power Connection to HUDCO Place, Andrews Ganj:

Housing & Urban Development Corporation Ltd. (HUDCO is pleased to allot to Delhi Electric Supply Undertaking (Delhi Electricity Supply Undertaking) sub-station site having plot area of 45 m x 75rn for establishing the 33 KV Grid Sub-station on a sub-lease basis at a nominal premium fee of Rs.1/- per annum. The broad terms and conditions are as follows;

1. The site allotted is on a sub-lease hold basis on the terms & conditions as may be approved by the Government of India.
2. The Grid sub-station building (only civil works) at the site will be constructed by HUDCO, as per the detailed designs to be provided by the Delhi Electricity Supply Undertaking.
3. The cost of establishing the Grid Sub-station shall be borne by the Delhi Electricity Supply Undertaking.

4. Delhi Electricity Supply Undertaking shall be liable to pay the property and other taxes, if any, on the allotted properties to the Municipal Corporation of Delhi or any other authority from the date of possession of the Site.
5. The maintenance of the sub-station building will be by the Delhi Electricity Supply Undertaking.
6. You shall not execute any construction or encroachment of temporary or permanent nature on the terrace of the sub-station.
7. The registration of the documents, if any, is required for the purpose mentioned in paragraph 1 above, shall be as per laws applicable in the National Capital Territory of Delhi. The stamp duty, registration charges, and other charges payable for the deed and registration will be borne by Delhi Electricity Supply Undertaking.
8. The possession of the Site will be handed over to you after paying the premium of Rs.1/- and execution of the Certificate of Provisional Entry as per the enclosed form.

The land for establishing the grid of electricity was allotted to Delhi Electric Supply Undertaking in September 1996, and the grid was completed in 1998. The question of MS Shoes had paid the entire amount of Rs. 100 Crores (US Dollar 24.23 million) *towards guest house blocks, they would have suffered without implementing the project of which the building plans' completion certificate was obtained as late as 1998, subject to the approval of the drainage plans which were approved finally on 7 September 1999. In the given circumstances in the prospectus of MS Shoes in the public issue, the project was to be made operational in one year of the allotment dated 31 October 1994. No investors could have waited for five years after an additional payment of Rs. 100 crores.*

Senior Vice President, Ansal Properties & Industries Ltd., Mr. Pradeep Seth, on 4 October 1996, to Mr. P.K. Garg, Chief (Disposal), HUDCO regarding Shopping Arcade at HUDCO complex Andrews Ganj New Delhi–rescheduling of payment of installment.

On receipt of your letter dated 7 September 1996, in which you did not fully appreciate our representation of 24 July 1996 and 27 August 1996 requesting for rescheduling of payment of second and third installment, and on the suggestion of your chairman, the undersigned and Mr. G.R. Gogia had meetings with you and Mr. Anup Aggarwal,

Executive Director (Legal) to arrive at some mutually agreed extension of time. During our discussions, we have been advised you are in a position to consider rescheduling the second and third Installment by three months if we do not press for losses arising due to delay in sanctioning of plans.

We understand our request relating to the rescheduling of payment was discussed in the meeting of the Board of Directors of HUDCO held on 26 September 1996 and the Board. We would like to resubmit the following to your consideration:

In your letter dated 7 September 1996, you have mentioned there is no relation between payment of installments and commencement of construction. In this connection, we would like to draw your attention to HUDCO's brochure issued before inviting the bids for the above project, where it is mentioned as under:

"June can take up the construction 1995 after the allottee obtains necessary approvals from the concerned authorities. If for any unforeseen reason, the possession of the site is not given to the allottee for construction purposes by June

1995, HUOCO will pay simple interest @6% to the allottee on the amount paid to date by the allottee."

"The construction will have to be completed within three years from the handing over of possession of the site."

The bid was accepted on 10 March 1995, and it was expected three months were sufficient to get the plans approved for the superstructure and commence construction by June 1995. The second and third installments were to be paid on 10 March 1996 and 10 September 1996, i.e., after 9 months and 15 months respectively from the date of commencement of construction. This facility was provided so that the construction could proceed at the site and allotted could book spaces and realize advances from prospective customers, and fully or partly finance the payment of the second and third installments from such advance payments/booking receipts. It will therefore be incorrect to state that there is no linkage between possession of the site, the commencement of construction, and payment schedule. Unfortunately, this could not happen, as HUDCO could only get its basement plans approved on 27 May 1996 after paying a compounding fee for getting the unauthorized constructions regularized, and construction could commence in July 1996 after a delay of thirteen months. You will therefore appreciate there is a definite commercial, technical, and moral linkage between the stages of construction, accrual of sales, and onward payments in any venture of this type and nature.

We would once again like to reiterate that the first extension of six months was granted on the fact that the sanctioning of the superstructure of the shopping arcade could not be processed by the Municipal Corporation of Delhi, as they wanted the earlier constructions of the basements, beneath the shopping arcade constructed by HUDCO, to be regularized and approved after the first extension of the same reasons for the delay in sanctioning of the plans continued. It was only on 27 May 1996 that the basement plans of HUDCO were approved by the Municipal Corporation of Delhi after HUDCO deposited a compounding fee. Thereafter, the Municipal Corporation of Delhi processed the plans for the shopping arcade and gave their approval on 10 July 1996. Since the same reasons continued to prevail even after the first extension, HUDCO should give further extension as sought by us, because the delay in sanctioning was for no fault of ours.

After the approval of the plans in July 1996, the construction work at the site is going in full swing, and mostly in two shifts. Part of the ground floor roof has already been cast, and work on a portion of the first-floor roof is in progress. This shows our earnestness and speed at which construction is progressing.

We need your support to decide our case on merits, fairly and equitably, so that the project does not suffer and HUDCO can realize its vision of a beautiful shopping arcade at HUDCO Place. It is an important project, and this landmark construction will be an important contribution by HUDCO and us to the citizens of Delhi. Hence, it is in our joint and expeditious interest to accept our request.

HUDCO considered there was definitely commercial, technical, and moral linkage between the stages of construction in the case of Ansals, but in the case of MS, Shoes kept their eyes and mind closed.

Chapter: Ten

HUDCO's Own Allotment Finalized on 15 October 1996
When MS Shoes Allotments Were Already Cancelled

Deputy Land and Development Officer, Ministry of Urban Affairs & Employment, Mr. L.D. Ganotra, on 15 October 1996, to Chief (Disposal), HUDCO regarding allotment of land to HUDCO at Pinjrapole, Andrews Ganj, New Delhi.

Regarding your letter No. HUDCO/AG/96 dated 24 April 1996 on the above subject, I am to say that the amendments in the terms and conditions which were communicated in the above letter have been accepted by the Ministry as under: -

Conditions No. Changes proposed by HUDCO

I. The word "within" 2 (Two) years from the date of handing over of the plot (2nd & 3rd line) may be deleted.

II. The word "separate books of accounts (1st line) may be changed to (separate account heads". The words should be kept in a separate bank account, and (10th & 11th line) may be deleted.

However, your request for amendment/deletion of Clause IX of the allotment letter is unacceptable.

HUDCO's own allotment of land by the Land & Development Officer was still not finalized, and the terms were amended in October 1996, but still the same was not accepted by HUDCO. It means HUDCO had no valid allotment until October 1996, as they were supposed to accept the terms within 30 days of the allotment letter dated 19 March 1996, in which the lease period was changed from 32 years to 99 years. Condition IX which was not allowed to be deleted by the Land and Development office, "The construction plans shall be got approved from the local body, DDA, DUAC, and the L & D O before undertaking any construction on the land". Was this done? Was it not a scam?

Senior Vice President (Marketing), Ansal Properties & Industries Limited, Mr. Pradeep Seth on 22 October 1996 to Mr. P.K. Garg Chief (Disposal) Housing and Urban Development Corporation Limited regarding Shopping Arcade at HUDCO Complex Andrews Ganj New Delhi

Rescheduling of Payment of Installments - This has reference to our Mr. Pradeep Seth's and Mr. Gogia's meeting with you, Mr. Anup Aggarwal Executive Director (Legal), and Mr. P.K. Agarwal, Deputy Chief (Finance) regarding rescheduling of payment for the second and third installments of the above project.

The committee agreed in considering the rescheduling of payments if we agree not to pursue further our claim towards damages and losses on account of delay in sanctioning of plans. This is to confirm that if we are given an extension of time, free of interest, in six months from 9 September 1996 to March 1997 against our claim for seven months for payment of the second installment and payment of 3rd installment, an interest-free extension of three months from its due date of 9 March 1997, i.e., up to 9 June 1997, then we would not claim any damages or losses on account of delay in sanctioning of Plans.

You have also asked us to confirm that ground rent is payable to us. We agree that ground rent will be paid by us as per terms of allotment and agreement to sublease dated 1 August 1995.

The Committee of HUDCO agreed to extend interest-free installments of both the installments not paid by Ansals for another six months. For all purposes, Ansals continued to get interest-free extensions, causing loss to the exchequer of more than Rs. 10 crores (US Dollar 2.82 million). *Considering the project to be in the public interest, commercial prudence was applied in the case of Ansals. In the case of MS Shoes, the project was not considered public interest, and no commercial prudence was applied in canceling and forfeiting the amounts paid by MS Shoes without giving possession of the land after receipt of the first installment. It was clear discrimination.*

Discrimination - *The effect of law or established practice that confers privileges on a certain class or that denies privileges to a certain class is discrimination under the Constitution of India. There are court decisions that prohibit discrimination in credit extension. The Constitution of India protects against discrimination. The differential treatment, especially failure to treat all persons equally, when no reasonable distinction can be found between those who are favored and those not favored.*

Moral philosophers have defined discrimination using a normative definition. Under this normative approach, discrimination is defined as wrongfully imposed disadvantageous treatment or consideration. This is also a comparative definition. An individual needs not to be harmed to be discriminated against. They simply need to be treated worse than others for some arbitrary reason.

Discrimination involves an element of unfavorable bias, and it is in that sense the expression must be understood in the context. Equal protection claims under Art. 14 are examined with the presumption that the State action is reasonable and justified. Discrimination means a difference in the treatment of two or more persons or subjects. The expression discriminates against means to make an adverse distinction concerning distinguishing unfavorably from others. A discriminator is a person unlawfully discriminated against. In the present case of MS Shoes, discrimination has been MS Shoes viz-a-viz Ansals.

Chapter: Eleven

HUDCO's Board Approved Another Interest Free Extensions of Ansals

The board of HUDCO in its 225th board meeting at Item No. 225.2.11 - Arcade at HUDCO, Andrews Ganj, New Delhi–M/s. Ansals letter dated 22 October 1996 regarding further extension of time for payment of 2nd and 3rd installments without interest.

The board in its 224th Meeting vide item No. 224.2.16 held on 26 September 1996 considered the legal opinion on the subject obtained from Shri Dipankar Gupta, barrister and Sr. Advocate, Supreme Court, and authorized the Chairman & Managing Director to constitute a Group to negotiate the matter with Ansals and re-submit the matter before the Board for consideration. In case it was necessary, Chairman cum Managing Director HUDCO constituted the Group as under:

1. Shri Anoop Aggarwal, Executive Director (Law)
2. Shri P.K. Garg, Chief (Disposal)
3. Shri P.K. Aggarwal, Dy. Chief (Finance)

The Group had a meeting on 22.10.196 with Shri Pradeep Seth and Shri G.R. Gogia from Ansals. No consensus was reached between HUDCO and Ansals regarding further extension of Second and Third Installments. However,

Ansals vide letter dated 22 October 1996, has intimated HUDCO reproduced below: -

"This is to confirm that if we are given an extension of time, free of interest in six months from 9 September 1996 to 9 March 1997 against our claim for seven months for payment of the second installment, and payment of 3rd installment, an interest-free extension of three months from its due date of 9 March 1997, i.e., up to 9 June 1997, then we would not claim any damages or losses on account of delay in sanctioning of the plan."

On the request of Ansals vide letter dated 21 February 1996 and 24 July 1996, the Board in its 218th Meeting (Item No. 218.2.12) held on 1 March 1996 and 223rd Meeting (Item No. 223.2.4) held on 23 August 1996 granted an extension by six months for the second installment without interest (in the 218th Meeting held on 1 March 1996) and six months for the third installment in the next Board Meeting held on 23 August 1996. It was not indicated in the decision whether the extension for the third installment was with interest or without interest. However, since the extension of time for the second installment was without interest, it is assumed six months' extension for the third installment accorded in the 223rd Board Meeting is also without interest.

Given the above Board's decision dated 23 August 1996, HUDCO vides letter dated 7 September 1996 informed Ansals that payments of the second installment and third installment were unrelated to any stage of development or construction, but to be fixed time payments. However, purely given the difficulties expressed by them, HUDCO agreed to grant them a final extension of time for payment of the third installment up to 8 March 1997.

The chronological order of details for sanction of building plans for Car Parking Basement and Shopping Arcade are given.

M/s. Ansals has yet to pay the annual ground rent amounting to Rs. 3.925 Crores (US Dollar 1.10 million), which is due from the date of possession, i.e., 10 November 1995, and has also not paid the second installment which was due on 9 September 1996 without interest. Ansals in its letter dated 22 October 1996 has stated that ground rent will be paid as per the terms of allotment and agreement to sublease dated 1 August 1995.

The financial implications on account of the extensions are given.

Since the Group reached no consensus, which had a meeting with Ansals on 22 October 1996, the Ansals' request for further extension of second and third installments was put up to the Board for consideration and further guidance in the matter. The Board may also confirm the extension of the third installment for six months, which was approved in the 223rd Meeting, was without interest.

The Board considered the above and approved.

HUDCO approved the extensions of both the installments interest-free to Ansals, purely given the difficulties expressed by them. HUDCO agreed to grant them a final extension of time for both the installments. In the meantime, Ansals continued to construct the property and sell the shopping arcade to prospective buyers, and started collecting the monies on further allotments to sub-sub-lessees. These extensions were subject to payment of ground rent due of Rs. 3.925 Crores (US Dollar 1.10 million) and a disclaimer on the non-judicial stamp paper. They will not claim damages for the non-disclosure of the illegal car park and other constructions of guest houses carried out in the Community Center.

In the first of the undertaking, Ansals did not issue the disclaimer agreement, and neither paid the ground rent, which reveals in the later correspondence between Ansals and HUDCO.

Chapter: Twelve

Fraudulent Concealment - Material Misrepresentation by HUDCO and Government of India

Executive Director, HUDCO, Mr. M.N. Joglekar on 29 October 1996 to Assistant Commissioner, Municipal Corporation of Delhi regarding Construction of type VI Housing, Guest Houses and Car Parking Basement of HUDCO Place, Andrewsganj, New Delhi: Completion.

HUDCO had taken up the construction of the above project in anticipation of sanction, as this was a time-bound project constructed for the Afro Asian Games. Recently, after the completion of the project, the Municipal Corporation of Delhi (Building Plans Dept., Town Hall) has regularized the construction and the necessary compounding fee deposited by us. The drawings submitted for regularization were the 'A Drawings' of the construction, and this was verified by the Engineers from the Municipal Corporation of Delhi Building Plans Department, during the inspection and subsequent regularization.

We were given to understand that this regularization was deemed to be completion, and accordingly, a meeting was convened with Mr. Sharma, Additional Commissioner, Municipal Corporation of Delhi, Town Hall, who suggested that the set of regularized drawings and one set for competition drawings be forwarded to your office for necessary action to obtain completion. We are pleased to forward the drawings necessary documents, as per the attached list, and request that you accord your approval at the earliest.

We also request that while the process of issue of completion certificate is being done, a NOC be granted for Delhi Electricity Supply Undertaking to provide electrical connection.

HUDCO being a huge company with a team of architects carrying out such huge constructions illegally and getting the building plans compounded, paying the compounded fee as penalties to Municipal Corporation of Delhi admitted in its letters that the buildings were constructed in anticipation of sanction. It is absurd to believe that HUDCO wrote to the Municipal Corporation of Delhi that the sanctions of the building plans were termed completion certificates of the buildings. HUDCO knew the truth that the building plans sanctioned were after payment of penalties, which clearly stated the buildings may be completed.

It is noted that the same was not disclosed to MS Shoes deliberately, intentionally, which was decided in the closed doors confidentially with the Ministry of Urban

Development that such disclosures be not determined while disposing of the properties. It was considered HUDCO has invested a huge amount in constructing the buildings, and the interest of 17% is being charged by HUDCO to the Government. It would be in the mutual interest to sell the properties without such material disclosures. This led to the concealment of material facts. These concealments have also been admitted by granting interest-free extensions to Ansals.

Concealment*–The act of refraining from disclosure, especially an act by which one prevents or hinders the discovery of something, which is also hiding the material facts. Concealment is an affirmative act intended or known to be light to keep another from learning of a fact of which he would otherwise have learned. Such affirmative action is always equal to misrepresentation and has any effect that misrepresentation would have. HUDCO was duty-bound to reveal the truth about the illegal buildings.*

Fraudulent Concealment *– The affirmative suppression or hiding, with the intent to deceive or defraud, of a material fact or circumstance that one is legally bound to reveal. It is the active concealment of a fact by one having knowledge or belief of the fact; (3) a promise made without any* *intention of performing it; (4) any other act fitted to deceive; (5) any such act or omission as the law specially declares to be fraudulent. The intentional failure to disclose a material fact, and especially a cause of action by one under a duty, to make such a disclosure to another who acts or fails to act in reliance and suffers a loss, is fraudulent concealment and leads to misrepresentation.*

Fraudulent concealment occurs when a party conceals or intentionally suppresses a material fact, which here HUDCO has deliberately and intentionally concealed they're not having title, and that the buildings were not having any sanctions of the local bodies, leads to fraudulent concealment and misrepresentation. A fraud victim can recover legal and punitive damages for fraud in a civil claim, holding the fraudster legally liable. In the present scam HUDCO along with, the Government has committed fraud with MS Shoes.

Material Misrepresentation *– The materiality of a misrepresentation is determined from the viewpoint of the maker, here HUDCO and Government of India under the Congress Government, while the justification of reliance is determined from the viewpoint of the recipient, here MS Shoes. The requirement of materiality may be met in two* *ways. First, a misrepresentation is a material, it would be likely to induce a reasonable person to manifest his assent. In the present case, HUDCO did material mis-presentations to induce MS Shoes to invest the amounts in illegal properties not disclosed by HUDCO.*

The white-collared Mr. V. Suresh, Corporate Planning Director, got himself promoted to the Chairman of HUDCO on 31 October 1996, on the retirement of earlier Chairman Mr. K.K. Bhatnagar. Mr. V. Suresh was politically connected, as he was doing favors to Government Officers, Ministers, as well as the officers of the Ministers, by providing free taxis billed to HUDCO, and cell phones and other gifts by him for many years. There were even newspaper reports exposing him later in the year 2002.

Times of India in the news of 7 June 2002 reported by Mr. Parul Chandra:

"How the Ministry got rid of HUDCO Chief ": reported that Mr. V. Suresh got all the favors from the Government by putting the bills of taxi and cell phone bills for Officers, the Ministers, and staff of the Ministers. Mr. V. Suresh had political connections, including in the Prime

Minister's office, who was removed by rolling back the retirement age at HUDCO from 60 to 58, but he would deny he had been removed. The board meeting of 7 June 2002 was scheduled for 4 June 2002, which was suspicious. The retirement age changed by the Ministry was to show the doors to Mr. V. Suresh by June 30, 2002. He was especially known to curry favors to most of the officials in the Ministry and the minister himself. He was caught footing the taxi bills for Rs. 11 lacs for an additional private secretary in the Ministry, providing office furniture, computer, and cook for the Minister. Mr. V. Suresh was termed as a liability both by the Central Vigilance Commission and Ministry, who had started probing charges of financial irregularities against him.

Another newspaper report in Financial Express on 6 June 2002 reported by Financial Express:

Rollback Blues: HUDCO Chief Retires: The Housing and Urban Development Corporations (HUDCO) most well-known face, V Suresh, made a quiet exit as chairman and managing director on Wednesday. But so will many others in the organization, since the reason for Mr. Suresh's exit applies to all of the rollbacks of the retirement age from 60 years to 58 years.

It was not a freak coincidence. Sources said that the Ministry of Urban Development, conducting a departmental inquiry against Mr. Suresh, issued a directive on the rollback of retirement age to make his exit from the organization a more respectable one. The HUDCO board of directors ratified the decision later. Since this decision has been implemented with immediate effect, more than a dozen HUDCO employees in its corporate office are rendered jobless overnight.

Mr. Suresh, who is well over 58 years, had finished his five-year tenure in HUDCO a few months back. He managed to get an extension until July 9. But with the rollback of retirement age, he had to go, said a source.

Mr. Suresh, who despite all charges can be credited with infusing competition for the housing finance sector by launching the HUDCO Niwas retail housing loan scheme, wanted to go strong with HUDCO for another two years.

The sources said he was regarded as friendly to urban development minister Ananth Kumar, and therefore could manage an extension. However, he fell out with Mr. Kumar recently, especially after the minister's own posting was in danger. There had been reports of Mr. Kumar being dropped in the long-expected Cabinet reshuffle. The ministry has got its joint secretary Pankaj Jain to take over Mr. Suresh's chair for the time being.

Interestingly, an official release, which begins with HUDCO being upgraded into schedule A company, inadvertently states, there is a need to bring in professionalism and dynamism in HUDCO operations and to reduce the formation of non-performing assets.

The organization will also be subjected to an inspection by the National Housing Bank.

The board has also decided to undertake structural changes by enhancing the powers of regional offices and doing away with the three-tier system. The zonal officers would henceforth have no role to play in sanctions and releases, but confine themselves to consultancy, business development, real estate development, default resolution, and carry out the financial, technical, and organizational audit of regional offices.

After retirement, Hirco Developments Private Ltd. announced in the year 2008, the appointment of V Suresh on their senior management team. He brings with him 43 years of experience in the public and private sectors. It is informed the company belongs to the Hiranandani group, who also remained as one of the directors of HUDCO for some time.

Chapter: Thirteen

Clear Scam and The Government Was Involved with HUDCO in the Whole Scam

The board approved the further extensions subject to approval of Government of India and subject to payment of ground rent dues of Rs.7.85 crores. (US Dollar 2.21 million)

The board of HUDCO in its 226th board meeting in item 225.2.11 meeting held on 15 November 1996 noted to avoid litigation, an early settlement should be negotiated and arrived at. The board further decided that the facts of the case, as indicated in the agenda, be studied further, and specific proposals are placed before the board for early decision, as desired by the board. The facts of the case have been studied in detail. The following facts are reiterated:

Handing over the possession of the shopping arcade site to Ansals for construction purposes.

As per the brochure of the shopping arcade site, the site should be given possession for construction purposes by June 1995, after the allottee obtains the necessary approvals from the concerned authorities. If for any unforeseen reason the possession of the site is not given to the allottee for construction purposes by June 1995, HUDCO will pay simple interest of 6% to the allottee on the amount paid to date by the allottee. The possession of the shopping arcade site was handed over to Ansals on 10 November 1995.

Delay in sanctioning of building plans of shopping arcade due to non-sanctioning of the building plans of car parking basement.

Municipal Corporation department vide letter dated 14 February 1996 informed that sanction of the building plans of the shopping arcade would be considered when the Municipal Corporation department regularizes/by compounded the constructed car parking basement. The Municipal Corporation department compounded the same vide letter dated 13 March 1996 and 8 April 1996. After regularization of the car parking basement plans. The Municipal Corporation department on the same day, i.e., 8 April 1996, forwarded the plans of the shopping arcade to the Delhi Urban Arts Commission and Chief Fire Officer. The Delhi Urban Arts Commission cleared the plan of the shopping arcade to vide letter dated 10 June 1996, and subsequently, Municipal Corporation department approved the building plans of the shopping arcade vide letter dated 11 July.

It may be observed from the above that the shopping arcade plans were held up due to the non-sanctioning of the car parking basement up to 8 April 1996. Therefore, from 8 April 1996 to 11 July 1996, was the processing taken by the Delhi Urban Art Commission/Micro Corporation department for sanctioning the building plans of the shopping arcade, which is entirely a matter between Ansals and the local authorities. This period has no linkage with the approvals of the local body to HUDCO for car parking basement construction.

The delay in sanctioning of the building plans of the shopping arcade due to non-sanctioning of a building plan of car parking basement work out to 5 months approximately from the date of possession of the site, i.e., 10 November to the date of regularization, i.e., 8 April 1996, of building plans of car parking basement by Municipal Corporation department, and 10 months 8 days from June 1995 to 8 April 1996.

The board had earlier approved an extension of the 2nd installment by six months, and the 3rd installment also by six months.

Keeping in view the clear directions given by the board, as well as the legal opinion earlier obtained on the subject, to avoid litigation and arrive at a negotiated settlement, and in commercial prudence. It is recommended the extension of 4 months 8 days can be given for the second installment. 2 months 4 days can be considered for the third installment.

However, because Ansals vide their letter dated 22 October 1996 (which was included to agenda item 225.211) had sought for six months additional interest-free extension for 2nd installment and three months additional extension for 3rd installment. HUDCO subsequently discussed the subject with Ansals. Accordingly, the revised communication received from Ansals on the subject is further given a confirmation for payment of ground rent amounting to Rs. 7.85 crores (US Dollar 2.21 million) for two years are to be received from Ansals.

Keeping in view the fact that this is a project implemented by HUDCO on behalf of the Government of India, and the total accruals coming from the implementation of this project will be utilized for general pool housing and financial implications involved in the extension, it is recommended that before the extension of time if approved by the board, is conveyed before a period of six months, government's consent is also obtained, and M/S Ansals has paid ground rent for two years amounting to Rs. 7.85 crores (US Dollar 2.21 million)

The board may also please confirm that the additional extension of time for the 3rd installment for six months, which was approved earlier in the 223rd meeting, and the subsequent decision to be taken for further extension for the 2nd and 3rd installment is without interest.

Executive Director, HUDCO, Mr. M. N Joglekar to the commissioner Municipal Corporation of Delhi in a letter on 21 November 1996:

We hereby give notice that I/we have completed the erection of the building executive of the works in plot no. Car Parking Basement Block No-HUDCO Place scheme Andrews Ganj. In pursuance of the sanction granted by the Authority vide File No- 1387/B/HQ/95/AE (ii)/241 Dated 28 May 1996, permission to occupy or use the building may be granted.

Sr. Vice President, Ansal Properties & Industries Ltd., Mr. Pradeep Seth on 22 November 1996 to Mr. P.K. Garg, Chief (Disposal), HUDCO Regarding Shopping Arcade at

HUDCO Place, Andrewsganj, New Delhi–Rescheduling of Payment of Installments.

Please refer to our letter dated 22 October 1996 and subsequent meetings with Members of Committee of HUDCO on 21 and 22 November 1996 regarding rescheduling of payment of installments of the above project.

In the meeting, you informed us it will not be possible to grant an extension of six months for payment of the second installment because our plans for the shopping complex were entertained by the Municipal Corporation of Delhi and forwarded to HUDCO on 8 April 1996. The Committee, therefore, felt that the maximum entitlement for an extension to us could be from 1 June 1995 to 8 April 1996, i.e., ten months and cight days out of which six months have already been granted, and therefore, the committee could consider further interest free extension of only four months and eight days towards payment of the second installments i.e., the second installment becomes due on 17 January 1997.

Although contractually there is a gap of six months between payment of second and third installments, we agree to a gap of four months and eight days between the second and third installments, i.e., third installments became due on 25 May 1997.

In case the above is acceptable to you, then we would not claim any damages or losses suffered by us on account of delay in sanctioning of our plans.

As desired, we reconfirm the ground rent will be paid as per terms of the letter of allotment and agreement to sublease dated 1 August 1995.

We hope the above will meet your requirements.

Senior Vice President (Marketing), Ansal Properties & Industries Limited, Mr. Pradeep Seth on 22 November 1996 to Mr. P.K. Garg Chief (Disposal) Housing and Urban Development Corporation Limited regarding Shopping Arcade at HUDCO Complex Andrews Ganj New Delhi

Rescheduling of Payment of Installments - Please refer to our letter dated 22 October 1996 and subsequent meetings with members of the Committee of HUDCO on 21 and 22 November 1996 regarding rescheduling of payment of installments of the above project.

In the meetings, you informed us it will not be possible to grant an extension of six months for payment of the second installment because our plans for the shopping complex were entertained by the Municipal Corporation of Delhi and forwarded to HUDCO on 8 April 1996. The Committee, therefore, left that the maximum entitlement for extension of us could be from 1 June 1995 to 8 April 1996 i.e., ten months and eight days. Out of which, six months have already been granted, the committee could consider a further interest-free extension of only four months and eight days towards payment of the second installments i.e., the second installment becomes due on 17 January 1997.

Although contractually there is a gap of six months between payment of the second and third installments, we agree to a gap of four months and eight days between the second and third installments i.e., third installments became due on 25 May 1997. In case the above is acceptable, then we would not claim any damages or losses suffered by us on account of delay in sanctioning of our plans.

As desired, we reconfirm the ground rent will be paid as per terms of the letter of allotment and agreement to sublease dated 1 August 1995.

Senior Vice President (Marketing), Ansal Properties & Industries Limited, Mr. Pradeep Seth, on 22 November 1996, to Mr. P.K. Garg Chief (Disposal) Housing and Urban Development Corporation Limited regarding Shopping Arcade at HUDCO Complex Andrews Ganj New Delhi.

Rescheduling of Payment of Installments - This has reference to our pending request for rescheduling the installments on the grounds enumerated in our previous letters.

We would request you to kindly expedite the decision on the request for an extension of time because our bankers from whom we are seeking loans require a letter of extension so that the case could be processed and put up before their respective Boards. Banks need time to process the loan applications, and we are afraid that the time is running out against the extensions likely to be given, and the purpose of seeking extension would be defeated if the extension letter is not received sufficiently before the date of expiry of the extended period.

We hope you will appreciate our earnest desire to raise resources to pay the subsequent installments and therefore your cooperation is solicited to send us the necessary extension letter at the earliest.

Senior General Manager (Marketing), Ansal Properties & Industries Ltd., Mr. H.K. Varma on 26 November 1996 to Mr. P.K. Garg, Chief (Disposals), HUDCO regarding Shopping Arcade at HUDCO Place, Andrews Ganj, New Delhi–rescheduling of payment of installments:

We invite your attention to our letter dated 22 November 1996 seeking extension of time for payment of further installments due towards Shopping Arcade at HUDCO Place.

In paragraph three of our letter under reference, while agreeing to a gap of four months and eight days for interest-free payment of the third installment, we had inadvertently typed the date as 25 May 1997, which is incorrect and is a typographical mistake.

You will appreciate we have already been granted time for payment of the third installment up to 8 March 1997, which was the mandatory six months gap allowed by you at the time of inviting bids. We intended to count four months and eight days from the due date for payment of the third installment i.e., 8 March 1997, which had already been allowed to us by HUDCO, and therefore, the date of interest-free payment of the third installment will fall due on 16 July 1997 instead of 25 May 1997.

We accordingly request our letter dated 22 November 1996 be deemed as corrected as above, and the due date for interest-free payment of the third installment be treated as 16 July 1997.

Chief (Disposal) to HUDCO to The Director (Land), Ministry of Urban affair & Employment Government of India Nirman Bhawan New Delhi on 28 November 1996 regarding Shopping arcade at HUDCO Place, Andrews Ganj.

The matter was placed before the Board in its 226th meeting vide item 26.2.7 held on 26 November 1996. The decision of the Board is reproduced below.

"The board deliberated on the proposal at length. The board, after detailed consideration, decided that a further extension of 4 months and 8 days for payment of 2nd installment (from 9 September 1996 to 17 January 1997) and further extension for 2 months and 4 days for payment of 3rd installment from 9 March 1997 to 13 May 1997 be granted to M/s Ansals, subject to obtaining a suitable and unambiguous disclaimer on stamp paper from the party for any claims and payment of ground rent for two years amounting to Rs. 7.85 cores (US Dollar 2.21 million) by the party.

The Board further decided that, as proposed in the agenda note, the matter is referred to the Government for approval, clearly bringing out the background on the project undertaken by HUDCO on behalf of the Government and the proposal.

It was further confirmed, because of the circumstances, that the board explained to the board from time to time that the intention of the board was for granting the extensions without interest.

It may be recalled that the Andrews Ganj project is implemented by HUDCO on behalf of the Government of India. As per the terms of the allotment letter, the total accruals coming from the implementation of the Andrews Ganj project (Shopping Arcade is also included) are to be utilized for General Pool housing. Financial implications are involved in the extension of second and third installments.

The matter is herewith forwarded to the Government for approval. A copy of the decision of the Board along with the agenda is enclosed (bearing page nos. B 22 to B 83). The financial implications of extensions are given on page B-65 of the agenda.

HUDCO's board agreed to extend both the installments interest-free due from Ansals until the date of regularization of building plans of car park basement and guest house blocks, but in the case of MS Shoes, the amounts were forfeited. It is a clear scam, and the Government was involved with HUDCO in the whole scam.

Chapter: Fourteen

HUDCO Inviting Bids for Hotel Land Disclosing the Lease Yet to Be Executed in HUDCO's Favor Which Was Not Disclosed When Bids Were Invited from MS Shoes

HUDCO floated a brochure to sell the hotel land along with the car park, against which they have received 40% of the amount from MS Shoes, and the litigations were still pending against HUDCO. But HUDCO decided to sell the 5-star hotel land along with a car park and floated the brochure disclosing that the allotment to the successful bidder will be subject to pending litigation with MS Shoes. The reserve price was doubled as compared to the previous brochure under which MS Shoes bids were accepted.

The Financial Institutions and the banks who had given bridge loans to MS Shoes by paying the amounts directly to HUDCO jointly wrote a letter dated 22 November 1996 to the Government and HUDCO not to re-tender the properties as the amounts of the banks and institutions are involved.

- **H O T E L S I T E**
- **HUDCO Place, Andrews Ganj, New Delhi.**
- Housing & Urban Development Corporation Limited HUDCO Bhawan, IHC Complex, Lodhi Road, New Delhi – 110 003.
- Hotel Site at HUDCO Place, Andrews Ganj, New Delhi a Unique Offer

INTEGRATED URBAN DESIGN- The HUDCO Place, an integrated urban design complex with design control, graphic design, landscape, parking, and other common services, is being developed by Housing and Urban Development Corporation Ltd. (A Government of India Undertaking) under direction from the Ministry of Urban Affairs & Employment. It is a perfect blend of traditional ambiance and up-to-date modern facilities. A spacious Central Plaza has been designed to create an environment of social interaction. A Five-Star Hotel, two clusters of centrally air-conditioned Guesthouses, each with six blocks, a Shopping Arcade, a Cultural Center, and a swimming pool are the highlights of this integrated urban complex. The two Guest House clusters on either side of the Central Plaza are designed as self-contained units with facilities comparable to Star Hotel.

LOCATION- Located in the heart of South Delhi, HUDCO Place is spread over 17.6 acres of land in the Andrews Ganj area, flanked by Khelgaon Marg and Josef Broz Tito Marg. HUDCO Place lies midway between Ring Road and Outer Ring Road to the South, making it eminently accessible and suitable for the location of a Commercial Center.

LANDSCAPE- A 19 acre stretch of land is demarcated as a Green Zone with parks. Jogging paths and water bodies, including musical fountains, lie in the vicinity of HUDCO Place, offering an added attraction.

HOTEL SITE - HUDCO offers a Five-Star Hotel Site for sale on a sub-leasehold basis, measuring about 3 acres (11480 sq. mt. approx.) of land with permissible buildable space of 25000 sqm. Plus, basement of 4000 sq. mt. and height restriction of 36 meters. However, the height of the Hotel may go beyond 36 meters for the provision of services, subject to the approval of the concerned Local Authority. The hotel will be provided with a basement car parking space with the capacity to park about 415 cars in a separate area (already constructed) adjacent to the Hotel Site. The proportionate cost of underground built car parking space will be Rs. 21.00 crores (US Dollar 5.92 million) (fixed) and this will be allotted on a license basis. The allottee may provide underground linkage from the Hotel with the Basement Car Parking space. However, the construction cost of such linkages shall be borne by the allottee. The linkage space (760 sq. meter Approx.) will be allotted @ Rs. 15,500/- per sq. Meter on a license basis.

- Reserve Price for the Hotel Site: Rs. 96.15 crores (Rs. Ninety-Six crores & Fifteen lacs only) (US Dollar 27.13 million)
- Earned Money for the Hotel Sire: Rs. 2.00 crores (Rs. Two Crores only) (US Dollar 0.56 million)
- Cost of built BASEMENT Parking Space for 415 Cars (approx.): Rs. 21.00 crores (fixed) (Rs. Twenty-one crores only) (US Dollar 5.92 million)

Additionally, the amount of license fee will be payable @ Rs. 10/- per annum for the Basement Car Parking space and the linkage space.

PAYMENT SCHEDULE PAYMENT SCHEDULE

(Hotel Site + Basement Car Parking Space)

a) Within four weeks from the date of allotment - 40%
b) Within four weeks from the date of allotment - 30%
c) Within four weeks from the date of allotment - 30%

TERMS AND CONDITIONS OF THE ALLOTMENT:

1. No extension of time will be allowed for the payment of the first installment. In case of default of the first installment on the date specified, the

allotment shall, without any further reference to the allottee, stand automatically canceled, and in such a case, the earnest money paid shall stand forfeited. The Earnest Money Deposit (EMD) of the allottee would be adjusted towards payment of the first installment. The second and third installments will have to be paid on or before the dates specified in the allotment letter. In the event of the allottee's inability to pay the second and third installments on the specified dates, the allottee will have the option to pay these within three months of the dates specified for payment of the second and third installments with interest calculated @ 20 percent per annum on the amount of the installment due. If the allottee fails to pay the second and third installments within the time permitted hereunder, the allotment shall stand automatically canceled without any further reference to the allottee, and in that event, 50% of the amount paid up to that date shall stand forfeited, and the balance 50% will be refunded to the allottee without interest. Thereupon, HUDCO will be free to re-auction the hotel site.

It is noted the time for payment of the premium as per the allotment letter shall be the essence of the contract, irrespective of whether the allottee has been able to start the construction on the allotted hotel site or not due to any reason whatsoever.

2. Immediately after the payment of the first installment, the allottee, with the help of HUDCO, shall take all required approvals in terms of Chapter XX C of the Income Tax Act and Urban Land (Ceiling & Regulation) Act so that there is no delay in handing over the possession of the plot. If this approval is not accorded, HUDCO will refund the amount paid without any interest, and the allottee shall not be entitled to claim any compensation or damages from HUDCO.
3. Upon the receipt of the first installment of the premium, both for the hotel site and the built car parking space, as indicated above, the Agreement to Sublease will be made available to the allottee for execution for the Hotel Site, and upon its execution and compliance of condition, as indicated in paragraph 2 above. The possession of the Hotel Site will be handed over to the allottee for raising construction

4. The Hotel building shall be constructed within the parameters of the approved Urban Design Form after obtaining required approvals for building plans, etc., by the concerned local authorities and the Delhi Urban Arts Commission. The height coverage in the basement and such related development controls shall be as per the operative norms of the statutory authorities.
5. Allottee shall obtain clearance for Five Star rating for the Hotel from the Department of Tourism/Government of India/Competent Authority, and shall be responsible for making all arrangements as are necessary for the maintenance of the Hotel building, including the firefighting system and the services.
6. Allottee shall have to arrange electric and water connections from the concerned authorities directly at his cost.
7. Allottee will be required to complete the construction of the Hotel Site within five years of the date of handing over possession of the Hotel Sire on a license basis for the construction of the Hotel building on the terms and conditions as may be specified by the Government of India / HUDCO.

In the event of non-completion of construction within the stipulated time. HUDCO may consider granting extension if exceptional and unavoidable circumstances have prevented the allotted to complete construction within the stipulated time. The decision of HUDCO regarding the extension of the exceptional and unavoidable circumstances will be final and binding upon the allottee. In case the construction is incomplete within the prescribed period or the extended period, as decided by HUDCO. HUDCO will have the integrity to take over the land, along with the unfinished building with material fixtures, if any, on the site, without payment of any compensation to the allottee.

8. The land for the Hotel Site is given to HUDCO by the Government of India in July 1990 on a long-term lease of 99 years. The land will in turn be leased to the allottee on a sub-lease basis, co-terminus with the 99 years lease period given to HUDCO. The Perpetual Lease for Hotel Site is yet to be executed by the Government towards HUDCO. The lease and sublease and Agreement to Sublease will be in the form approved/specified by the Government. All costs for the preparation of the

required documents stamp duty, registration charges, and other levies of any kind whatsoever will have to be borne by the allottee.

9. Allottee shall pay annual ground rent to HUDCO at the rate of 2-1/2% of the premium for land for the Hotel site from the date of handing over possession of the Hotel site. The ground rent shall be revised periodically following the terms and conditions of the sub-lease deed. Property taxes and other municipal levies shall be borne by the allottee from the date of possession of the site.
10. Habitat Service Center (DSC), a Social registered under the Societies Registration Act, 1860, or any other agency identified by HUDCO, will be a maintenance agency for the common area/services. The allottee shall deposit maintenance charges with HUDCO, including depreciation (if any) for the common (car parking basement, roads, external lighting, etc.) of the complex with HUDCO in advance every quarter until maintenance arrangements are handed over to the Maintenance Society proposed to be formed by all the allottees following the provisions of the Delhi Apartment Ownership Act or any other agency established as

per the terms and conditions of the perpetual sub-lease document. The allottee shall be deemed to have agreed to become a member of the Maintenance Society and abide by its bye-laws. The tentative expenses are estimated to be around Rs. 50/- per sq. meter per annum of the buildable space (i.e., 25,000 sq.mt.) for the Hotel. An initial interest-free deposit equivalent to two quarters (i.e., Rs. 6.25 lakhs) will have to be deposited at the time of payment of the second installment for the Hotel Site, to be used as a Corpus fund for maintenance purposes by society.

11. Allottee shall not have any authority to sell, transfer, assign, or otherwise part with the possession without the prior permission of the Lessor/HUDCO. Allottee may, at the discretion of HUDCO, be permitted to raise a loan only for construction of the building and equipment, to mortgage the premises subject to such terms and conditions, including recovery of 50% unearned increase in the value of this land, as will be laid down in the lease documents, and subject to the first charge of HUDCO for the unpaid cost of land for

the Hotel Site, as well as other dues payable hereunder.

12. The Hotel site and the building constructed thereon shall not be used for a purpose other than a Hotel. Similarly, car parking spaces shall be used only as car parking and for no other purpose.
13. Allottee shall be permitted to use the permissible percentage of total covered areas for activities/trades, ancillary to the Hotel, as approved by the concerned local authorities.
14. Allottee shall not deviate in any manner from the layout plan nor after the size of the Hotel Site for the said purpose either by sub-division, amalgamation, or otherwise failing, which HUDCO in its discretion will be entitled to cancel the sub-lease and forfeit the amount paid by the allottee.
15. Allottee may license out the spaces meant for activities/trade up to permissible limits ancillary to the Hotel only, and for such purposes for which they are meant.
16. Allottee shall ensure the licenses of the space carved out of the area meant for activities/trade, ancillary to the Hotel, observe the general conditions of the sub-lease entered into between

allottee and HUDCO, and the lease-deed entered into between the HUDCO and the Government of India. The licenses of the spaces meant for activities/trade, ancillary shall not use or be permitted to be used the spaces referred to above or any portion thereof for any purpose whatsoever other than the prescribed use.

EARNEST MONEY

Earnest money must accompany the offer, as mentioned above. The earnest money would be refunded within a maximum period of 30 days from the date of opening of bids, without any interest to the unsuccessful bidders. The earnest money should be in a Demand Draft drawn towards "Housing & Urban Development Corporation Ltd." payable at New Delhi. If for any reason the EMD is not refunded within 30 days from the date of opening of the bids, simple interest @ 6% would be payable beyond 30 days.

Interested parties may send their offer in a sealed cover in three envelopes put together in a fourth sealed envelope.

- **ENVELOP I:** Earnest Money
- **ENVELOP II :** Technical information about the party containing viz:
    a) Name of the offeror and address
    b) Present Business
    c) Brief History of the offeror, with particular reference to financial parameters (enclose copies of Annual Report, Audited Balance Sheet/Profit and Loss Account of the last three years).
    d) Details of collaboration proposed, in any
    e) Experience in managing the business
    f) Any other relevant detail
- **ENVELOP III:** Price Offered
- **ENVELOP IV:** Will be opened only to those parties who have paid the requisite earnest money.
- **ENVELOP III**: Will be opened only after Envelop II is found to be in order.

Telephone - 091-11-464 9610 | Fax–091-11-469 7378/462 5308

The last date for submission of an offer is 29 November 1996 up to 2.30 PM. The offers will be opened on the same day at 3.00 PM.

Any further details can be obtained from the above address.

HUDCO reserves the right to reject any or all offers without assigning any reason. In that case, HUDCO will refuse the earnest money within 30 days of the date of rejection of the bids without any interest, and after 30 days with simple interest @ 6% p.a.

Any conditional offer will automatically stand rejected.

The said hotel site is a subject matter of litigation. However, the Honorable Division Bench of the Delhi High Court has, on request of HUDCO, to enable re-auction of the property, vacated the interim orders of status-quo. For any further clarification, please contact at the address given above.

HUDCO declared in the brochure disclosing that the said hotel site is a subject matter of litigation. However, the Honorable Division Bench of the Delhi High Court has, on request of HUDCO, to enable re-auction of the property, vacated the interim orders of status-quo. HUDCO still deliberately and wrongfully disclosed the High Court had enabled re-auction of the property. There is no doubt that the interim orders of the status quo were vacated, but

HUDCO took no permission from the Court for re-auction of the hotel property.

HUDCO in the present brochure disclosed that the lease had not been executed towards HUDCO. In the case of MS Shoes, HUDCO did not require such disclosure, which was a material fact to be disclosed. HUDCO even in the present brochure disclosed that the Government had given the land to them in July 1990 on a long-term lease, which means six years' lease had already expired, which was not disclosed in the brochure under which the bids of MS Shoes were accepted. This aspect is further admissions by HUDCO, which establishes the non-disclosures by HUDCO concealing material facts, as until then HUDCO did not have the allotment of 99 years' lease in their favor.

The Financial Institutions and the banks who had given bridge loans to MS Shoes by paying the amounts directly to HUDCO jointly wrote a letter dated 30 November 1996 to the Government not to re-tender the properties and keep them in abeyance as the amounts of the banks and institutions are involved. Since HUDCO did not stop re-tenders top to re-tender the properties, the banks and financial institutions filed the recovery proceedings against MS Shoes, restraining them from selling any properties.

Chapter: Fifteen

Leela Hotel's Proximity with HUDCO's New CMD Earlier Corporate Planning Director, Mr. V. Suresh

Leela Hotels were eager to bid for the 5-star hotel land against the above brochure. The director of Leela Hotels Limited, Mr. Vivek Nair, is known to the Minister Mr. M. Arunachalam, who was at the relevant time the labour minister. He met the minister as Mr. V. Suresh, the Corporate Planning Director, informed him orally that in the last tender of the Guest House blocks. Mr. M. Arunachalam, the then Minister of Urban Development, had to stop the tenders by directing HUDCO on 14 June 1996.

The call was received from the Minister's office that Mr. Pavan Sachdeva should meet Mr. Vivek Nair, as he is interested in a settlement of 5-star hotel land in litigation with MS Shoes. Pavan Sachdeva met him at the Taj Hotel in his suite where he was staying. Mr. Vivek Nair informally sought all the information from Mr. Pavan Sachdeva and used the same to bid for the property of 5-star hotel land with a car park. At this time, Mr. Pavan Sachdeva did not know the problem of the land use, non-sanction of layout plans, and that the car park was illegal since HUDCO had concealed all these facts, including the title, towards HUDCO.

Thereafter, Mr. Vivek Nair also met the Commissioner Municipal Corporation of Delhi, Mr. Vinod Duggal, about the sanction of the building plans for the hotel.

Mr. Vivek Nair advised Mr. V. Suresh, the Corporate Planning Director, who was the real villain behind the fall of MS Shoes, said that HUDCO will apply to dismiss the suit. Mr. Vivek Nair also took the legal advice of the Lawyers and met the Lawyers of HUDCO to bid for the property. Mr. V. Suresh assured Mr. Vivek Nair that he will get the suit of MS Shoes dismissed.

Due to the inference of Mr. Vivek Nair in proximity with Mr. V. Suresh, Corporate Planning Director, who was solely responsible for the Andrews Ganj Project, the bids being invited on 29 November 1996 were postponed to 26 December 1996 with a proposal that HUDCO would get the suit of MS Shoes dismissed.

Now thereafter, Mr. Vivek Nair of Leela Hotels continued to pursue a dismissal of the suit of MS Shoes.

Mr. Pavan Sachdeva requested Mr. M. Arunachalam to call Mr. V. Suresh to stop the re-tender. Mr. V. Suresh was called by Mr. M. Arunachalam, he in an egoistic manner told "Five-Star hotel is gone to Mr. Vivek Nair" "Now he should only try to save guest house blocks".

On the insistence of Mr. Vivek Nair having the smartest relation with Mr. V. Suresh, HUDCO file an application on 5th December 1996 in the High Court of Delhi, being I.A. No. 12352 of 1996 in Suit No. 275 of 1996 for dismissal of the suit of MS Shoes, stating:

In any event, even on the pleadings in the suit, the reliefs of declaration and consequential relief of permanent injunction claimed by the MS Shoes cannot be granted in law. The HUDCO most respectfully submits the allotment originally been towards the MS Shoes has been terminated on account of default by the MS Shoes in payment of the installments within the time specified in the letter of allotment. That because of the cancellation of the letter of allotment, concerning the hotel site and car parking space, the suit itself has become infructuous and is liable to be dismissed.

That the HUDCO, being a company owned by the Government of India, is desirous to re-auction the property in the public interest. However, it is submitted that when the HUDCO attempted to re-auction other properties of

Guest House Blocks situated at the HUDCO Place, which was allotted to the MS Shoes and is a subject matter of Suit No. 1062/95 pending in this Honorable Court, the re-auction was unsuccessful, although the response to an advertisement issued was excellent, the interested parties not being desirous of participating in the bid given the pendency of the litigation which was, as duty-bound, disclosed in the brochure prepared for the purpose

The pendency of the litigation is causing grave and irreparable loss and injury to the HUDCO in as much as, on account of the pending suit, it is being unable to freely re-auction the property to obtain the best price as it is bound to do in the public interest. It is further submitted the HUDCO has made capital investments in the property, which it must recover immediately, so that other projects of the HUDCO are not jeopardized. It is further submitted the HUDCO is also having to unnecessarily bear other additional costs towards maintenance, and other levies, etc. on the suit properties, and would have to continue to do so until it is re-auctioned.

That the continued pendency of the litigation, although the MS Shoes is not entitled to any of the reliefs sought in the plaint, and that the suit is not only infructuous, but also vexatious and frivolous, because the MS Shoes is in breach of its obligation under the letter of allotment, and the letter of allotment stands validly terminated, is causing irreparable loss and injury to the HUDCO who is unable to re-auction the said property.

That given the above facts and circumstances, it is most respectfully submitted it would be in the interest of justice to dismiss the suit.

HUDCO admittedly stated the suit of MS Shoes had become infructuous since the relief of declaration sought in the suit cannot be granted, as the allotment stands canceled and the amounts stand forfeited.

Noting of the ministry: Mr. Dhiman, Under Secretary, Ministry of Urban Development–8 December 1996 put up the note to the Joint Secretary of the Ministry for extension of Ansals installments:

The project was entrusted in 1990, through the time various developments have taken place, and while in the intervening period, a sizeable realization has been created by the HUDCO, it is observed the project has not been going smoothly because, in the process, the hotel project and the Community Center Project, which was through the auctions bids taken by the MS Shoes, has gone in litigation, and the party having made payment 50% of the amount has not been in a position to pay the subsequent dues, from which the HUDCO has canceled the allotment.

Further, in some cases, due to a resultant delay in submission/approval of the plans in respect of the components to be constructed by HUDCO, i.e. two-story basement and construction of Shopping Plaza thereon, it is understood the bidders have been claiming an extension of time for payment of the due installment without levy of interest, the HUDCO has accepted which request without prior approval of the Government, and thus resultant loss of the interest as would have been payable by the parties due to deferred payments.

Earlier, the progress of the project was being monitored by the Empowered Committee, but later it was decided the project will be monitored by the board of directors of the HUDCO, which will be apprising the Ministry of various developments through the monthly reports. However, these reports have not been forthcoming regularly, and on certain occasions when the matter was raised through the Parliament Questions or litigation ensured, information was even furnished to the Ministry as and when required.

To date, it is anticipated that major components of the project, i.e., Hotel Site, Community Center, is already locked in litigation, and the matter of Shopping Arcade, auctioned at Rs. 168.80 Crores (US Dollar 47.64 million), 50% of the amount was received on 6 April 1995, but the second installment by six months, i.e., up to 9 September 1996, without seeking the prior approval of the Ministry.

In the meantime, the allotted institution approached the HUDCO for the execution of the supplementary lease deed, but in the absence of the lease deed being executed by the Land & Development Office, action on that account could not be taken by the HUDCO. The ministry even examined the matter, and the Land & Development Office was requested to execute the lease deed to enable the HUDCO to take action for the execution of the sub-lease. However, the file was received back from the Land & Development Office on 25 November 1996.

On getting a reference from HUDCO, intimating that the board of directors in its meeting held on 26 November 1996 decided that a further extension of 4 months and 8 days for payment of the second installment from 9 September 1996 to 17 January 1997, and extension of 2 months and 4 days for payment of the third installment (from 9 March 1997 to

13 May 1997) being granted to Ansals, subject to obtaining a suitable and ambiguous disclaimer on stamp paper from the party for any claims and payments of ground rent for two years amounting to Rs. 7.85 Crores by the Party. The extension has been approved without a levy of interest.

Accordingly, the decision of the board has been referred to the Ministry on the plea that total accruals coming from the implementation of the Andrews Ganj Project must be utilized for general pool housing, and that financial implications are involved in the extension of second and third installments.

This matter was briefly discussed with Joint Secretary (Urban Development) when Executive Director (Legal) HUDCO at the instance of Chairman-cum-Managing Director, HUDCO, called on Joint Secretary (Urban Development). It was believed the issue involves heavy financial implications, and a decision thereon would require the concurrence of the Finance Ministry vis-à-vis, taking into consideration relevant factors, including the legal overtones. The representation of the HUDCO mentioned the party after 9 December 1996, i.e., the date allowed obtaining payment may even institute legal proceedings for not granting an extension of time, and this project may also undergo problems.

After detailed deliberation on the subject matter, it was held the entire position needs to be gone into before a final decision on deferring indictment payment is endorsed, because it has financial implications to the tune of about Rs. 11 Crores (US Dollar 3.01 million).

In the above background, it is held we should ask for the Status Report from the HUDCO in respect of different facets of the project, and then take a view about the future course of action in consultation with all concerned, including finance, law, etc.

Noting on 9 December 1996 of Mr. Dhiman, Under Secretary, and Ministry of Urban Development to the Joint Secretary:

This relates to the grant of extension for payment of 2nd & 3rd installment by M/s. Ansals in respect of Shopping Plaza, Andrews Ganj, New Delhi. In this connection, the preceding note from the middle of page 61/N onward may kindly be identified.

After recording the note, the position was reviewed with Mr. P.K. Garg and Mr. Anup Aggarwal of HUDCO. A brief note furnished by HUDCO is placed at Slip 'X'. The financial implications on account of extension of time given to Ansals Properties for deferment of installment contained in the 'D' placed at Slip 'Y' and cash flow statement as on 31 March 1996 is placed at Slip 'Z'.

Consequently, it would reveal the party has already been allowed an extension of time by six months up to 9 September 1996 in respect of the second installment. As regards the third installment which was due on 9 September 1996, an extension has been granted up to 8 March 1997, whereas interest liability is Rs. 69,54,994 and Rs. 46,36,630 per month in respect of the amount payable on account of second and third installments.

The board of directors of HUDCO has already recommended an extension of time for payment of the second installment from 9 September 1996 to 17 January 1997, and an extension of time for two months 4 days for payment of the third installment from 9 March 1997 to 13 May 1997, subject to obtaining a disclaimer and payment of ground rent for two years amounting to Rs. 7.85 Crores (US Dollar 2.21 million) by the party.

In this connection, it may be stated that deferring payment of installment results in denial not only of the principle, but also a waiver of the interest which otherwise would have been levied, and non-payment thereof could even result in the property. The HUDCO has apparently allowed the extension after negotiating with the party, which would have otherwise claimed damages for not being in a position to execute the project due to delay. In getting sanctioned by the HUDCO through the Municipal Corporation of Delhi of the basement portion of the Shopping Arcade Plaza, on which the construction was to commence after the basement has been constructed.

While the delay in making available the possession of land is to the extent of about 5 months, the party has already been allowed an extension of time by six months, and thereafter any extension normally would have attracted the provision of payment of interest. However, the plea taken by the party appears their money amounting to Rs. 85 Crores was locked, and the construction process has been delayed on account of the non-availability of the site for executing further construction, for which they are legally entitled to claim damages if the matter is agitated before the legal forum. As a settlement, HUDCO through its board of directors has recommended further extension is referred to above without recovering the interest vide para 3 above.

In the given situation, it would have been appropriate to allow extension without levy interest in respect of the second installment by six months only, and the party asked to make payment on the due date, i.e., 9 September 1996, and thereafter the party could be allowed to compel payment of the second installment on payment of interest with effect from 9 September 1996 plus penal interest on or before 8 March 1997.

However, there appears to be some rationale in deferring the third installment, because the construction process has, in a way, been shifted by six months. Therefore, in respect of the third installment, an extension of time could be allowed for six months from 9 September 1996 on the apology of extension granted earlier for six months in respect of payment of second installment & party may be allowed to compel payment of the third installment without interest up to 8 March 1997.

In this connection, it may be submitted HUDCO had recommended an interest-free extension of the second installment up to 17 January 1997, and in respect of the third installment from 9 September 1996 to 13 May 1997.

Submitted for kind consideration and orders whether we may take action with respect to W. R. T. para 7 and 8 above.

Joint Secretary (Urban Development) on 9 December 1996, this deals with the grant of extension for payment of 2nd and 3rd installments by Ansals in respect of Shopping Plaza in Andrews Ganj to HUDCO. The preceding notes explain in detail the background. The review of the entire project should be taken up in its entirety in light of the various recent developments/litigations. As regards the extension of time for payment of installments, the HUDCO shall have to explain why the Government was not involved with him in the decisions regarding deferment earlier.

While deciding the issues related to the payment of 2nd and 3rd installments vide suggestions recited in paragraphs 7 & 8 of the note above, the element of delay in handing over the site, and in getting the plan approved for the basement to need to be discussed.

Mr. B.R. Dhiman, 9 December 1996–The case was briefly discussed with Joint Secretary (Urban Development) when a director (Land), director (Finance), and the undersigned were present.

It was decided that an interim reply could go to HUDCO, intimating that the matter is under consideration by the Government.

After brief deliberations, it was believed that allowing extension to compel payment of the second and third installment by HUDCO needed to. The de-linked from the review of the Project and a decision taken quickly in the light of this, the preceding note may kindly be identified, and the proposal contained therein para 7 is submitted for consideration and approval.

The Director (Land): Preceding notes may kindly be seen, marked to Joint Secretary

Joint Secretary (Urban Development) submitted to Joint Secretary (Finance) may please see for concurrence on the proposal at para 7 & 8 on page 65/ante.

The Joint Secretary (Finance) sent the note back on 10 December 1996, writing "please examine".

Under Secretary, Ministry of Urban Affairs & Employment, Mr. B.R. Dhiman, on 9 December 1996 to Chief (Disposal), HUDCO regarding Shopping Arcade at HUDCO Place, Andrews Ganj, New Delhi slotted to M/s. Ansals – regarding further extension of time for payment of 2nd and 3rd installments.

I am directed to refer to the correspondence resting with your letter No. HUDCO/AG/SA/96 dated 28 November 1996 on the above-cited subject matter, and to say that the matter is under consideration of the Government.

*A Newspaper report appeared in Pioneer reported by Mr. Punnoose Tharyan: "**Ansals pay peanuts for HUDCO land," "Rs. 100 per month for 1169 sq. meter in South Delhi":***

"If the Housing and Urban Development Corporation (HUDCO) is to be believed, land prices have crashed in the capital, or else why would they rent out 1,169 square meters of land in South Delhi for a measly Rs.100 per month?"

Accordingly, to a License deed signed between HUDCO and Ansals, the Delhi-based construction firm (a copy of which owns the reporter), Ansals were given a license to use

1,169.42 square meters at Delhi's Andrews's Ganj area for Rs. 100 per month for three years.

Incidentally, the current price prevailing in the area for the land is around 90 crores, for which Ansals have had to pay only Rs 1200 annually. And as if to emphasize their so rosiness. HUDCO has said in its deed that the above license fee shall be payable for the entire three years period in advance at the time of handing over the space through a bank draft payable at Delhi. The total amount in question is a mere Rs. 3600.

It needs to be pointed out that this license deed executed on 10.11.1995 by HUDCO and Ansals Properties & Industries Limited (APIL) is through the representative of the president of India.

The land was given at a site adjacent to another site, which was allotted to Ansals for a shopping arcade, which Ansals procured for around Rs.168 crore (US Dollar 46.49 million).

And whereas to construct the shopping arcade and execute the other related works efficiently, the licensee (Ansals) has approached the licensor (HUDCO) for grant of license to use some space in the said complex for construction of the shopping arcade, a construction office, and for stacking building materials and working area around the proposed shopping arcade structure, the license deed said.

Ever since it was given a license for the land, Ansals have put the 1,169 square meters to their fullest advantage, so much so that they continue to use it commercially for selling their shop offices which are to come up at their adjacent land. This exercise was vegan as early as November 1995, when the business group was allotted a shopping arcade site

Ellis Richard the UK-based property broker roped in by Ansals is selling space for Ansals from the authorized site. Attractive brochures printed on behalf of the Ansal were procured by the Pioneer from the site. The brochure has the address of Ellis Richard, and one of the contact addresses given includes that of the site, which was originally licensed for stacking construction material.

The brochures which give details of the space prices contain addresses of various Ansal offices.

These include that of its registered office in Delhi, the site office (though it does not specifically mention it is a site office), and offices in Bangalore, Mumbai, the UK, Dubai, Kuwait, and Bangkok. Point 11 of the deed of so says that the license shall be liable to cancellation in case of breach of any terms and conditions on the part of the licensee.

The Licensor shall however give a notice of seven days in writing calling upon the licenser to show cause on account of breach of any terms and conditions.

But then it can be pointed out that HUDCO has been causing the cancellation threat frequently in all its communications to the Ansals concerning the allotment of the shopping arcade sites. Surprisingly. It never carried these threats out despite several slips' ups on the part of the builders. ``

The above reveals the favoritism by HUDCO, which I would name as a scam by HUDCO. What is the opinion of the readers?

Ansals were well-known builders in Delhi who had proximity with all the Officers of the Ministry of Urban Development and HUDCO's Officers, including the board members. Ansals were granted extensions to further interest-free installments on the plea of approval from the Government. The noting of Mr. B.R. Dhiman put up to higher officers is interesting to observe that the monthly loss of interest has been shown in lacs, while the ground rent due is shown in crores, the trick of the officers placing the note for approval. However, it seems Joint Secretary Finance sent back the note for examination again.

Chapter: Sixteen

HUDCO Earned 13% P.A Monthly Compounded Interest on The Surplus of The Amount Received from MS Shoes

The Competition Certificate of the car park basement allotted to MS Shoes was rejected in December 1996, while the allotments of MS Shoes were canceled on 1 January 1996, given which in any case HUDCO could not have demanded the 2nd installment from MS Shoes nor could have canceled the allotments of MS Shoes. The buildings were constructed with many violations which required compounding or rectifications, and in any case, HUDCO was liable to be prosecuted by the Municipal Corporation of Delhi for building an illegal car park basement at HUDCO Place, Andrews Ganj.

Zonal Engineer (Building)/Central Zone, Municipal Corporation of Delhi on 13 December 1996 to M. N Joglekar, the Executive Director Housing & Urban Development Corp. Limited., regarding Rejection of occupancy certificate in respect of the premises' car parking basement, HUDCO Place, Andrews Ganj filed no. 70/CC/96.

I am to inform you that your application dated 21 November 1996 for the grant of occupancy certificate for the above premises is refused due to the following defects/deviations from the sanctioned building plans in question.

1. Photographs of the building duly attested by the architect signed by owner-front, side, and top view-not submitted.
2. No objection certificate from Chief Fire Officer as per condition laid down as per Chief Financial Officer communicated to you, as mentioned in the sanctioned letter, be submitted.
3. Three sets of completion drawings be submitted.
4. The one set of drawings submitted with the Completion Certificate is simply a copy of the sanctioned plan, as such three sets of completion drawings are submitted.
5. C & D forms will be compounded after compliance with the above.
6. Structural stability certificate is submitted.

Note: However, the case can be considered for the grant of a Completion Certificate if the deviations mentioned from items no. 1 to 6 are regularized with payment of a compounding fee, and the deviations from items No. 1 to 6 are removed /rectified being noncompound able. This may be noted that in case you fail to comply with these instructions, we will be constrained to launch prosecution against you under section 346 of the Delhi Municipal

Corporation Act, 1957 for occupying the premises without obtaining the occupancy certificate, and to take deliberation action u/s 343/344 of the Delhi Municipal Corporation Act on the above-listed observations.

Ms. Neena Garg, Director (Finance) from Finance Ministry on 19 December 1996 regarding extensions granted to Ansals:

The issue relates to handling over the shopping arcade premises at M//s. Ansals without any encumbrances. Apparently, the only hitch in handing over the site was clearance/regularization of car parking space by the Municipal Corporation of Delhi.

It is not clear as to how and why HUDCO undertook the construction of basement parking without getting the plans approved/sanctioned by the Municipal Corporation of Delhi.

Despite the above HUDCO, having handed over the site to Ansals on 10 November 1995 should have, as a proper financial procedure, insisted upon Ansals to pay penal interest on delayed payment on 2nd and 3rd installments, even if they were liable to pay 6% interest to the over the site in time.

The reasons for granting interest-free extension by the HUDCO board have not been clearly brought out, except for some mention of damages (not quantified) to be claimed by Ansals.

Keeping in view, HUDCO has provided the Municipal Corporation of Delhi clearance for the Shopping Arcade site only on 8 April 1996. This could be considered the critical date for all purposes, including the levy of ground rent and the date on which 1st installment was due. Therefore, the 2nd installment should be due only after 11 months, i.e., March 1997, and the 3rd installment six months thereafter. Thus, this date should also be reckoned with the levy of ground rent, unless the party has already agreed to pay the ground rent from 10 November 1995. However, we may agree to the negotiated dates of HUDCO, as brought out in paragraph 9, provided the party does not claim interest and damages on the 1st installment lying with the Government. The Director placed the positive note as Ansals approached her, but the Joint Secretary refused to comment.

The above note was put up to Joint Secretary (Finance) on 23 December 1996, who disagreed to comment on the proposal as a member of the HUDCO board of directors. It will not be in order for me to make any comments. The case may kindly be submitted to Additional Secretary/Secretary.

Chief Disposal, Housing & Development Corporation Limited, Mr. P. K Garg to Mr. R. P Shroff, General Manager, Hotel Leela venture Ltd. on 20 December 1996 regarding clarification given by HUDCO during the pre-bid meeting for the hotel site.

I am enclosing herewith the clarification given by HUDCO on the issues raised by the prospective buyers during the pre-bid meeting held on 12 December 1996.

In the pre-bid meeting held on 12 December 1996, the issues raised by the prospective bidders were clarified as follows:

1. HUDCO is unaware of any fee to be paid to the competent Authority for obtaining various approvals under the Urban Land court fee of Rs 10/- on every application filed with the competent Authority. The prospective bidder may also like to check this independently themselves.
2. HUDCO will have no objection to allowing the solicitors of the prospective bidders to inspect the

HUDCO court case file, however, no extracts will be allowed to be taken from the file.

3. HUDCO will not indemnify any successful bidder in case the High Court or any other Court passes any judgment against HUDCO in the suit filed by an earlier allottee, namely, M/s MS Shoes East Ltd.
4. In case the prospective allottee secures payment of the entire consideration towards the price of the hotel site, even before the hotel building is complete. HUDCO may consider granting the sub-lease documents, subject to the condition that the hotel building will have to be constructed within five years from the date of allotment failing, which HUDCO will be entitled to cancel the lease and resort to the remedies available to it.
5. Clause 7 in the HUDCO brochure seeking bids for the hotel site is a standard condition, and it will not be possible for HUDCO to delete this condition. However, as mentioned, the brochure in exceptional and unavoidable circumstances which have prevented the allottee to complete the construction of the hotel site within the stipulated periods HUDCO can always consider an extension. Further, HUDCO will have no objection to giving the notice

to the lender of the ultimate allottee before it exercised its right to cancel the allotment sublease in case requested.

6. It was clarified that the foreign company will have to obtain and submit the required approvals at the time of preparing the bid. Further, it was clarified that the foreign company will not be permitted to bid in the name of another Indian company on its behalf, as any transfer by the Indian company towards the foreign company will amount to transfer necessitating the payment of the unearned increase, as stipulated in the brochure.
7. Against what has been stated under Item No 10 (page 10) of HUDCO replies circulated at the pre-bid meeting concerning the maintenance of the common services in the car parking basement, it is clarified the maintenance agency will be maintaining the common areas and services on behalf of the allottee. The maintenance society, as far as possible, will take insurance against the fire, etc., of the equipment installed in the common areas, and for which it shall be responsible to the extent of the insurance cover. It is needless to mention that insurance in any case will have to be

taken on behalf of the allottee and funded out of the maintenance fund charged to the allottees. For any other incident, efforts will be made to determine if the ultimate responsibility of the damages, if any, will have to be shared by the allottees themselves.

8. In the layout plan approved by the Municipal Corporation of Delhi and Delhi Urban Art Commission, the site proposed for auction has been sanctioned as the site for a hotel. The allottee may construct on the allotted site a hotel building with a star rating and not necessarily a 5-star rated hotel.
9. The two basements may be constructed at 4000 sq. meter. Each is approved by concerned local authorities, i.e., Municipal Corporation of Delhi & Delhi Urban Art Commission, etc., provided the same is not counted towards the FAR. The FAR (Buildable area) and ground cover should not exceed more than 25000 sq. meter. And 4000sqmt. Respectively, both the parameters have already been approved by the Municipal Corporation of Delhi/District Urban Art Commission, while sanctioning the layout plan of the HUDCO place Andrews Ganj.

Chief Disposal, Housing & Development Corporation Limited, Mr. P. K Garg to Mr. B. R Dhiman, under Secretary (land), Ministry of Urban Affairs & Employment on 23 December 1996 regarding the use of land as a resource for supplementing. This is in continuation of our letter No. HUDCO AG/EP/96 dated 4 October 1996. Enclosed please find herewith the status of payment, Andrews Ganj. The Community Center project was on 20 December 1996.

This is for your kind information and further necessary action, please.

Status of payment, Andrews Ganj (Community Center) Project

(IN RUPEES)

Property/Allottee	Total Cost	Paid	Balance Due
Guesthouse / Restaurant, Kitchen/shops			
A-2 first Floor Tamil Nadu Electricity Board	27,285,520	21,828,416	5,457,104 (On Possession)
A-2 Second Floor Haryana Government	22,011,000	19,807,150	2,203,850 (On Possession)
A-2 Third Floor Evvell lignite Corporation Ltd.	18,996,000	17,096,400	1,899,600 (On Possession)

5-Block Karnataka Government	99,645,464	86,643,487	13,001,997 (On Possession)
6-Block Indian Oil Corporation Ltd.	91,343,478	79,319,982	12,023,496 (On Possession)
Natural Center Site Phoenix Overseas Ltd. Penal Interest paid	77,000,000	56,500,000 988,800	20,500,000 (Last Installment)
Shopping Arcade Site M/s Ansal Properties & Industries Ltd.	1,688,093,200	844,046,600	844,046,600

Telephone Exchange Mahanagar Telephone Nigam Limited	22,500,000	22,500,000	
Sub- Total	2,046,874,662	1,148,730,835	899,132,627

Disputed allotted Properties (allotted to M/s MS Shoes East Limited) The case is pending in the High Court, Delhi.

Guest House (9 Block) Restaurant / Kitchen (9 Block)	990,100,000	396,040,000	594,060,000

Shops (25Nos) Hotel Site & Car Parking	781,000,000	270,400,000	510,600,000
Final Interest paid for Guest Hotel Site		20,737,533	
	1,771,100,000	686,813,533	1,104,660,000
Total	3,817,974,662	1,835,544,368 (Amount received by HUDCO)	2,003,792,627

Allotments canceled.

The above establishes HUDCO had received Rs. 68,68,13,533/- (US Dollar 21.89 million) *from MS Shoes, which was forfeited illegally, deceivingly received the amount without the title in their favor and without disclosing that the buildings were illegal, unauthorized, and had no sanctions of plans.*

Chief (Disposal), HUDCO, Mr. P.K. Garg on 30 December 1996 the Director (Land), Ministry of Urban Affairs & Employment regarding Use of land as a resource for supplanting General Pool Accommodation–Status of Andrews Ganj Project

Enclosed please find herewith the following:

1. Details of the direct implementation of the Project by HUDCO. HUDCO Place, Andrews Ganj.
2. Cash Flow Statement for the project from the year 1989-90 to 31 December 1996.
3. Revised cost estimates for Andrews Ganj Project.
4. Status of receipts of Andrews Ganj up to 30 December 1996

This is for you or enhancing information and necessary action, please.

1. Cash Flow Statement for the Andrews Ganj Project from the Year 1989-90 to 31 December 1996.
2. Total Expenditure on the project

   77,83,50,877.71 (US Dollar 21.97 million)
3. Since its inception, i.e., 1989-90
4. Up to 31 March 1996
5. Total Interest charged by HUDCO

   16,29,01,822.11 (US Dollar 4.60 million)
6. On the investment @ 17% p.a.
7. HUDCO's overheads @ 1.5% of the

   1,16,75,263.17 (US Dollar 0.32 million)
8. Expenditure incurred
   A. Total 1+2+3

      95,29,27,962.99 (US Dollar 26.89 million)
9. Installment Receipts from the
10. Sale of Properties

    1,80,64,61,383.95 (US Dollar 50.89 million)

11. Interest @13% on the Properties

    11,42,94,706.53 (US Dollar 3.22 million)

    A. Total 4+5

       1,92,07,56,090.48 (US Dollar 54.21million)

12. Net Surplus HUDCO has on 1 March 1996 (B-A)

    96,78,28,127.48 (US Dollar 27.31 million)

    i. I.e., Rs. 96.78 Crores (US Dollar 27.31 million)

Note:

1. The interest payable to the Government on surplus is issued on the maximum interest rate offered by the State Bank of India on deposit, 13% at present.
2. The method of calculation of the interest and HUDCO's as per the decision letter no. J-13014/6/90-LD dated 14 September 1995.

The above reveals HUDCO charged the interest @ 17% p.a. on the investments made, and after realizing the amounts from MS Shoes on the surplus amount, they continued to earn 13% p.a compounded monthly from 1995 itself.

Chapter: Seventeen

Scam By HUDCO and Government of India Under Congress Government

The favorable note was put up by Director (Finance) on 31 December 1996 to the Additional Secretary for approving the extension of interest-free installments of Ansals:

May kindly peruse note 1 Director (Finance) on page 67/- only. The proposed paragraph may be approved, as there has been a delay on the part of HUDCO.

It is also for consideration if HUDCO should be asked to compensate for the loss caused due to their not taking prior approval from the Municipal Corporation of Delhi of the basement plans. This could be if approved, four dealt with separately.

Signed (Director, Finance)

Please get the statement showing what must be done/paid as per the original agreement/terms, what proposal to be done now, and the reasons, therefore, item wise statement required.

We may discuss thereafter in the procure of HUDCO representative & - Director/Finance,

Signed (Additional Secretary -Urban Development) - 3 January 1997

Reference Prepare, A statement is placed below as desired

Secretary may kindly consider the time and date convenient for discussion may also be indicated, so that Chairman Cum Managing Director, HUDCO, is requested to depute a representative.

Signed (Additional Secretary-Urban Development)-8 January 1997

*A newspaper report in Economic Times appeared on 8 January 1997 concerning Ansals who have failed to make payments on due dates and have applied for an extension of time. It has also been mentioned that in the case of M/s. MS Shoes no extension of time was given by the HUDCO. The Newspaper Report by Mr. Shubham Mukerjee reporting in Economic Times "**Favor not granted to MS Shoes" "Ansals fail to pay HUDCO fee again":***

"The Ansal group has failed to meet the December 31 deadline to pay the second installment for the shopping cum office complex at the HUDCO Place in Andrews Ganj.

According to sources, the Ansals have sought an extension of six months. This will be the third time the company has sought this deferment from HUDCO.

HUDCO sources say a decision to this effect will be taken at a board meeting on January 29. Though HUDCO has extended the favor to the Ansals. It had earlier canceled allotments of MS Shoes when it failed to pay the bid installments on a date for the hotel properties in the same complex.

HUDCO has since forfeited the amount paid by MS Shoes for the four-star hotel cum guest house property and the five-star hotel property coming up at the same complex and has also re-tendered the two sites.

HUDCO director finance regarding other sub-leases referred to a similar case as an exceptional benefit for Ansal when a similar exception was not granted to MS Shoes. He refused to make further comments on the issue, Chairman V Suresh could not be contacted as he is on an official tour. Ansal officials confirmed that they have sought a six-month extension for payment of the dues. They however refused to comment on the reasons for seeking an extension. The Ansals who had won the award for the plaza through a competitive bid were to pay around Rs 150 crores.

According to the payments schedule, 50 percent of the amount was to be paid within four weeks of receiving the allotment letter, which the company has since already paid. The property was allotted in March 1995.

The Ansals were supposed to pay a further 30 percent within 12 months of receiving the letter, and the third installment of 20 percent within 18 months both remained unpaid to date. Since then, the company has managed to get two extensions in June and September, sources stated.

Meanwhile, the Ansals are facing problems in selling the shop and office spaces in the complex, from the high rates being demanded by the company. Ansals officials say there are few buyers because the entire amount must be paid in white."

Ansals failed to pay their second installment, HUDCO understanding their difficulties extending interest-free installments, but on the other side canceled allotments of MS Shoes when the same car park was unauthorizedly allotted to both like Ansals had 210 car parks in the basement and MS Shoes had 415 car parks in the same basement. What do you think readers imagine? Is it not a scam or a scandal by HUDCO?

Reference to the note was placed as follows by the Under Secretary in the Ministry on 13 January 1997: -

1. The issue relates to the auction of the Shopping Arcade in Andrews Ganj Project to M/s. Ansal Properties & Industries was briefly discussed by Secretary (Urban Development) on 8 January 1997, when Additional Secretary (Urban Development), Joint Secretary (Urban Development), and undersigned were present. It was desired that for proper appraisal of the situation, connecting documents should be obtained from the HUDCO w.r.t. allotment of land, agreement for sub-lease and subsequent development w.r.t. request received for an extension for payment of installments, the reaction of the HUDCO thereon, action was taken for submission/sanction of building plans for basement area by HUDCO and Shopping Arcade area by the Ansal. It was desired that the correspondence exchanged in this regard need also be referenced.
2. In the above background, the matter has been discussed Chief Disposal, HUDCO, and a statement indicating the sequence of events from 10 March 1995 to 7 September 1996 duly referenced and supported by the documentary information is placed at Slip 'K' the same may be perused.

3. The collection of the relevant documents reveals the allotment of the Shopping Arcade was constructed on 10 March 1995, and as per terms of the letter, the party was to pay an amount of Rs. 168.81 crores (US Dollar 46.49 million) in installments representing 50%, 30%, and 20% of the total amount. The installments were payable on or before 6 April 1995, and the same was paid by the party in time, amounting to Rs. 84.40 crores (US Dollar 23.24 million).
4. As per the allotment letter and agreement for sub-lease executed on 1 March 1995, the second installment was payable on or before 9 March 1996, and the third on 9 September 1996.
5. The possession of the land was to be handed over by June 1995, and any delay in doing so would attract payment of 0.6% of the amount deposited by the party. Under the terms of allotment, the building plan was submitted to HUDCO by M/s. Ansals in July 1995 for forwarding the same to Municipal Corporation of Delhi. However, these were not initially forwarded to Municipal Corporation of Delhi by HUDCO on the plea that this was possible only after signing the agreement to sub-lease deed,

which was executed on 1 August 1995. Thereafter, the building plans of Ansals were forwarded to the Municipal Corporation of Delhi by HUDCO on 28 August 1995, but the same was returned vide the Municipal Corporation of Delhi letter dated 14 February 1996 informing that sanction of the Shopping Arcade would be considered when basements constructed by HUDCO are regularized/compounded following the building bylaws, among other objections with the Bldg. plan for the Shopping Arcade.

6. As regards the sanction of the building plan for the basement, it may be stated that though the construction of the basement was started by HUDCO in the year 1993-94, the building plans of the basement area were submitted to the Municipal Corporation of Delhi by HUDCO only on 8 November 1995. The construction of a basement was being executed by HUDCO without the approval of the Municipal Corporation of Delhi on submission of the building plans for the construction of a shopping plaza by Ansals. The Municipal Corporation of Delhi asked HUDCO to pay the compounding fee before the plans could be

sanctioned for the basement and entertained for the shopping area. Municipal Corporation of Delhi vide letter dated 13 March 1996 asked HUDCO to pay 7.6 lacs as regularization fee for car parking basement. The same was paid by HUDCO on 20 March 1996. On 8 April 1996, the Municipal Corporation of Delhi requested HUDCO to pay an additional compounding fee of Rs. 3.25 lacs, which was paid to the Municipal Corporation of Delhi on 18 April 1996. The HUDCO is yet to obtain clearance from Fire Officers & completion certificates from the Municipal Corporation of Delhi.

7. Thus, the compounding fee was determined for the basement area on 8 April 1996. The building plans for Shopping Arcade furnished by the Ansals through HUDCO were forwarded on 8 April 1996 by the Municipal Corporation of Delhi to the Delhi Urban Art Commission and Chief Fire Officer for consideration and approval, and the same for Shopping Arcade was approved by the local body on 11 July 1996. sanction of Shopping Arcade plans of Ansals was held up due to non-sanctioning of the car parking basement up to 8 April 1996.

8. The party delay in sanction of the building plan requested for deferment of the second installment by thirteen months, including six months of both the installments.
9. Keeping in view the various developments from time to time, the entire matter was examined by the Board of Directors of HUDCO in its meeting held on 26 November 1996, and it was construed that delay in sanctioning of the building plans worked out to 5 months approximately from the date of possession of the site, i.e. 10 November 1995 to the date of regularization, i.e. 8 April 1996, of the building plan for car parking basement by Municipal Corporation of Delhi, and 10 months 8 days from 1 July 1995 (i.e. the date of which possession was to be handed over) to 8 April 1996 (i. The Board had earlier approved extension of the 2nd installment by six months & 3rd installment also by six months, thus deferring payment of the 2nd & 3rd installments to 9 September 1996 and 8 March 1997 respectively.
10. Keeping in view the various factors, HUDCO obtained the legal opinion from Shri Dipankar K. Gupta, who advised that keeping in view the

relevant factors negotiated arrangements should be resorted to. The matter was discussed with the party, who vide their letter dated 22 November 1996, agreed to an interest-free extension of the second installment up to 17 January 1997 and up to 13 March 1997 in respect of the third installment. Accordingly, the Board of Directors in its last meeting has recommended an interest-free extension of the second installment by 10 months & 8 days, and the third installment by 8 months & 12 days i.e., up to 17 January 1997 and 25 May 1997 (Slip 'O') respectively.

11. In this context, it may be mentioned that as per terms of allotment/agreement to sublease, the payment of installments was fixed time payment and not related to the stage of construction developments. The HUDCO could allow 6% compensation to the party for the delay in making the site available for construction. However, due to delay in sanction of the basement, the building plans of the party for the shopping arcade thereon were not entertained by the Municipal Corporation of Delhi.

12. In all, there has been a total delay of 9 months & 8 days between the day when the possession was to be handed over, i.e., 1 July 1995, and the date of sanction of the basement plan, i.e., 8 April 1996. Even then, the building plans for a shopping arcade were submitted & scrutinized by the Municipal Corporation of Delhi & returned vide Municipal Corporation of Delhi letter dated 14 February 1996 with a proviso that the same could not be entertained without the regularization of the basement. If we take 8 April 1996 as a crucial date, the party is at the most entitled to an extension of time by 9 months & 8 days for the second installment which should have accordingly been paid up to 17 December 1996 without interest and with interest thereon, w.e.f. 18 December 1996 to 18 March 1997, and ask the party to obtain payment of the ending installment with interest up to 16 March 1997 as per terms of allotment, failing which the allotment will lapse. Similarly, the third installment will be payable by 13 May 1997. There is no need to shift the installment by a corresponding period of 3 months

and 8 days. This installment will also be payable with interest @ 16.48% on 13 August 1997.

13. Normally HUDCO should have Normally allowed extension after recovery of interest @ 16.48% on the amount payable, simultaneously allowing 6% compensation on the amount deposited, w.e.f. 1 July 1995 to 8 April 1996. In the above background, it may also be submitted that deferment of the 2nd installment involves monthly interest @ Rs. 69.54 lacs (US Dollar 0.19 million) and for the 3rd installment @ Rs. 46.36 lacs (US Dollar 0.12 million). Thus, there is an approximate loss of interest to the tune of about 10 crores. During this period, interest on the amount deposited by the party, i.e., Rs. 84.40 crores (US Dollar 23.24 million), has accrued to HUDCO, being credited to the surplus.

14. However, keeping in view the legal opinion and the recommendations of the Board of Directors of HUDCO, and also the fact that first deferment by six months in respect of both the installments has been communicated to the party by the HUDCO, re-opening of the matter at this stage will not seem desirable because the party have a sound

case with delay in entertaining of their building plans by the Municipal Corporation of Delhi, which has ultimately resulted in deferring the entire execution of the project, thus their claims for damages to some extent merit consideration: -

15. In the above circumstances, it is for consideration orders whether we may: -

    i. the party may be allowed compensation @ 6% to the amount deposited by it, w.e.f. 01 July 1995 to 8 April 1996, and while doing so, asked to obtain the payment of the installments as due as per the original schedule of payment, and for the delay as has taken placed asked to pay interest at the prescribed rates:

Or

ii. The first decision of the Board of Directors of HUDCO to allow interest-free extension of time for payment of the second installment up to 9 September 1996 and the third installment up to 8 March 1997, which has been covered to the party as well, maybe endorsed and the party asked to pay interest in respect of the second installment w.e.f. 10 September 1996 to 17 January 1997.

Or

iii. Whether given net delay of 9 months and 8 days occurred between the deemed date of possession, i.e., 01 July 1995 to 8 April 1996 (date of sanction of basement plan) extension of time for payment of the second installment as now recommended free of interest up to 17 January 1997 could be allowed interest-free (by adding 9 months and 8 days) up to 17 December 1996. The third installment up to 13 May 1997 may be allowed interest-free, as approved by HUDCO. The party will, however, be allowed to pay both installments within 3 months with interest as per provisions of the allotment letter.

16. The above proposal is subject to the party executing a disclaimer clause plus payment of up-to-date ground rent from the date of possession, i.e., 10 November 1995. Further, it may be mentioned that in the Economic Times dated 8 January 1997, it has been reported M/s. Ansals have failed to make payments on

due dates and have applied for an extension of time. It has also been mentioned that in the case of M/s. MS Shoes no extension of time was given by the HUDCO. This aspect also may be kept in view while deciding the matter. Press clipping to place at Slip 'N'.

Submitted for consideration and orders. Signed by (B.R. Dhiman-Under Secretary)

The position wrt para 16 portion 'XX' above has been checked up with HUDCO from a perusal of the ppo at flag 'P'. It seems that in the case of MS Shoes, the extension was allowed by the Court, but the party could not secure payment. Hence, the position is slightly different in the case of Ansals, where construction has been delayed due to the delay in construction of the basement on which the Shopping Arcade was to come up.

The above was discussed with the Secretary (Urban Development) on 13 January 1997, when it was noticed that opting (iii) above seems appropriate seems a current situation. Signed by (B.R. Dhiman, Under-Secretary) - 17 January 1997

Interestingly, it is obvious in the proximity of Ansals with the officers of HUDCO and Ministry that the proposal of extension of interest-free extensions was considered. Even the secretary agreed to option iii above, and it was admitted that yes, building plans of car park sanction were not sanctioned due to which extensions be given. But in the case of MS Shoes, the plea of HUDCO was accepted that the High Court had given an extension to MS Shoes to deposit the amount when the truth is the amount of Rs. 35 Crores (US Dollar 9.63 million) *deposited by MS Shoes was not accepted by HUDCO and the demand draft of Rs. 90 Crores* (US Dollar 24.78 million) *offered in the Court was not accepted by HUDCO because the value of the properties had doubled, and HUDCO, as well as Government, became greedy to realize extra amounts.*

Isn't it a SCAM by HUDCO and Congress Government leading to the disaster of MS Shoes?

Leela Hotels, who was the highest bidder in the bids invited on 26 December 1996, continued to press wise HUDCO to delay the allotment until the case of MS Shoes is dismissed, as per the application filed on 5 December 1996 by HUDCO in the suit filed by MS Shoes.

Chapter: Eighteen

Intellectual Advice of Dr. Sarabjeet, Advocate to Pavan Sachdeva, CMD, MS Shoes

Mr. Pavan Sachdeva had sleepless nights when HUDCO moved the application that the suit pending before the High Court has become infructuous, as the relief sought of mandatory injunction cannot be granted since the cause of action does not exist. After reading the newspaper report on 8 January 1997, it revealed to Mr. Pavan Sachdeva that Ansals were being given extensions of installments.

His Solicitors, Dutt & Menon, also raised their both hands that nothing can be done now and the suit is bound to be dismissed. Mr. Pavan Sachdeva started thinking of an alternative. He met on 12 January 1997, one of his friends, Dr. Sarabjeet, who was an Advocate, took the advice from him. Mr. Pavan Sachdeva, on the other side, was facing demands raised by the Municipal Corporation of Delhi for property tax for allotment of 5-star hotel land, car park, restaurants, kitchen, guest house blocks, and shops.

The demands of the Municipal Corporation of Delhi for property tax were to the tune of Rs. 7.00 Crores rateable value and the attachment of bank accounts notices were received from the Municipal Corporation of Delhi. MS Shoes did not have possession of the properties, and the properties were canceled as well, and we're not liable for payment of property tax, legally or otherwise.

The advice he received from Dr. Sarabjeet was valuable, as he advised that he challenge the cancellation as illegal, null, void, along with the possession. Municipal Corporation of Delhi be also arrayed as the first party, and the mandatory injunction suit is filed.

*Another Newspaper Report was reported on 17 January 1997 by the Chief Financial Reporter of Nav Bharat Times in Hindi. "**HUDCO sent the Andrews Ganj land extension approval to Government:***

The news in Hindi newspapers was that HUDCO has granted interest-free extensions to Ansals, subject to approval by the Government, but HUDCO confirmed the extension to Ansals through a letter in writing that the board has approved the extensions of installments.

*Another Hindi Newspaper reported "**HUDCO has sent to the Urban Development Ministry for approval in respect of Ansals":***

I could not translate Hindi to English, but the crux of the news was that the HUDCO board approved the extensions and sent it to the Government for approval, and clarified that the court had granted extensions to MS Shoes, besides the case of Ansals, is not the same.

*Mr. Punnoose Tharyan again reported on 18 January 1997 in Pioneer "**HUDCO defers action against Ansals,**" **"Real Estate giant defaults on installment for shopping plaza,":***

"Housing and Urban Development Corporation Ltd. has deferred taking any action against the Ansals for default of installment payment towards a shopping-cum-office complex at the HUDCO Place in South Delhi.

The Ansals had failed to pay the December 1996 deadline in paying the second installment for the shopping complex and had sought an extension of six months for paying up the said amount.

According to highly paced matters, the HUDCO board, which met on January 15, this year, not only deferred deciding on whether to cancel or retain the Ansal bid but also referred the issue to the Urban Development department in the Urban Affairs Ministry.

On one hand, while HUDCO has forfeited the first installment of around Rs. 70 crores (US Dollar 19.75 million) of MS Shoes for defaulting in the second installment towards the hotel site at ANDREWS GANJ LAND SCAM

On the other hand, it was soft-pedaling with the Ansals. MS Shoes had, it may be recalled, bid for the hotel property at a site adjacent to the shopping arcade bagged by the Ansals for the shopping complex.

The HUDCO board meeting held on Wednesday was attended by HUDCO Chairman Suresh, the Finance Director Sundershan, and directors Kirti Shah and BM Reddy. The Government directors on the board were conspicuous by their absence.

All efforts to elicit the views of Mr. Suresh failed despite a fax questionnaire being sent to him. This was attempted after the Chairman's office made it clear that Mr. Suresh would respond in written questions.

Surprising, HUDCO is soft-pedaling on taking any action against Ansals, even though the allotment for the complex had been constructed in the conditions along with several others that any delay beyond three months for payment of the installments would entail cancellation of allotment and/or forfeiture of the total amount deposited till date.

Of late, HUDCO has come under sharp criticism from a few prominent members of Parliament who have been advocating that HUDCO should refrain from re-tendering the hotel site in South Delhi since it would ultimately result in a loss of Rs. 300 crores of public money given to the previous allottee (MS Shoes) against the same project as unsecured loans by financial institutions and banks.

In two letters dated 4 January and 8 January, 1997 addressed the Prime Minister, who still holds the Cabinet portfolio of the Urban Affairs Ministry, a prominent Rajya Sabha member belonging to the Samajwadi Party has pointed out that "HUDCO is a government subsidiary and the norms and decisions of this subsidiary should be uniform and equal. But unfortunately, the then Chairman of this organization. Mr. K.K. Bhatnagar was moving HUDCO as an empire of his. Certain wrong decisions are taken to favor some people and to punish some other people are continuing.

One letter was sent on to say that "Even after repeated requests from financial institutions about the amicable settlement of balance payments of MS Shoes East Ltd., which was highlighted by several papers, nothing had been done till today to save public money. If the wrongdoings of the previous Chairman-cum-Managing Director are not undone by the present setup and if it continues with this unfortunate legacy, then I have my own apprehension about the future of HUDCO vis-à-vis the allottees".

A similar request had also been determined by another MP, Mohan Rawle, to the Prime Minister to HUDCO to fully finance the MS Shoes hotel project by passing on part Pari passu charge to the financial institutions/banks against the unsecured loans.

It was only after repeated requests from a BJP Member of Parliament last year that the then Minister of Urban Affairs Mr. M. Arunachalam had expressed in a confidential note in the public interest, it would be appropriate to stop the tenders of all concerned properties until further directions.

A public notice for cancellation of tender is issued in leading newspapers immediately."

It is understood HUDCO was courteous and obliging to Ansals. Their project was considered in the public interest at Andrews Ganj, but MS Shoes project in the same place was considered differently. My dear readers, what is it? Isn't it a scandalous attitude of a government-owned Company, and the Government of Congress was hand in glove with HUDCO?

Another Newspaper report appeared in NavBharat Times on 19 January 1997, ***"Why is HUDCO being sympathetic to Ansals":***

*Another report appeared in Financial Express reported on 20 January 1997 by Mr. Vishal Bakshi "**HUDCO seeks Ministry's Advice on Ansals Issue**":*

"The Housing and Urban Development Corporation HUDCO has decided to seek advice from the Ministry of Urban Affairs on the contentious issue of granting an extension to the Ansal group for the balance payment.

The Ansal group was to pay the balance of 50 percent of the total land price at Rs. 160 crores (US Dollar 45.15 million) *by March last year, but was granted an extension until June 1996, and then again until December 1996. Ansals have once against sought an extension until June this year, HUDCO sources said.*

HUDCO has put the ball in the ministry's court, as it is already in the thick of controversy for giving two extensions totaling nine months to Ansals, while it did not accept MS Shoes East Limited's application for granting an extension in the Rs.170 crores hotel project at the same site.

Sources in Ansals claimed the extension was sought given the poor stage of the capital market, from which it could not raise funds as planned interestingly. MS Shoes had also asked for an extension on similar grounds, but its application was rejected.

Second, the price asked by Ansals for the shopping cum commercial complex from prospective customers also did not evoke much response, company sources said.

At a board meeting of HUDCO last week, it was decided to seek the Ministry's advice but ruled out the cancellation of the allotment of land to Ansal as of now. Sources said that according to the agreement between HUDCO and Ansals, there was no provision of granting an extension after payment of the first installment."

HUDCO was controlling all ministry officials through their Chairman cum Managing Director V. Suresh, who used to oblige all by footing the taxis bills and phone bills, in respect of which he was caught and shunted out, but by then it was too late for V. Suresh made use of all the officers, even the minister's officer on special duty. V. Suresh had also used taxi bills being paid by Ansals and getting their extensions approved from the Government. My dear readers, what is it?

V. Suresh should have been punished criminally if it was the USA. He was totally a scandalous man.

Chapter: Nineteen

Fresh Suit 1/1997 In Respect of Five-Star Hotel Land and Suir 2/1997 Regarding Guest House Blocks Filed by MS Shoes challenging Cancellation Letter as Illegal, Null & Void

Dr. Sarabjeet prepared the suit, taking about ten days to prepare the suit which was filed on 24 January 1997 before the Trial Court at 'Tis Hazari, Delhi, and Mr. Pavan Sachdeva appointed Dr. Sarabjeet's brother whose name was Mr. Rakesh as his Counsel to appear.

The suit was filed on 24 January 1997 in the Court of District & Sessions Judge, Delhi by MS Shoes against Municipal Corporation of Delhi and HUDCO in respect of Five-Star Hotel Land:

Petition seeking restraint against Corporation from charging House–Tax and declaring the impugned letter as null and void, and directions there too;

That MS Shoes is a public limited company incorporated under the Companies Act, 1956, having its registered office at 5, NWA, Punjabi Bagh, New Delhi -26. The Chairman and Managing Director are duly authorized to institute and verify the present plaint.

That the Municipal Corporation of Delhi is the Municipal body of Delhi, given the due powers to act following the law. The Municipal Corporation of Delhi is liable to be sued for and against through its commissioner. The

HUDCO is a Company incorporated under the Companies Act.

1. That MS Shoes, having attended a high efficiency and an impressive level in his business regarding manufacturing and export of leather shoes and other footwear components, decided to diversify its operation by entering into an integrated hotel project. That Municipal Corporation of Delhi is the municipal body to collect/charge house tax from the residents of Delhi, as per the provisions of the DMC Act. Section 114-119 of the Delhi Municipal Corporation Act is clear to show the responsibility of the Municipal Corporation of Delhi. The Municipal Corporation of Delhi has wrongly assessed the house tax in respect to suit property by rateable value to the tune of Rs.3,90,50,000/- (US Dollar 1.07 million).
2. That the HUDCO, the alleged lessee in respect of a piece of land at Andrews Ganj, New Delhi, had allotted the said piece of land for putting up a 5-Star hotel. It was in June 1994 that the HUDCO invited bids for the said hotel projects, which included guest houses, shops, restaurants, etc. The MS Shoes

had given his bid for setting up the said 5-Star hotel project. The bid of MS Shoes was opened on 15 July 1994, and his offer was found most competitive, and the same was duly accepted. The site in question was allotted to the MS Shoes for 5-Star hotel and car parking site for total consideration of Rupees seventy-eight Crores and ten lacs only, it included Rs. Fourteen Crore (US Dollar 3.85 million) for the car parking site.

3. That the MS Shoes vide its letter dated 31 October 1994 accepted the terms and conditions, and the letter of allotment dated 31 October 1994 was issued. The MS Shoes had paid the first installment amounting to Rupee's Twenty-Five Crores Four Lacs earnest money deposited earlier. The MS Shoes also paid Rs. two lacs fifty thousand to the HUDCO's maintenance agency.
4. That HUDCO was to provide an agreement for sublease to the MS Shoes and further to hand over the site along with car parking space to the MS Shoes, to enable him to raise construction for the 5-Star hotel project. The HUDCO kept on avoiding too; to comply with its part of the Settlement/Agreement. The HUDCO neglected to

execute the necessary documents. The terms and conditions of the allotment letter and the further agreement clearly indicate the possession of the hotel side and car parking space was to be granted before the payment of the second installment. The Minister also restrained the allotment of the suit property.

5. That Municipal Corporation of Delhi has even produced an assessment of the guest house block in HUDCO Place, Andrews Ganj, New Delhi, towards the MS Shoes. The Municipal Corporation of Delhi has thereby started pressing for the demand in furtherance of the said assessment. It is pertinent to state that the HUDCO has vided its letter dated 31 January 1996, which demanded the further installment fail, which the allotment would stand forfeited. The MS Shoes represented against the said act. The MS Shoes clearly stated he was not liable to pay any interest, and further he was unable to pay the second installment from the act and conduct of HUDCO, part of the agreement. The MS Shoes was compelled to file a suit before the Honorable High Court of Delhi on 30 January 1996. In the said suit, MS Shoes had prayed for restraints

against the HUDCO for cancellation of allotment pronounced towards the MS Shoes. The said suit was based open to the facts and circumstances before the cancellation of allotment. But now the HUDCO has gone to the extent of cancelling the allotment, and even the fresh hid has been invited.

6. That is pertinent to point out that MS Shoes paid the 1st installment amounting to Rs.25,04,00,000.00 (US Dollar 6.89 million) along with agreed interest on 31 January 1995, 28 February 1995, and 1 March 1995. The said amount included Rs.23,64,00,000.00 (US Dollar 6.51 million) as a first installment for the allotment of the Hotel Site (after adjusting Rs.2,00,000.00 (US Dollar 0.55 million) Earnest Money deposited earlier). The HUDCO has now invited fresh tenders to re-allot the property, against the law. The HUDCO was to give possession by February 1995 to the MS Shoes, and the next installment was payable 6 to 8 months later, i.e., in October 1995. Infect, the second installment was payable in January 1996 after three months' grace period, along with interest. Now the HUDCO illegally wants to give away the allotment

in someone else's favor, thereby causing an irreparable loss and injury.

7. The HUDCO had issued a letter received by MS Shoes on 2 May 1996, which purported to be a cancellation letter. The MS Shoes time and again requested the HUDCO to examine the facts of the case, but to no avail. The HUDCO has in a similar matter given twice-time extensions to Ansals, whereas they have canceled the allotment of MS Shoes without any reasons.
8. That the Lease Deed has not been firmly executed even towards the HUDCO. Huge money of the financial institution, i.e., banks, etc., are involved in the project, and as such the arbitrary act of HUDCO will cause an irreparable loss and injury. The HUDCO being a financial institution cannot act in such a manner when the MS Shoes has already paid 40% of the total money. All these facts clearly show the HUDCO never had any intentions to comply with its part of the agreement.
9. That the MS Shoes is entitled not to pay the second installment to the HUDCO until the possession is being handed over to the MS Shoes in respect to the suit site. Alternatively, HUDCO is under obligation

to comply with the terms of the agreements. The HUDCO has not even initiated fulfilling its role by taking necessary steps, like income tax clearance, etc.

10. That the act and conduct of the HUDCO & Municipal Corporation of Delhi is arbitrary, illegal, and uncalled-for. The MS Shoes has got a legal right, and he has no other remedy except to approach the Honorable Court in such circumstances. The HUDCO & Municipal Corporation of Delhi is bent upon acting following their whims without following the established principle and norms. The HUDCO & Municipal Corporation of Delhi has no legal right to take such uncalled steps.
11. That the MS Shoes has fallen a victim to the earlier mentioned act and conduct of the HUDCO & Municipal Corporation of Delhi, without none of his faults. The HUDCO & Municipal Corporation of Delhi are acting beyond their scope with the sole motive to cause serious loss to the MS Shoes.
12. That the HUDCO & Municipal Corporation of Delhi, if not curtailed, would cause damage to the legal authority of the MS Shoes, and that too, with

none of the authority to check them. The HUDCO & Municipal Corporation of Delhi has no right, title, or interest to act following impugned order/letter/demand. The demand of the HUDCO & Municipal Corporation of Delhi is unjustifiable and needs to be set aside bypassing required orders to protect the MS Shoes. The HUDCO & Municipal Corporation of Delhi has the sole motive to cause harassment to the MS Shoes.

13. That in case the HUDCO's threat materializes, the MS Shoes would suffer an irreparable loss and injury which cannot be compensated in any manners.

14.. That the cause of action arose towards the MS Shoes and against HUDCO & Municipal Corporation of Delhi on all occasions as and when the impugned demand was raised by the HUDCO & Municipal Corporation of Delhi. The cause of action also arose in May 1996, and further on 26 December 1996 when tenders were invited. The threat of HUDCO to re-allot the suit property is still surviving, and as such the cause of action is contained and subsisting.

1. That for jurisdiction, this court has all the right and title to adjudicate upon the present suit, as the parties to the suit reside in Delhi and the cause of action arose in Delhi.
2. That for court fees relief of Declaration is valid at Rs.1,05,000/- on which court fees Rs.3368/80p are paid, and for permanent injunction and mandatory injunction, the suit is valued at Rs.200/- and Rs.130/- respectively on which court fees have been paid.

It is therefore prayed that a decree of declaration may kindly be passed towards MS Shoes, declaring the letter (impugned) dated 2 May 1996 as null and void. It is also prayed HUDCO be directed by the government injunction to deliver possession of the property to the MS Shoes and restrain HUDCO to re-allot the suit site.

It is prayed that the Municipal Corporation of Delhi is restrained from raising/ charging house tax demands in respect to suit property from the MS Shoes, in the interest of justice, with suitable directions thereto.

Any other order or relief Honorable Court may deem fit and proper in the circumstances may be granted towards the MS Shoes and against the HUDCO and Municipal Corporation of Delhi.

The above suit was numbered as suite no. 1/1997 and was listed before Additional District Judge, Mr. R.S. Arya` who granted an ex-parte interim injunction on 25 January 1997 directing HUDCO to maintain status-quo in respect of the allotment of the site in question at Andrews Ganj of 5-star hotel land with car parking.

Pioneer Newspaper Reported on 25 January 1997
"HUDCO advised to grant an extension to Ansals,"
"Ansals defaults on installments for office complex":

"The Minister of Urban Affairs has advised the Housing and Urban Development Corporation (HUDCO) to grant an extension until 17 April 1997 to Ansals to pay up the balance Rs. 50 crores (US Dollar 13.779 million) toward an allotment of a shopping-cum-office complex at HUDCO Place in South Delhi.

The Ministry's views had been sought on the contentious issue by the HUDCO board at a meeting on 15 January this year.

Ansals were allotted the property in South Delhi by HUDCO in March 1995. According to the schedule, 50 percent of the amount was to be paid within four weeks of receiving the allotment letter which the company duly paid. While 30 percent was to be paid within 12 months as part of the second installment, while another 20 percent was to be paid as part of the third installment in 18 months. The company has however not been abiding to pay up the balance amount and has been granted two extensions in time in June and September 1996. Now it is reliably learned the company had sought another six months postponement to repay the balance amount.

Sources close to Ansals told The Pioneer the company had sought the extension because there was a delay of five months in handing over the site to the company by HUDCO. Moreover, the buildup site which was provided to Ansals, on which the shopping arcade was to be built, did not have the requisite permission from the Municipal Corporation of Delhi. It took over a year for HUDCO to regularize the site, after which only Ansals could start construction. The sources added from HUDCO may be further noted that the grounds for seeking as well as granting extension were made on valid and transparent reasons and that no favors were sought or granted by the company. Ansals were given what was their legitimate due.

In the meantime, the postponement of payment time for the Ansals has raised eyebrows for those in the MS Shoes camp who are crying foul over the decision of the Urban Affairs Ministry. MS Shoes sources said that the company HUDCO had been allotted a hotel by complex site at the company at a site adjacent to the one allotted to Ansals. But they were not too lucky with HUDCO, which has since forfeited the first installment paid by the group.

The Urban Affairs Ministry had intervened on behalf of MS Shoes and had advised HUDCO in June 1996 that it was "in the public interest". It would be appropriate to stop the tenders of all the concerned properties until further directions. A public notice for cancellation of tender is issued in lending newspapers immediately. The advice had fallen on deaf ears, and to date, MS Shoes perceives it had been at a disadvantage compared with Ansals. But MS Shoes has recently received a shot in the arm in support from several MPs who have shown their concern at the way HUDCO had forfeited the first installment."

Despite such controversies being raised in the news, HUDCO continued to favor Ansals granting discriminatory treatment to MS Shoes. I read the constitution of India; it says equal rights to all who are equally placed. But in the Andrews Ganj land scam, there was no such principle followed. I would simply say it is a scam definitely. I am sure readers will agree with it.

Another suit like the above suit was filed for Guest House blocks, Shops, and Restaurants against Municipal Corporation of Delhi and HUDCO, which was numbered as suite no. 2/1997 and was listed on 27 January 1997, and the interim order was passed by the Court of Additional District Judge Mr. R.S. Arya to maintain the status-quo in respect of Guest House Blocks, Restaurants & Shops.

Chapter: Twenty

Withdrawal Of Previous Suits by MS Shoes

After getting the status-quo order from the Court of Mr. R.S. Arya, MS Shoes filed an application on 30 January 1997, being I.A. No. 930 of 1997 in suit no. 275/1996 in respect of 5-star hotel land. The said application was for withdrawal of the suit, disclosing that the fresh suit has been filed for substantial relief.

Application on behalf of MS Shoes under section 151 CPC:

The MS Shoes has instituted the aforesaid suit for declaration and injunction, permanent and mandatory, and the same is pending before this Honorable Court. For the sake of brevity and to avoid prolixity, MS Shoes craves leave to refer and rely upon the said suit.

1. The cause of action that arose for the said suit was that without performing the obligations enjoined upon the HUDCO under the allotment letter dated 31 October 1994, the HUDCO was wrongfully asking the MS Shoes to make payment and perform its obligations failing, which the HUDCO is threatened to cancel the contract.
2. The MS Shoes also sought a decree of permanent injunction against the HUDCO, restraining the

HUDCO from canceling the allotment letter dated 31 October 1994.

3. During the pendency of the present suit, the HUDCO terminated the contract by letter dated 2 May 1996. Further, MS Shoes has also received notice of house tax from the Municipal Corporation of Delhi. The MS Shoes, therefore, had to file a suit to challenge the cancellation letter and the notice of the Municipal Corporation of Delhi.
4. The said letter of cancellation could not be challenged in Suit No. 275 of 1996, as it is a consequent event. Given the subsequent events and the stand taken by the HUDCO, the MS Shoes, by way of abundant caution, filed a fresh suit pending in the Court of Mr. R.S. Arya, Judge, Delhi being Suit No. 1 of 1997.
5. It is stated the above-mentioned suit, i.e., Suit no. of 1997 is a comprehensive suite, and inter alia includes the entire cause of action pleaded before this Hon'ble Court in the present suit. Given the above, MS Shoes may be permitted to withdraw the present suit to avoid multiplicity of litigation, and pursue reliefs relating to the entire cause of action in Suit No. 1 of 1997.

In the premise, it is prayed this Honorable Court may be pleased to:

a) Permit the MS Shoes to withdraw suit No. 275 of 1996 pending before this Honorable Court for the reasons mentioned in paragraphs 5 and 6.
b) Pass such further orders/orders as this Honorable Court may deem fit and proper in the facts and circumstances of the case.

After getting the status-quo order from the Court of Mr. R.S. Arya, MS Shoes filed a similar application on 30 January 1997, being I.A. No. 944 of 1997 in suit no. 1062/1995 in respect of Guest House blocks, Restaurants, Kitchen & Shops. The said application was for withdrawal of the suit, disclosing that the fresh suit has been filed for substantial relief.

Application on behalf of the MS Shoes under section 151 CPC:

1. The MS Shoes has instituted the aforesaid suit for declaration and injunction, permanent and mandatory, and the same is pending before this Honorable Court. For the sake of brevity and to

avoid prolixity, MS Shoes craves leave to refer and rely upon the said suit.

2. The cause of action in the said suit is from the fact that the time not being the essence of the contract, terms of which were incorporated in the allotment letter dated 31 October 1994. The MS Shoes is entitled to an extension of time for payment of the second installment. The MS Shoes also sought relief from forfeiture and a decree of permanent injunction against the HUDCO from canceling the allotment letter dated 31 October 1994 concerning the suit property.
3. During the pendency of the sit-by letter of canceling dated 1 January 1996, the HUDCO canceled the allotment dated 31 October 1994, in pursuance of the said cancellation letter. The HUDCO is also attempting to re-tender the said suit property.
4. Meanwhile, MS Shoes also received notice of house tax from the Municipal Corporation of Delhi.
5. Further, the HUDCO moved an application in the present suit stating that the suit has become infructuous, inter alia, because the contract has already stood rescinded. Given the subsequent event and the stand taken by the HUDCO, the MS Shoes,

by way of abandoning caution, filed a fresh suit pending in the court of Shri R.S. Arya, Judge, Delhi being Suit No. 2 of 1997.

6. It is stated that the above-mentioned suit, i.e., Suit no. 2, of 1997, is a comprehensive suite, and inter alia includes the entire cause of action pleaded before this Honorable Court in the present suit.
7. Given the above, MS Shoes may be permitted to withdraw the present suit to avoid a multiplicity of litigation, and pursue reliefs relating to the entire cause of action in Suit No. 2 of 1997.

In the premises, it is prayed this Honorable Court may be pleased to:

a) Permit the MS Shoes to withdraw suit No. 1062 of 1995 pending before this Hon'ble Court for the reasons mentioned in para 5 and 6.
b) Pass such further orders/orders as this Honorable Court may deem fit and proper in the facts and circumstances of the case.

HUDCO opposed the withdrawal of the suit before the High Court, but the High Court passed an order in the case of Guest House Blocks on 13 February 1997 in suit no.

1062/1995 allowing I.A. No. 944/1997 when lawyers present were Mr. Mukul Rohatgi, Sr. Advocate with Mr. Vibhu Bakhru and Ms. Anuradha Dutt for MS Shoes. Dr. A.M. Singhvi, Sr. Advocate, ASG with Mr. C. Mukhopadhaya and Mr. Manish Kumar for HUDCO.

Learned Counsel appearing for the MS Shoes states the MS Shoes seeks to withdraw the present suit unconditionally and in terms of Order 23 Rule 1 CPC. Since MS Shoes is withdrawing the suit unconditionally, the suit stands dismissed as withdrawn. The Parties shall bear their own costs.

All the pending applications also stand disposed of accordingly.

(DR. M.K. SHARMA), JUDGE

HUDCO had itself filed an application that the suit has filed for a mandatory injunction of the installment has become infructuous, and no relief can be granted as the allotment stands canceled. The only legal way was to challenge the cancellation letter as illegal, null & void, and the reason to restrain the Municipal Corporation of Delhi to demand property tax on these properties. The fresh suit was filed as a new cause of action had arisen. But HUDCO for withdrawal of the suit continued to oppose the application. This was the type of attitude of HUDCO towards MS Shoes.

The installments of Ansals were being extended, but the amounts received from MS Shoes were forfeited, which were received fraudulently by concealing material facts of the buildings constructed illegally without any approvals of Municipal Corporation of Delhi, FIRE department, Delhi Urban Art Commissions. Besides, there was no electricity connection available as the land was yet to be allotted to Delhi Electric Supply Undertaking, further without title towards HUDCO due to which the first step of permission of authorities under the Income Tax Act under section 269 (UC) was not granted, but the 2nd installment was demanded which legally could have not been demanded.

Chapter: Twenty-One

All Government Officer Were Desperate to Approve Ansals Interest Free Extensions of Instalments which was Approved by Five Officers in a Day

HUDCO was aware that the layout plans approved were conceptual, and still, the revised layout plans were required to be approved, which was concealed from MS Shoes. In the absence of approval of revised layout plans, the building plans for the hotel could not be approved. It is understood that until 1997, i.e., until this date, revised layout plans were not approved. It is still to be seen when the revised layout plans would be approved? Conceptual,

Executive Director (Design and Development), M.N. Joglekar, letter on 17 February 1997 to The Town Planner Town Planning Department Municipal Corporation of Delhi. Regarding: - Submission of revised layout plan about HUDCO Place Project at Andrewsganj.

The layout plan about the project cited above was approved by Municipal Corporation of Delhi, Town Planning Department earlier vide their letter no. TP/Municipal Corporation of Delhi/3541/94 dated 12 May 1994 copy of the letter enclosed herewith. Due to various technical, administrative, and management issues, changes/revisions have been incorporated in this revised layout plan.

There are two type-IV and two type-V housing pockets, in addition to one pocket for transit housing. The configuration of the layout concerning one type–IV and two type-V blocks has been modified. There are some unimportant changes in the layout of the transit housing pockets. The location of the primary cum nursery school has changed.

The location of two nursery school sites has also been changed. The building's detailed drawings about the circular shopping Centre have already been approved by the Building Section. Municipal Corporation of Delhi. The final form/configuration of this building component is reflected on this/revised plan.

The above changes have been done keeping in view the maximum permissible ground coverage and FAR, change and height of the building, etc.

You are requested to kindly accord approval to this revised plan, to enable the Building Section of the Municipal Corporation of Delhi to proceed with the approvals on the detailed building components.

We are also enclosing herewith three copies of Proforma sheets duly signed, and a draft processing fee No.484149. Dated 30 January 1997 for a value of Rs.7200/-.

The Under Secretary put up a detailed note Mr. B.R. Dhiman to the Joint Secretary, which was sent to the Additional Secretary and the Secretary, finally to the Prime Minister's office, Mr. Deve Gowda, for consideration on 25 February 1997 in respect to extensions of installments to Ansals:

This pertains to HUDCO's proposal recommending the extension of time to M/S Ansals for payment of second and third installments for' the Shopping Arcade at HUDCO Place, Andrews Ganj, New Delhi. The options available are indicated in paragraph 15 on pages 72-73/N. In addition, there is a fourth option by which the Government can accept HUDCO's proposal conveyed in their letter dated 28 November 1996 too. HUDCO have based their proposal on their commercial judgment and the legal opinion of Mr. Dipankar P. Gupta, Barrister and Senior Advocate, Supreme Court of India. Shri Gupta has opined that if litigation results at this stage, either by way of cancellation of the agreement or claim for damages or otherwise, the project, in the public interest, will suffer. He, therefore, recommended this is a case that ought to be negotiated and settled at this stage. It can be reasonably anticipated that action as per the options indicated in paragraphs 15(I) or (ii) would lead to litigation, the result of which, according to Shri Dipankar P. Gupta, is practically impossible to assess and predict. HUDCO's proposal was discussed with the Secretary (JD) and it was observed that instead of the period of ten months and eight days taken into account therein (between- June 1995 to 8 April 1996), the actual delay was nine months and eight days (1 July 1995 to 8 April 996). The proposal at para 15 (111) on page 73/N, based on this assessment, may be approved subject to the condition that M/s Ansals must drop all their claims for damages or, otherwise, on account of any alleged delay on the part of HUDCO which may have occurred till date, apart from payment being composed of up-to-date ground rent from the date of possession, i.e., 10 November 1995.

The adverse financial implications for the Government, reflected in para 13 on page 72/N, is a consequence of the failure on the part of HUDCO to obtain the requisite building permissions from the Municipal Corporation of Delhi on time. Therefore, as opined by the Additional Secretary (UD) on page 68/N, HUDCO may be asked to compensate the Government for this loss. However, this issue may be dealt with separately.

As regards the news item referred to in Para 16 on P.73/N, given the material on the subject received from HUDCO, it is apparent that M/s. Shoes Ltd. also was given an extension of time by the Delhi High Court, despite which they failed to pay and consequently the allotment was canceled.

Under the queries raised by the PMO via their note on page 76/N, we had requested HUDCO clarify the position whether the proposal strictly requires approval of the Government, or as done in the past, the Board of Directors of HUDCO is empowered to do so. Further, the legal and financial implications were also inquired into, inter alia, indicating whether the proposed action would have any adverse implications on similar cases in the complex.

In response to this reply received from the HUDCO, it is placed at Slip 'FR'. –Based on the information furnished by HUDCO Vis-à-vis various developments here, the position w.r.t. queries raised by the PMO vide note at page 76/N is clarified seriatim as under: -

The HUDCO is executing the project on behalf of the Government. In the matter of planning, development, execution, and disposal of various components and other related issues, the HUDCO has been associating the Ministry as and when considered necessary. Accuracy on account of the disposal of various components are kept in separate non-lien accounts. After adjustment of the expenses incurred, surplus from the Project is available to the Government for the execution of general pool accommodation on identified projects. The decision to allow extension of time of M/sandals, without levy of interest, due to certain factors, affected the surplus available to the Government, therefore reference has been made to the Government and approval solicited by the HUDCO before granting a further extension.

As per terms of allotment of Shopping Arcade site towards M/s. Ansals possession was to be handed over by June 1995. This could be done only on 10 November 1995. However, the building plans submitted by the party for Shopping Arcade, to be constructed over the car parking and basement, were not entertained/processed by the Municipal Corporation of Delhi and were linked by the local body with the sanction/approval of the building plans of the car parking/basement area executed by the HUDCO, plan of which was regularized on 8 April 1996. Thus, the plans of M/s. Ansals for Shopping Arcade were processed by the Municipal Corporation of Delhi, and clearances were given in July 1996.

Keeping in view the delay in handing over possession, entertaining the plans, and processing thereof due to non-sanction of the car parking/basement area by the Municipal Corporation of Delhi, following which M/s. Ansals plans were not entertained, the party requested for the corresponding deferment of second and third installments without levy of interest. HUDCO examined this matter and the opinion of Sr. Counsel (Shri Deepankar Gupta, Ex-Attorney General of India) was obtained who suggested resolving the matter amicably. Accordingly, HUDCO proposed an extension of time for deferment of second and third installments up to 17 January 1997 and 13 May 1997, which involved notional non-accrual of interest amounting to Rs. 10.9 crores (US Dollar 3.00 million).

The matter was examined in the Ministry, keeping in view the various factors, including the fact that the delay in the sanction of the car parking basement area had a direct bearing on the sanction/execution of the project by M/s. Ansals and delay cannot be attributed to them, therefore, as suggested by the Board of Directors of the HUDCO, it was believed that though the proposed extension resulted in non-accrual of interest to the tune of Rs. 10.9 crores (US Dollar 3.00 million) as per recommendations of HUDCO, it was decided to allow interest-free extension in respect of second & third installments interest-free up to 16 December 1996 and 13 May 1997, respectively. This modified proposal also results in non-accrual interest to the tune of Rs. 10.22 crores (US Dollar 2.81 million).

This aspect was examined in consultation with associated Finance, keeping in view the fact that the party is entitled to 6% interest on the amount deposited by them, i.e., Rs. 84.4 crores (US Dollar 23.24 million) for any delay in handing over the site, and thus non-accrual loss could be 10.48% in the shape of interest. The accruals from the disposal of various components have been kept in separate non-lien accounts and have been deposited in fixed-term accounts, yielding interest @ 13% to the Government on the surplus. The entire proposition as suggested by HUDCO, as per the opinion of the Sr. Counsel was considered rational to settle the issue from prudential norms, as in simple terms, the entire process involved foregoing of 16.48% interest and accrual @ 19% (i.e., 13% on fixed deposits + 6% as interest on the amount deposited by the party). Thus, the opinion of Sr. Counsel being for settlement after discussion with the party and proposal conforming thereto, reference to the Law Ministry was not considered necessary.

Thus, the proposal for extension was considered reasonable in consultation with associated finance and recommended accordingly.

As regards the implication of the proposal on similar cases, it is submitted that the Community Center Complex consists of various components, namely: -

i. Built up Guest House Blocks and Hotel Site (Land) allotted to M.S. Shoes. Handing over of land was related to securing payment of the prescribed installment and clearance under income tax. Further, in respect of the Guest House Complex allotted to M.S. shoes, possession was to be handed over on obtaining full payment/on completion of buildings. Due to non-compliance with these requirements, allotments have been canceled.
ii. In the case of M/s. Ansals the possession of space for the construction of the Shopping Arcade was to be made available by June 1995, after receipt of the 1st installment and related clearances which were received.
iii. As regards the Cultural center allotted to M/s. Phoenix Overseas Ltd. in October 1994. The agency has already paid first and second installments and

related clearances, and the possession are being handed over to them.

In the above background, the case of MS Shoes and M/S. Ansals is strictly not at para, because MS Shoes have not been in a position to secure payment and furnish the requisite clearances in time, even though the extended time was allowed by the court, whereas in the case of M/s. Ansals the delay is attributable to the delay in the sanction of the plans of the car parking/basement area on which construction of the Shopping Arcade was to take place. Hence, the two situations cannot be equated, and the stand could be taken appropriately accordingly.

Further, it is reported MS Shoes has filed fresh suits in which they have procured status quo w.r.t disposal of properties under the fresh bids invited, and contended their case for an extension of time has been rejected/allotment canceled, whereas the same has not been done in the case of M/s. Ansals. Although the two situations cannot be equated, nothing can be predicted about the outcome of the court cases. However, the above background case can be defended appropriately.

In all important matters, the final decision is taken with the approval of the cabinet minister, and therefore this being an important case, it was considered necessary that the Honorable Prime Minister is also apprised before the final decision is conveyed to the HUDCO.

Given above, the case is submitted for an attentive perusal of the PMO. Signed by (B.R. Dhiman), which was further discussed with the Secretary Urban Development and Joint Secretary, Urban Development on 28 February 1997:

The issues raised in the PMO's U.D. note dated 13 February 1997 at page 76/N have been discussed and clarified in the notes on pages 80-83/N, which may please be checked.

The project (construction of Shopping Arcade at the site by the allottee to whom the site was handed over by HUDCO on 10 November 1995) is already in progress. Given the delay in handing over the site, HUDCO had allowed a six-month extension without payment of interest.

M/s. Ansals, however, insisted on the further extension without payment of interest from the deemed date of possession, i.e., 30 June 1995 to 8 April 1996, when their plans were processed by the Municipal Corporation of Delhi.

HUDCO considered the matter and obtained a legal opinion. In the circumstances explained in the note on pages 80-83/N, as well as keeping given the legal opinion of Shri Dipankar P. Gupta, Barrister and Senior Advocate (former Solicitor-General of India) that this is a case which ought to be negotiated and settled at this stage itself in the public interest (rather than entering into litigation), HUDCO recommended further extension without payment of interest up to 17 January 1997 and 13 May 1997 for payment of 2nd and 3rd installment respectively due to delay in entertaining/processing of plans for a shopping arcade

Keeping in view the fact that there was no delay of 9 months & 8 days (from the deemed date of handing over, i.e. 30 June 1995 to 8 April 1996 when the plans of the party were processed), it was suggested that for payment of 2nd installment without interest period should not be more than 9 months & 8 days, and therefore interest-free extension for payment of 2nd installment was recommended up to 17 December 1996 vide para 15 (iii) of note at page 73/ante, whereas interest-free extension in respect of 3rd installment was allowed up to 13 May 1997, as recommended by HUDCO.

Considering the decision on HUDCO's recommendations is yet to be conveyed to HUDCO, and the date for securing payment of 2nd installment with interest as well, i.e. 17 March 1997, is quickly approaching and the allottee would require a reasonable period to take payment, it is observed while retraining the interest-free period up to 17 December 1996 in respect of 2nd installment, the period for obtaining payment of 2nd installment with interest may be allowed up to 17 April 1997, i.e. 4 months instead of 3 months as per terms and conditions of allotment letter. Accordingly, the following proposals for further extensions are for approval: -

i. Extension of time to M/s. Ansals for payment of the second installment from 9 September 1996 to 17 December 1996, interest-free and with interest @ 16.48% up to 17 April 1997.
ii. Extension of time to M/s. Ansals for payment of the third installment from 9 March 1997 to 13 May 1997, interest-free and with interest @ 16.48% up to 13 August 1997.

iii. The extensions of time proposed at (i) and (ii) above will be granted to M/s. Ansals subject to the following conditions: -

a) M/s. Ansals shall furnish a suitable and unambiguous disclaimer on stamp paper for all their claims for damages or otherwise on account of alleged delays on the part of HUDCO which may have occurred till date; and

b) M/s. Ansals shall compel payment of ground rent from the date of possession, i.e., 10 November 1995.

The proposals in paragraph 7 above are submitted for approval.

Signed by B.R. Dhiman - 28 February 1997 Approved by Joint Secretary (Urban Development)–28 February 1997, approved by Joint Secretary (Finance)- 28 February 1997, approved Additional Secretary (Urban Development). Mr. Hamender Kumar–28 February 1997, approved by Secretary (Urban Development) Mr. J.P. Singh–28 February 1997, approved by Minister of State, Urban Affairs & Employment, and the file was sent on the same day to the Prime Minister' Mr. Deve Gowda.

The above noting in detail submitted and approved by all Government Officers for extension of installment to Ansals were approved the same day and sent to the Prime Minister, who was holding charge of Cabinet Minister of Ministry. Ansals were having close proximity to all the officers, as they had the urgency, explained in their letter dated 28 February 1997. Ansals raised the loan to pay the 2nd installment, while the terms of the allotment letter did not permit raising loans for payment of the installments. Ansals' proximity with HUDCO's officers was that they had obtained the promise that they would permit Ansals to raise loans against the 2nd installment.

Now Ansals were aware that since the file has been sent to the Prime Minister on 28 February 1997 and it will take time, they shot a letter of 28 February 1997 to HUDCO.

Assistant General Manager (marketing), Ansal Properties & Industries Limited, Mr. Vivek Juneja to Mr. P. K Garg, Chief (disposal), HUDCO, Lodhi Estate, New Delhi on 28 February 1997 regarding rescheduling of payment of installment. This is a reference to our various letters on the above subject, ending with the last letter dated 23 January 1997 requesting you to expedite communication of the decision taken by the Board of Directors of HUDCO on the above subject in their meeting held on 26 November 1996.

We reliably understand the board has decided to extend the date for payment of the second and third installments.

Our bankers need a time extension letter so that the loan applications furnished by us could be processed and sanctioned. You will appreciate that bankers need time to process the loan application, and time is running out, and the purpose-seeking extension could be defeated if the extension letter is not received sufficiently before the date of expiry of the extended period.

We once again request you to kindly expedite communication of the extension of time at the earliest, enabling us to make arrangements with the bankers.

At the request of Ansals, they have disclosed they knew that the board had approved the extensions of installments to be paid. Interestingly, to date, only the 1st installment was paid as was paid by MS Shoes, but the allotments of MS Shoes were canceled and the amounts forfeited in early 1996 itself.

Another newspaper report appeared reporting "**Land deal between HUDCO and Ansals," "Company Affairs Department probing alleged violations":**

"The Department of Company Affairs (DCA) at the –behest of the Prime minister's office is scrutinizing alleged violations in the land deal between Housing and Urban Development Corporation (HUDCO) and Ansals.

HUDCO had canceled the land deal with Pavan Sachdeva promoted MS Shoes, citing inordinate delay in paying up the second installment by the company, and reallocation of the site to Ansals.

Earlier it's a last-ditch effort to revive the contract with HUDCO MS Shoes. They had written a note to the Prime Minister's Office accusing of partisan behavior and requesting an inquiry.

MS Shoes in its petition accused HUDCO of giving preferential treatment to Ansal Properties and Industries Ltd by accepting its payment even after the due date with interest while condoning the delay on the grounds of depressed market conditions.

The Housing and Urban Development Corporation had allegedly backed its decision to revoke the contract with MS Shoes, as it was incurring financial losses due to the avoidable delay in payment of the entire price of the contract.

MS Shoes alleged that undue favoritism was shown on Ansals by granting it an extension for a second time to repay Rs.150 crore (US Dollar 42.33 million) for the shopping plaza in the complex earlier allotted to the former.

MS Shoes further stated its bid for the five-star hotel complex along with parking space was accepted as it was the highest.

The site acquisition followed in 1994 after the incumbent decided to diversify into the hotel industry under the aegis of MS World link Hotels Limited.

Towards this end, the public equity capital of Rs.700 crore (US Dollar 197.57 million) was floated, but it failed and finally landed the promoters in a financial quandary.

In these circumstances, it was forced to seek extra time for payment as a relief against forfeiture.

It also suggested an alternative proposal to tide over the pending payment by asking for rescheduling the payment in quarterly installment along with the interest against a straight second lump-sum installment.

Meanwhile, MS Shoes had already paid the first installment consisting of 40% of the Rs.178 crores (US Dollar 50.23 million) property project.

The contract was further given out to the new partners against the wishes of the Ministry of Housing and Urban Development.

The petitioners also attempted to consolidate their argument by highlighting the name of shareholders and financial institutions whose money amounts to Rs.70 Crore had been sunk in the project.

Despite strong representation from concurring banks and financial institutions, HUDCO was ahead with retendering of four- and five-star hotel sites in January this year. Which was earlier allotted to MS Shoes Limited."

I as an author do not understand a Prime Minister of India sending a company affairs department to probe the violations by Ansals? What company affairs must do with such probes? It sounds weird of the Prime Minister directing such to the company department? I feel this is also part of the scam, as it makes no sense in a probe by a department that has nothing to do with Andrew Ganj Scam by HUDCO. It seems here also some games was played by V. Suresh or someone else.

Chapter: Twenty-Two

Court Held Callousness of HUDCO and Government Towards MS Shoes Forfeiting 40% Of the Consideration

HUDCO applied to vacate the interim order of Status-quo passed on 25 January 1997 by the Court Mr. R.S. Arya. HUDCO was in a hurry to issue an allotment letter to Leela Hotels. In their application and reply, they specifically stated MS Shoes is not equally placed as Ansals, since MS Shoes has been facing a Central Bureau of Investigation case since April 1995.

*Business Times Bureau, the reporter Mr. Prabhakar Sinha reported on 13 March 1997 "**HUDCO allows an interest-free charge to Ansals":***

"New Delhi. Housing and Urban Development Corporation Limited. (HUDCO) is not charging any interest on delayed payment of the second and third installments for the lease of space earmarked for shopping cum office at Andrewsganj in New Delhi to Ansal Properties and Industries Ltd (APIL).

HUDCO has already granted the six-month interest-free extension to APIL from the due date for the second installment on March 9, 1996, and for the third installment on September 9, 1996, for Rs.50.64 crore (US Dollar 14.29 million) and Rs.33.76 crore (US Dollar 9.52 million). Ansals were allotted the property for Rs.168.80 crore (US Dollar 46.49 million).

However, HUDCO had rejected similar requests made by financial institutions (FIS) and banks like the tourism Finance Corporation of India, Industrial Development Bank of India, State Bank of Patiala and others to grant a similar extension to MS Shoes for its hotel project proposed to be set up at the site allotted by HUDCO and canceled the allotment.

If HUDCO had accepted the proposal given by financial institutions and banks, they could have recovered their dues on MS Shoes. Financial institutions had stated they were endeavoring to examine the proposal received for meeting commitments of the company to HUDCO in respect of balance consideration payable for the properties.

In the case of APIL, HUDCO is considering giving them another interest-free extension, as they could not pay the amount on the due date. HUDCO chairman and managing director V. Suresh said the extension was granted because of the delay in handing over the possession of the space to APIL by five months in October 1995.

He said the other reason for the extension was the delay in the regularization of construction of the car parking basement by the municipal Corporation of Delhi, over which the shopping arcade was to be built. Ansals have demanded the interest on their first installment of Rs.84.60 crore (US Dollar 23.24 million) paid on April 6, 1995, for the period of delay of around one year in providing the regularization certificate by MCD.

In the case of MS Shoes, according to the allotment letter issued by HUDCO, the second installment of around Rs.35 crore (US Dollar 9.63) would have been due after handing over the site to the developer, but instead of handing over the land, HUDCO canceled the allotment based on the delay in payment of the installment.

Mr. Suresh said MS Shoes case was different from the Ansal case. The total cost of the lease for the five-star property at Andrews Ganj to MS Shoes was around Rs.64 crore (US Dollar 18.07 million), of which Rs 25 crores is paid as the first installment on January 31, 1995."

Rs. 10 Crores loss was accepted by the Government, relaxing two installments interest-free, and not only that if they had canceled Ansals allotment like MS shoes, but HUDCO and Government could also have earned the appreciation of this property as well. But no MS Shoes as per HUDCO was not equally placed as that to Ansals, as MS

Shoes CMD, Pavan Sachdeva was facing a CBI probe of his public issue, which the competitors had registered to destroy him. But readers will soon know God's game. Ansals also got trapped in a CBI case, and their all directors were either absconding or behind the jail.

But HUDCO's scam continued destroying MS Shoes totally to get themselves undue rich, and yes, they did succeed till today, ei. 2021 as MS Shoes continued to struggle to await justice. But which justice will get time to hear was a question to ratify HUDCO Scam?

It seems Leela Hotels or HUDCO got near Mr. R.S. Arya and got the stay vacated despite various observations of the Court in favor of MS Shoes. The order was passed on 17 March 1997, disposing of the application of HUDCO and the application of MS Shoes.

It is observed that Mr. R.S. Arya accepted the documents placed on record by MS Shoes, which had suit no. 275/96 filed before the High Court, orders passed in suit no. 275/1996 and FAO (OS), First Appeal No. 22/1996, copy of the application of HUDCO seeking dismissal of the suit being infructuous and that cause of action does not remain, further the application of MS Shoes seeking withdrawal of the suit no. 275/1996 which disclosed the fresh suit on a fresh cause of action has been filed. There was no concealment, only that withdrawal of the suit order was not passed since HUDCO opposed MS Shoes' application. Hence, there was no concealment by MS Shoes in suit no. 1/1997 filed before Mr. R.S. Arya.

MS Shoes applied to the Court to summon the file of Ansals, which was declined to be produced by HUDCO for their ulterior motives.

In the Court of Shri R. S. Arya, Additional District Judge, Delhi in Civil Suit No. 1/1997 order passed on 17 March 1997 disposing of Order 39 Rule 1 and 2 of Civil Procedure Code, the application of MS Shoes filed along with the suit and application of HUDCO under Order 39 Rule 4 of Civil Procedure Code vacating interim order dated 25 January 1997:

I have heard arguments addressed by Mr. R.K. Anand, Senior Advocate, counsel for MS Shoes, and Dr. A.M. Singhvi, Sr. Advocate, Additional Solicitor General of India, counsel for HUDCO on application under Order 39 Rules 1 and 2 CPC of MS Shoes, and on application under Order 39 rule 4 CPC of HUDCO. The arguments could be concluded in ten dates falling between 5 February 1997 to 6 March 1997. I have also perused the written notes of arguments of the parties. I have thoroughly perused the pleadings of the parties and documents placed on record. I have given thoughtful consideration to the points of arguments advanced by the Learned Counsel for the parties.

It is also relevant to record here that during arguments, the Ld. Counsel for MS Shoes also applied to Order 11 Rule 14 CPC calling upon HUDCO to produce the file relating to allotment of the shopping arcade to Ansals and terms and conditions contained in the letter of allotment, the agreement to sublease, and the extension sought for and granted to Ansals by HUDCO, which application was opposed, and HUDCO filed a reply in opposition thereof. The application of MS Shoes shall also be discussed in this order of mine.

The relevant and material documents placed on record by the parties which need to be scrutinized and then discussed for effective disposal of the instant applications are detailed as under: -

i. Letter of allotment dated 31 October 1994 from HUDCO.

ii. Letter of cancellation of allotment dated 2 May 1996 from HUDCO,

iii. Letter from HUDCO dated 31 January 1996 calling upon MS Shoes to coerce payment of the 2nd installment failing, which suffers automatic cancellation of the allotment,

iv. Copy of the plaint in suit no. 275/96 filed in the Honorable High Court;

v. Order passed by the Honorable High Court dated 31 January 1996, 2 February 1996, 20 February 1996, 21 March 1996, 16 April 1996, and 17 May 1996 in Suit no. 275/96;

vi. Orders passed by Honorable High Court dated 12 April 1996, in FAO (OS) 131/96 against order date 31 March 1996 in suit no. 275/96;

vii. Order dated 10 April 1996 in FAO (OS) 22/1996.

viii. Letter of the Ministry of Urban Development New Delhi dated 15.6.1993; (HUDCO has filed all these above documents).

ix. A confidential letter dated 14 June 1996 issued from the office of Minister of Urban Affairs and Employment stopping the tenders of all the concerned properties, including the suit property in the public interest;

x. Letters from the financial institutions addressed to the Ministry of Housing and Urban Development, Government, of India, showing concern and anxiety to protect the substantial amount of public funds involved and recovery of loans advanced by institutions, with an appeal to issue urgent instructions to HUDCO to keep the re-tendering in abeyance;

xi. A blank proforma for agreement to sublease supplied by HUDCO along with a letter of allotment;

xii. Letter dated 25 October 1995 from MS Shoes to HUDCO calling upon HUDCO to take steps for obtaining necessary approvals and hand over possession;

xiii. Letter dated 30 January 1996 from MS Shoes to HUDCO in addition to the above letter dated 25 October 1995;

xiv. copy of an application under section 151 CPC dated 30 January 1997 filed in suit no. 275/96 by MS Shoes herein seeking permission to withdraw the suit;

xv. copy of an application under section 151 CPC filed by HUDCO herein in suit no. 275/96 in Honorable High Court seeking dismissal of the suit as having become infructuous; (the above documents from no. ix to xv having been filed by MS Shoes)

Let us take first the alleged abuse of the process of law and conduct of MS Shoes. Since the relief of injunction is purely discretionary and equitable, the conduct of MS Shoes seeking such relief plays a vital role, and further, it is supposed to be not abusing the process of law. The abuse of the process of law is imputed and ascribed on account of the institution of the present suit, while suit no. 275/96 was pending before the Hon'ble High Court. The said suit was between the same parties which are here except Municipal Corporation of Delhi-Defendant no. 1. The said suit related to the same subject matter, and there was also a declaration sought to the fact that the dates for determining subsequent installments as per the schedule of payment in the letter of allotment be deemed to be extended, and HUDCO herein be restrained from canceling the letter of allotment. It is a matter of record MS Shoes has suppressed the material facts in respect of said suit no. 275/96. I find only a halfhearted pleading in paragraph no.7 of the plaint disclosing the filing of the suit before the Hon'ble High

Court dated 30 January 1996, with prayer for issuing restraint on cancellation of allotment, and the said suit is based upon the facts and circumstances before cancellation of allotment, and the present suit having been filed after the cancellation of allotment.

I have given thoughtful consideration to this point of contention. What are the present facts of that suit no? 275/96? It has not been disclosed to me by either of the parties since no document has been placed on record, except a copy of an application for withdrawal of the said suit, and one more copy of the application of the HUDCO herein seeking dismissal of the said suit no. 275/96 as having become infructuous? But what actually happened to these applications is not disclosed to me specifically whether they said was allowed to be withdrawn with permission to file the present one, or it was simply allowed to be withdrawn without such permission, or it was dismissed as having become infructuous has not been disclosed to me. The pendency or non-pendency of that suit is a matter of concern for this court, particularly when the provision of Order 2, rule 2, of the Civil Procedure Code is sought to be made applicable to the present suit. The ld. Counsel for MS Shoes has relied upon AIR 1970 SC 1059 to show the meaning of course of action, and AIR 2948

Calcutta 97 to show what is the bar under Order 2, rule 2, Civil Procedure Code.

So far as AIR 1970 SC 1059 is concerned, it has been laid down therein that where the cause of action based on which the previous suit was brought does not form the foundation of the subsequent suit, and in the earlier suit, MS Shoes could not have claimed the relief which he sought in the subsequent suit, order 2 rule does not bar MS Shoes' subsequent suit 2 Civil Procedure Code (Judgment of Mysore High Court reversed).

As to AIR 1948 Calcutta 97, MS Shoes filed a suit pleading that he has a reasonable apprehension that the HUDCO was harboring the intention of causing injury to his reversionary rights in certain articles, and asked the court to prevent the HUDCO from carrying into effect the wrongful intention. In the subsequent suit, the cause of action pleaded was that after the institution of the previous suit, the HUDCO destroyed his reversionary rights to those articles by her wrongful acts.

"Held, that the cause of action in the two suits was different, and therefore, Order did not bar the subsequent suit 2, rule 2, Civil Procedure Code."

From this whole discussion and observation, I come to form the opinion that at this stage, the suit does not seem to be barred by the provision of section 41 (h) of the Specific Relief Act and the application for an interim injunction can be decided to ignore section 41 (h) of the Specific Relief Act. It is also relevant to record here that so far, no deed concerning the land allotted by the Government of India to HUDCO vide letter dated 15.6.1993 inclusive of the suit land does exist executed between the Government and HUDCO - meaning thereby the President has yet to execute perpetual lease deed in favor of HUDCO. This being the case, the plea of the counsel for MS Shoes that the filing of a suit for specific performance will be premature at this stage holds good.

The fifth point of law raised by HUDCO relates to the suit having been improperly valued and insufficient pecuniary jurisdiction. The ld. Counsel for HUDCO has also cited judgments reported as AIR 1960 Asam 65 and AIR 1978 Delhi 114, which I have perused. The ld. Counsel for HUDCO has argued that in sum and substance the suit is one for specific performance and possession of the suit property, which requires valuation and court fees payable on the true nature of relief claimed, and as the suit, in reality, a suit for specific performance, court fee would be payable ad valorem on the market value of the property on the date of filing of the suit, following section 7 (x) of the Court Fee Act 1870. The court fee is paid accordingly, the pecuniary jurisdiction of this court to entertain and adjudicate this suit shall stand ousted since the value of the land and contract consideration issued in crores.

After giving thoughtful consideration to this point of law raised by the Ld. Counsel for the HUDCO, I referred to my above observations made while discussing the legal point relating to a suit allegedly being barred by the provision of section 41(h) of the Specific Relief Act. Therefore, this issue of valuation and court fees becomes unnecessary at this stage for deciding the application under Order 39 Rules 1 and 2 of CPC. Valuation and court fees must be examined at a later stage. So far as the relief for possession is concerned, prima facie, at this stage, I believe that in the event of finding the cancellation of allotment or MS Shoes being illegal and void, the simple mandate directing the parties to act according to the terms and conditions of the allotment letter will suffice.

The sixth point of law raised by the Ld. Counsel for HUDCO is that MS Shoes is guilty of gross latches in impugning the letter of cancellation and seeking to stay the allotment of the suit property. In support of this contention, the Ld. Counsel stated that the letter of cancellation was issued on 2 May 1996, and the re-allotment of the plot was advertised on 17 October 1996. The last date of submission of tenders was finally, after extension, fixed 31 December 1996. MS Shoes, having full knowledge of all these, filed the present suit only. In January 1997 when the entire process up to the stage of valuation of tenders was complete, and only the approval of the board of directors was required to allow the property towards the highest tenderer. Reference has been made to the decision reported AIR 1979 SC 1628 and AIR 1987 SC 251. I have perused the relevant paragraphs of the judgments. The counsel for MS Shoes has contended the judgment cited was passed in a written petition, an extraordinary constitutional remedy, whereas the remedy reported to by MS Shoes is a statutory remedy providing for the filing of the suit within the prescribed period of limitation. The contention of the counsel for MS Shoes carries weight. The judgments cited by the counsel for HUDCO were passed in written petitions. No limitation applies to writs, whereas the same applies to suits. Therefore, MS Shoes can't be held guilty of laches. Moreover, the facts of the above-cited cases are distinguishable from those of the present case of MS Shoes.

The seventh point of law raised by the Ld. Counsel for HUDCO relates to the timely payment of installments being the essence of the letter of allotment dated 31 October 1994. The ld. Counsel for HUDCO has vehemently argued the terms for the letter of allotment read with the circumstances, including the insistence of the HUDCO vide letters dated 18 October 1995 and 31 January 1995 for payment of the 2nd installment, without interest on 31 October 1995 or with interest as per clause 5. (ii) and (iii), on or before 31 January 1996 clearly establishes the intention that timely payment of the installments was the essence of the contract.

To appreciate this contention of Ld. Counsel for HUDCO, I have specifically thoroughly pursued the allotment dated 31 October 1994. The schedule for payment of the installments is laid down in paragraph 5. (ii) and (iii). The payment for Hotel Site is given under category (A) and car parking space under category (B). The dispute is concerning the payment of the 2nd installment payable before the end of one year of the date of the allotment letter (i.e., before 31 October 1995). This second installment could also be paid with interest at 16% for three months if the payment is made after the due date.

I am in agreement with the contentions of the counsel for HUDCO in respect of timely payment of installments being the essence of the letter of allotment, as also supported by judgments reported in (1995) Supp. 2 SCC 33, AIR 1993 SC 1742, and AIR 1965 Mad. 352. But this letter of allotment is to be read and not in parts. If time is an essence of the contract in respect of the payment of installment, equally is important the handing over of the possession of the suit land to MS Shoes, as is specifically laid down in paragraph 5 (ix) of the said letter of allotment. Let it be reproduced.

"Upon the receipt of the first installment of the premium both for the Hotel site and the Car Parking space, as indicated in para 5(vi), the agreement to sublease will be made available to you for execution for the Hotel Site, and upon its execution, the possession of the Hotel Site will be handed over to you for raising construction."

The parties failed to execute all required documents for obtaining approval of the competent authority under the Urban Land (Ceiling and Regulation) Act 1976, and also the appropriate authority in terms of Chapter XC of the Income Tax Act, and this agreement to sublease which was to be made available to MS Shoes for execution for the

Hotel Site, and upon its execution, the possession of the Hotel Site was to be handed over to MS Shoes for raising construction. After reading part 5 (vi), (ix) and para 6 of the letter of allotment dated 11 October 1994, I come to form the opinion that as regards execution of required documents as aforesaid, both the parties were required to act in concert and co-operation, which concert and co-operation were lacking between the parties. However, this is a matter to be proved or disproved on merits at the closest proper stage. Further, it is relevant to record here that the Ld. Counsel for HUDCO has stated that without prejudice to the rights of HUDCO, it is submitted that given the clearances of Urban Land Ceiling Authority and Income Tax Clearance under form 37(I) (which clearance would be deemed to have been received within four months of such application, i.e. sometime in May 1996, and MS Shoes' failure to have deposited the amount directed by the Honorable High Court, MS Shoes can't seek shelter under clause 5 (iv) of the letter of allotment dated 31 October 1994. The council further stated that no clearance of the Urban Land Ceiling authority is required in respect of the Government Land. Having considered the above statement of counsel for HUDCO, I again say it is all due to the non-cooperative attitude of the parties that resulted in the cancellation of the allotment, causing heavy financial loss to the Government and MS Shoes as well. Had the parties acted timely in the corporation, the agreement would have materialized. Had MS Shoes got possession of the suit land, the financial institution would have certainly invested money in the project, and thus MS Shoes could have saved himself from the cancellation of the allotment in his favor. It is admitted that 40% of the total consideration of the transaction amounting to more than Rs.25 crores (MS Shoes padded US Dollar as the first installment which amount belongs to various financial institutions, and those institutions have also come in court with their respective reply to an application under Order 1 rule 10 of the Code of Civil Procedure for being impleaded as a party in the suit. HUDCO, HUDCO, given clause 5(iii), has canceled the allotment and forfeited the total amount deposited to date by MS Shoes. This act of forfeiture on the part of HUDCO is a hasty step in ignoring the undeniable fact that the forfeited money circulating in crores belongs to public institutions. This does not become of a hundred percent Government-owned entity (HUDCO) to forfeit this amount hastily, knowing fully well that in the same allotment letter dated 31 October 1994 is also provided in the end in para no.7 "that in the event of non-payment of the above-said amounts by the date specified and return of the proforma of an agreement to sublease duly signed, the acceptance of the offer may by you (MS Shoes) shall stand rescinded without further reference to you, and the earnest money of Rs. Two crores only (US Dollar 0.55 million) paid by you (MS Shoes) shall stand forfeited." After reading para no.7 and para no.5(iii), I am of the considered opinion that the HUDCO, being a hundred percent Government-owned agency and entity, acted with callosity towards MS Shoes in forfeiting the entire amount of the first installment, thus rendering MS Shoes to get ousted from the business world, and further rendering the financial institutions who advanced the said forfeited amount, to accompany and watch their money snatched away without any fault of them. The financial institutions have repeatedly written to the Ministry of Housing and Urban Development, Government of India, vide their letters dated 22 November 1996, 30 December 1996, 13 June 1996 to protect their money paid to HUDCO. This is part of the project cost launched by HUDCO, inclusive of the project of the Five-Star-Hotel Site, the subject matter of the suit, and further requested to issue instructions to HUDCO to keep the re-allotment in abeyance. Acting upon these letters also request made by the members of parliament, the then

Minister of Urban Affairs vide his order dated 14 June 1996 was pleased to stop the tenders of all the concerned properties at the disposal of HUDCO, inclusive of the suit land until further orders and public notice for cancellation of the tender was ordered to be issued in leading newspapers immediately. The copy of the letter is placed on record, and so are placed the various said letters written by the financial institutions. This order staying tenders by the then Minister concerned was reached after about one month of the cancellation of the allotment of MS Shoes.

The purpose of recording these facts is the Government itself, being the complete owner of the property in question, was not pleased with the act of HUDCO since it was not in the interest of public money to reschedule the payments towards these projects. These are the reasons which establish the act of HUDCO. In forfeiting, the entire amount of the first installment was a callous act and not justified. The HUDCO should have been @constructed with (illegible) of the earnest money of Rupees Two crores, as was provided in paragraph 7 of the letter of allotment. The HUDCO will be responsible for encouraging unnecessary litigation since huge amounts of financial institutions are involved.

So far as the blank proforma for sublease agreement is concerned, the supply of the same and the terms and conditions mentioned therein are not denied by the parties, but what denied HUDCO is its authenticity since the same is black, unsigned, and unexecuted. Certainty the said proforma is blank and unsigned, yet the fact remains it did not reach the HUDCO as required under the terms and conditions of the allotment letter towards MS Shoes, for which is responsible the non-cooperative attitude between the parties, as also observed by me above while discussing the above law points. Had it been executed, HUDCO would not have denied its terms and conditions. If this form is perused along with the aforesaid two letters of allotment, one dated 15 June 1993 by the Government of India and the other dated 31 October 1994 by HUDCO towards MS Shoes, it will stand borne out that the President has yet to execute the perpetual lease deed towards HUDCO and thereafter both the President and the corporation shall be in a position to execute the sub-lease deed towards the intended sub-lease after the President has executed the perpetual lease deed towards corporation and that the intended sub-lessee has paid fully the premium and other amounts as payable in terms of the letter of allotment and agreement to sublease. These documents have not yet been executed, and therefore, no such contract existed between the parties inviting the intervention of Article 299 of the Constitution.

Now I come over to the triple test, which MS Shoes is confronted with to fulfill and get through the same. So far as the first test, MS Shoes having prima -facie case in its favor is concerned. From the discussion and observation of the above law points, it can be safely concluded MS Shoes has a prima facie case worth being judged on facts. Factually, the suit of MS Shoes is prima facie sound, but the same sounds not if seam in the perspective of my observations on abuse of process and conduct of MS Shoes, and further observations made while discussing Order 2, Rule 2, of the CPC, and also while discussing section 10 of the CPC. The crux is the proper course for MS Shoes was to amend the previously instituted suit no. 275/96 before the Honorable High Court. As regards the balance of convenience, it is admitted fact that forty percent of the total consideration has been paid by MS Shoes towards the 1st installment, which amount is beyond Rupees Twenty-Five crores, and the same having been forfeited wrongly, putting MS Shoes and the financial institutions in a disadvantageous position. What has HUDCO lost? It is told on behalf of HUDCO that on account of the ex-party status quo order remaining in force, the HUDCO is suffering the loss of about four/five lacs daily, which it would have earned in the absence of the same since the highest bidder M/s. Leela Hotels and Convention Centre Ltd. have made an offer of Rupees two hundred seventeen crores and eighty-five lacs only, and on the allotment to him, HUDCO would be entitled to receive forty percent of the tender amount, i.e. a sum Rupees eighty-seven crores and fourteen lacs only within thirteen days of the allotment on which amount the HUDCO would have earned interest to the tune of Rs. four, five lacs daily.

I have given thoughtful consideration to this point of contention. HUDCO forgets the amount of MS Shoes forfeited by it, and on which amount he has been earning interest, but remembers that money which is not still in his pocket, although likely to come if the ex-party status quo order is vacated. If vacated, MS Shoes shall certainly suffer an irreparable loss from his business career. MS Shoes would have saved himself from being ruined of his business career had he remained serious and sincere in discharging his obligations of the agreement, particularly when he happened to catch a straw thrown by the Honorable High Court to save him from being drowned in an ocean of commerce, but MS Shoes preferred not to deposit Rupees fifteen crores and preferred to leave the saving straw for being drowned. I would also like to add here that the HUDCO was not in a mood to save MS Shoes. Had the mood been favorable to MS Shoes, the HUDCO would have granted some more reasonable extension for securing payment of installment, as it did in the case of Ansals. Although MS Shoes had moved an application under Order XI, Rule 14 CPC seeking production of the allotment letter and the extension application made by Ansals and grant of extension by HUDCO, the same was hastily opposed by HUDCO on legal grounds, and the result remained that the HUDCO did not like to produce the same. Although the same is not needed by me now, given my above-detailed observations on facts and law, the presumption can be drawn from the negative attitude of HUDCO it granted extensions to Ansals, whereas the same was refused to MS Shoes.

Therefore, the application under Order 39 Rules 1 and 2 CPC of MS Shoes is dismissed, and the ex-party status quo order dated 25 January 1997 is vacated.

In the last, it is made clear this order of mine shall not tantamount to any expression of opinion on the merits of this case.

Announced in open court.

Dated: 17 March 1997, Additional District Judge, Delhi

The Court held that in the previous suit MS Shoes could not claim the present relief, as the previous suit does not form the foundation of the subsequent suit, given the present suit is not barred in law.

On the other side, the court held the previous suit no. 275/1996 has not been disclosed since no documents have been placed on record. The Court neglected to check the item (iv) of the documents relied on the judgment which was the complete set of suit no. 275/1996 filed by MS Shoes. The application of HUDCO the suit 275/1996 became infructuous, and MS Shoes' application before the High Court for withdrawal of the suit had also been filed, but the court held it has not been disclosed what happened to these applications? The court neglected that there were no orders passed on these applications, and hence nothing else was required to be disclosed, as they were pending before the High Court.

The Court held that the relief of possession is not required, since if in the event of finding the cancellation of allotment or MS Shoes being illegal and void, the simple mandate directing the parties to act according to the terms and conditions of the allotment letter will suffice.

Court held that time was not the essence of the contract in respect of payment of installments. Equally important was handing over the possession of the land to MS Shoes, as laid down in the terms of the allotment letter.

Court held that HUDCO is a 100% Government-owned agency that has acted with responsibility towards MS Shoes in forfeiting the entire amount of its installment by snatching away the amounts of the financial institutions who advanced the amounts who have written to the Government several times to keep the re-allotment in abeyance.

The Court also held Members of Parliament and the Minister of the Government also stopped the re-tendering after the cancellation of allotment of MS Shoes, which shows the Government was not pleased with the acts of HUDCO towards MS Shoes. HUDCO will be responsible for encouraging unnecessary litigation since huge amounts are involved.

Court also observed the lease deed was yet to be executed by the Government in favor of HUDCO, and even after the payments were made by MS Shoes, the lease deed was not executed, neither agreement to sublease was executed, as in the absence of the lease, the same could not be done. No such contract existed between the parties, inviting the intervention of Article 299 of the Constitution.

Court also concluded MS Shoes has a prima facie case worth being judged on facts, and the suit is prima facie sound. On the other, held that the discretionary power of stay cannot be used, as suite no. 275/1996 was not disclosed.

Court also held that HUDCO, after receiving the amount beyond Rs. 25 Crores (US Dollar 7.05 million), has wrongly put MS Shoes and financial institutions in a disadvantageous position. What HUDCO has lost? HUDCO's statement that they are suffering a loss of Rs. Four / five lacs daily due to the stay as Leela Hotels and Convention Center Limited has made an offer of Rs. Two Hundred and Seventeen Crores and HUDCO must receive 40% of this amount from Leela Hotels within 30 days, on which HUDCO could earn an interest of Rs. four, five lacs daily.

Court also held the negative attitude of HUDCO towards MS Shoes, and on the contrary, extending Ansals extensions, but refusing MS Shoes.

Chapter: Twenty-Three

Ansals Interest Free Extensions of Instalments Loss of Rs. 10.90 Crores (US Dollar 3.00 million) Or Rs. 300 Crores (US Dollar 82.62 million) to Government Exchequer

The pressure of Ansals and their proximity with HUDCO's Officers and Government Officers were working to approve the interest-free extensions to be granted to Ansals, causing loss to the exchequer of Rs. 10.90 Crores (US Dollar 3.00 million). The loss was not Rs. 10.90 Crores (US Dollar 3.00 million), rather the appreciation of the shopping arcade land allotted to Ansals above the car park, which was a loss of Rs. 300 Crores (US Dollar 82.629 million).

The Ministry of Urban Affairs and Employment, the justification note put up on 28 March 1997 for extending interest-free extensions to Ansals:

Sub: Shopping Arcade space (Over Basement Car Parking space) allotted to M/s. Ansal Properties & Industries Ltd – Extension of Time for Payment of Installments

1. HUDCO Place (Community Center), Andrews Ganj Project is being implemented by HUCCO under the direction of the Ministry of Urban Affairs & Employment. The net resources generated from the development and disposal of the Project are to be utilized for the construction of maximum different houses/flats under the general pool residential accommodation. The Community Center Project

consists of 12 Blocks of Guest Houses, a Hotel Site, a Cultural Center Site, and a Shopping Arcade Site over the constructed Basement by HUDCO.

2. The space for the Shopping Arcade was allotted to M/s. Ansal Properties & Industries Ltd. (Ansals) vide Allotment Letter dated 10 March 1995. As per the Allotment Letter, the payment of Rs. 168.81 crores (US Dollar 46.49 million) to HUDCO were to be paid by M/s. Ansals in three installments as under: -

    i. within 4 weeks from the date of allotment letter (i.e., on
    ii. or before 6 April 1995) (Rs.84,40,46,600/-) (US Dollar 23.24 million) -50%
    iii. within 12 months from the allotment letter (i.e., on or
        a. before 9 March 1996) (Rs. 50,64,27,960/-) (US Dollar 13.95 million) -30%
    iv. within 18 months from the date of allotment letter (i.e., on or before 9 September 1996) (Rs. 33,76,18,640/-) (US Dollar 9.30 million) – 20% Rs.168,80,93,200/- (US Dollar 46.49 million)

Out of the above, the first installment of 50%, i.e., Rs. 84.40 crores (US Dollar 23.4 million) was by Ansals. The due date on 6 April 1995.

3. The Allotment Letter mentioned HUDCO will execute all required documents for obtaining the approval of Competent Authority under the Urban Land (Ceiling & Regulation) Act, 1976, and appropriate Authority's approval in terms of Chapter XX C of the Income Tax Act, and that only after obtaining required approvals HUDCO would execute the agreement to sublease and handover possession of the Shopping Arcade space allotted. However, HUDCO, being one of the organizations exempted to hold excess land in terms of section 19 of the ULC Act, did not require any approval from the Competent Authority to transfer the property in question to Ansals. The other approval under chapter xx C of the Income Tax Act was obtained both by HUD0 and Ansals in June 1995. Thereafter, the agreement to lease was executed between HUDCO and Ansals on 1 August 1995. The possession of the Shopping Arcade Space was handed over to Ansals on 10 November 1995.

4. As per the brochure of the Shopping Arcade space issued by HUDCO while inviting offers/bids, the possession of the space was to be given by June'95 for construction purposes. The construction was to be started after the Allottee obtained necessary approvals from the concerned authorities. The Municipal Corporation of Delhi (Municipal Corporation of Delhi) linked the sanctioning of the Shopping Arcade plans of Ansals with the regularization/ sanctioning of the plans for the Car Parking Basement, which was constructed by HUDCO, which was regularized by the Municipal Corporation of Delhi on 8 April 1996. After regularization of the plans of the Car Parking Basement, the Municipal Corporation of Delhi processed the plans of Ansals for the Shopping Arcade. Therefore, there was a delay in sanctioning the plans of the Shopping Arcade of Ansals due to the non-regularization/sanctioning of the building plans of the Car Parking Basement constructed by HUDCO. Therefore, the initial extension for six months (without interest) was granted to Ansals for the payment of Second and Third installments by the Board of Directors of HUDCO in their meeting

held on 1 March 1996 and 23 August 1996, respectively. Accordingly, the repayment date for the second installment was due on 9 September 1996, and the third installment was due on 9 September 1996, and the third installment was due on 9 March 1997. The same decision was conveyed to Ansals by HUDCO. The interest in this period as per the terms of the allotment letter dated 10 March 1995 works out to Rs.6.96 crores (US Dollar 1.91 million) approximately.

5. M/s. Ansals insisted on HUDCO for a further extension on similar grounds. In this context, HUDCO obtained the opinion of Shri Dipankar Gupta, Barrister and Senior Advocate of the Supreme Court. Shri Gupta opined that if litigation results at this stage, either by way of cancellation of the agreement or claim of damages or otherwise, the project which is in the public interest, will suffer. He, therefore, recommended this is a case that ought to be negotiated and settled at this stage itself. Negotiation may consider the extension on the condition that Ansals would drop all their claims for damages or otherwise on account of alleged delays

on the part of HUDCO, which may have occurred until date.

6. The matter for a further extension was considered by the Board of Directors of HUDCO in their Board meeting held on 26 November 1996. The Board of Directors, keeping in view the legal opinion given by Shri Dipankar Gupta, Barrister, and applying Commercial Prudence, recommended further extension of a second installment by 4 months 8 days without interest (i.e., 9 September 1996 extended to 17 January 1997) and 2 months 4 days for a third installment without interest (i.e., from 9 March 1997 to 13 May 1997). The further extension with interest in a further period of 3 months is also permissible, as per the terms of the allotment letter dated 10 March 1995. The loss of interest due to the proposed extension, as recommended by the Board of Directors of HUDCO, works out to Rs.3.95 crores (US Dollar 1.08 million) as per the terms of the allotment letter dated 10 March 1995.
7. The extension already granted by HUDCO in Para 4 above, and the present extension proposed by HUDCO totals 10 months 8 days for the second installment and 8 months 4 days for the third

installment. It may be mentioned here that the Municipal Corporation of Delhi started processing Ansals's building plans of the Shopping Arcade after 8 April 1996, i.e., the date on which HUDCO's plans for the car parking basement were regularized (by Municipal Corporation of Delhi). As the deemed date of possession for installment was by June 1995, the delay on account of non-sanctioning of HUDCO's plans for car parking basement was 9 months 8 days, i.e., 1 July 1995 to 8 April 1996.

8. . HUDCO's proposal for an extension of time (Para 6 above) was examined in this Ministry (Page 69-85/N). In the circumstances stated at X on page 81/N, it was recommended Ansals may be given an extension of time for payment of the second installment: for 3 months 8 days instead of 4 months 8 days recommended by HUDCO without interest, and two months 4 days for the third installment, as recommended by HUDCO's Board of Directors. For the reasons mentioned in Para 7 on pages 84-85/N, it was recommended further extension, with interest, may be given up to 4 months for the second installment, and 3 months

with interest in the third installment. As the extended time for payment of a second installment with interest will expire on 17 April 1997, and as a decision on HUDCO's proposal is unlikely to be taken before that date, it is proposed this time may be extended by one more month, i.e., up to 17 May 1997. This will not result in any additional loss of interest to the Government. The loss of interest due to the extension proposed by the Ministry works out to Rs.3.25 crores (US Dollar 0.89 million) approximately as per the terms of the allotment letter Rs. 69.54 lacs (US Dollar 1.96 million) per month for 2nd installment and Rs.46.36 lacs (US Dollar 0.12 million) per month for 3rd installment).

9. The extension recommended by the Ministry (in para 8 above) is subject to a suitable and unambiguous disclaimer on stamp paper by Ansals for all their claims for damages or otherwise on account of alleged defaults on the part of HUDCO which may have occurred till date, and that the party shall make payment of the ground rent from the date of actual possession, i.e., 10 November 1995.

10. Recently there have been reports in the newspaper alleging that HUDCO has adopted a dual policy in extending the time for payment of installments for its project at Andrews Ganj. This issue was raised in Parliament, and a copy of the reply in respect to Rajya Sabha Starred Question No. 371 for 20 March 1997 explains the Position (Slip 'XX'). As is evident, unequal alleged treatment does not arise.

11. When 'this proposal' was submitted to the Honorable Prime Minister (as UDM), PMO directed this Ministry (Page 86/N) to obtain the views of the Ministry of Finance on the loss to the Government of the decisions recommended in paragraph 7 on pages 84-85/N. In this context, the proposal of this Ministry recommending further extension of time up to 17 May 1997 for payment with the interest of the second installment, as recommended in paragraph 8 of this note above, may also be noted.

12. In the circumstances stated above, the views of the Ministry of Finance are solicited on the financial implications of the proposal in paragraphs 8 and 9 of this notes.

Signed by Mr. Ashok Arora, Section Officer (Land) March 1997. Put up to Joint Secretary (Urban Development) who approved same day, put up to Additional Secretary (Urban Development), Mr. Hamender Kumar who approved same day, put up to Joint Secretary (Finance) who on 31 March 1997 referred a reference has also been designated as decided by Prime Minister's Officer, which was marked to Additional Secretary (Expenditure) in the Ministry of Finance and was sent to examine.

Chapter: Twenty-Four

Leela Hotels Were Allotted Five-Star Hotel Land Subject to Outcome of Suit 1/1997 of MS Shoes

HUDCO hurriedly allotted the five-star hotel land to Leela Hotels Limited without waiting for the appeal (CM Main) MS Shoes filed their freedom since after the allotment to Leela Hotel's third-party interest would be created.

The Chief (Disposal), HUDCO on 31 March 1997 issued an allotment letter to M/s. Leela Hotels & Convention Center Ltd. Regarding Allotment of Hotel Site measuring 11480 sq. meter (approx.) at HUDCO Place, Community Center Andrews Ganj, New Delhi.

Please refer to your financial bid for the Hotel Site that opened on 31 December 1996.

1. Housing & Urban Development Corporation Ltd. (HUDCO) is pleased to accept your offer and allot the above Hotel Site to you for Rs. 201.00 Crores (Rupees Two Hundred One Crore only) (US Dollar 55.35 million). On a perpetual sub-leasehold basis. The site has permissible buildable space of 25,000 sq. Mtrs. and permissible basement of 4000 sq. meter.
2. We are also pleased to allot to you the underground car parking space with the capacity to park about 333 cars on a separate area in the underground car

parking space (adjacent to the Hotel site) on a license basis at a fixed cost of Rs. 16.85 crores (Rupees Sixteen Crores Eighty-Five Lakhs only) (US Dollar 4.64 million). Further underground linkage space of about 60 sq. mt. (approx.) @ Ra. 15,500/- per sq. meter is also allotted to you on a license basis. In addition, the license fee will be Rs. 10/- per annum for the Car Parking Basement and underground linkage space.

The broad terms and conditions for the allotment are as under: -

i. You shall compel the payment of premium, i.e., consideration of Rs. 201,00,00,000/- (Rs. Two Hundred One Crore only) (US Dollar 0.55 million) for the allotment of the Hotel site and Rs. 16,85,00,000/- (Rupees Sixteen Crore and Eighty-Five Lakhs only) (US Dollar 4.64 million) for the allotment of car parking space and Rs. 9,30,000/- (Rupees Nine lacs thirty thousand only) (US Dollar 0.24 million) for the allotment of 60.00 sq. mt. (approx.) of linkage space, i.e., a total of Rs.217,94,30,000/- (Rupees Two Hundred Seventeen Crores Ninety-Four

Lacs Thirty thousand only) (US Dollar 60.02 million). The payment shall be determined in the following manner:

PAYMENT SCHEDULE

a) Within four weeks of the date of this allotment, letter (i.e., before 28 April 1997) – 40% (Rs. 87,17,72,000) (US Dollar 24.00 million)
b) Within one year from the date of this allotment, letter (i.e., before 31 March 1998) 30% (Rs. 65,38,29,000) (US Dollar 18.01 million)
c) Within two years of the date of this allotment, letter (i.e., before 31 March 1999) 30% (Rs. 65,38,29,000) (US Dollar 18.01 million)

Rs. 217,94,30,000 (US Dollar 60.02 million)

The above payments shall be made through demand drafts drawn towards HUDCO payable at New Delhi.

ii. No extension of time will be allowed to you for the payment of the first installment. In case of default of the first installment on the date specified, the allotment shall, without any further reference to

> you. Stand automatically canceled, and in such a case, the earnest money paid shall stand forfeited. The Earnest Money Deposited (EMD) paid by you would be adjusted towards payment of the first installments. The second and third installments will have to be paid on or before the dates specified in the allotment letter. In the event of your inability to pay the second and third installments on the specified dates, you will have the option to pay these within three months of the dates specified for payment of the second and third installment with interest calculated @ 20 percent per annum on the amount of the installment due. If you fail to pay the second and third installments within the time permitted hereunder, the allotment shall stand automatically canceled without any further reference to you, and in that event, 50% of the amount paid up to that date shall stand forfeited, and the balance 50% will be refunded to you without interest thereupon HUDCO will be free to re-auction the hotel site.

Please note the time for payment of the premium as per the allotment letter shall be the essence of the contract, irrespective of whether you have been able to start the construction on the allotted hotel site or not due to any reason whatsoever.

iii. Immediately after the payment of the first installment you, with the help of HUDCO, shall take all required approval in terms of Chapter XX C of the Income Tax Act, so that there is no delay in handing over the possession of the plot. If this approval is not accorded, HUDCO will refund the amount paid without any interest, and you shall not be entitled to claim any compensation or damages from HUDCO.

iv. No approval under the Urban Land (Ceiling & Regulation) Act is needed for transferring the Hotel site by HUDCO to you. If any approval under the said act is needed, it will be obtained by you at the appropriate time.

v. Upon the receipt of the first installment of the premium for the hotel site, the built car parking space, and the linkage space, as indicated above. The Agreement to sublease will be made available to you for execution for the Hotel Site, and upon its execution and compliance of condition, as indicated in paragraph (iii) above, the possession of the Hotel

Site will be handed over to you for raising construction.

vi. The Hotel building shall be constructed within the parameters of the approved Urban Design Form after obtaining required approvals for building plans etc. from the concerned local authorities and the Delhi Urban Arts Commission. The height, coverage in the basement, and such related development controls shall be as per the operative norms of the statutory authorities.

vii. You shall obtain clearance for Five Star rating for the Hotel from the Department of Tourism/Government of India/Competent Authority and shall be responsible for making all arrangements as are necessary for the maintenance of the Hotel building, including the firefighting system and the services.

viii. You shall have to arrange electric and water connection from the concerned authorities directly at your cost.

ix. (ix) You will be required to complete the construction of the Hotel Building within five years of the date of handing over possession of the Hotel site on a license basis for the construction of the

Hotel building on the terms and conditions as may be specified by the Government of India/HUDCO. In the event of non-completion of construction within the stipulated time. HUDCO may consider granting an extension if exceptional and unavoidable circumstances have prevented you from complete construction within the stipulated time. The decision of HUDCO regarding the exceptional and unavoidable circumstances will be final and binding upon you. In case the construction is not completed within the prescribed period or the extended period, as decided by HUDCO, HUDCO will have the right to take over the land along with the unfinished building with materials, fixtures, if any, on the site without payment of any compensation to you.

x. The land for the Hotel Site was given to HUDCO by the Government of India in July 1990 on a long-term lease of 99 years. The land will in turn be leased to you on a sub-lease basis, co-terminus with the 99 years' lease period given to HUDCO. The Perpetual Lease for Hotel Site is yet to be executed by the Government in favor of HUDCO. The lease and sub-lease and Agreement to Sublease will be in the form approved/specified by the Government. All costs for the preparation of the required documents, stamp duty, registration charges, and other levies of any kind whatsoever will have to be borne by you.

xi. You shall pay annual ground rent to HUDCO at the rate of 2-1/2% of the premium for land for the Hotel site from the date of handing over possession of the Hotel site for construction. The ground rent shall be revised periodically following the terms and conditions of the sub-lease deed. Property taxes and other municipal levies shall be borne by you from the date of possession of the site.

xii. The Habitat Services Center (HSC), a Society registered under the Societies Registration Act 1860, or any other agency identified by HUDCO will be the maintenance agency for the common area/services. You shall deposit maintenance charges with HUDCO, including depreciation (if any) for the common services (car parking basement, roads, external lighting, etc.) Of the complex with HUDCO in advance every quarter until maintenance arrangements are handed over to the Maintenance Society proposed to be formed by all the allottees of the Community Center, HUDCO Place, Andrews Ganj, following the provisions of the Delhi Apartment Ownership Act or any other agency established as per the terms and conditions of the Perpetual Sub-lease document. You shall be deemed to have agreed to become a member of the Maintenance Society and abide by its bye-laws. The tentative expenses are estimated to be around Rs. 50/- per sq. Meter per annum of the buildable space (i.e., 25,000 sq. mtr) for the hotel. An initial interest-free deposit equivalent to two quarters (i.e., Rs. 6.25 lakhs) (US Dollar 0.16 million) will have to be deposited at the time of payment of the second installment for the Hotel Site, to be used as a Corpus Fund for maintenance purposes by the society.

xiii. You shall not have any authority to sell, transfer, assign, or otherwise part with the possession without the prior permission of the lessor/HUDCO. You may, at the discretion of HUDCO, be permitted to raise a loan only for construction of the building and equipment, to mortgage the premises subject to such terms and conditions, including recovery of 50% unearned increase in the value of this land, as will be laid down in the lease documents, and subject to the first charge of HUDCO for the unpaid cost of land for the Hotel Site, as well as other dues payable hereunder.

xiv. The Hotel site and the building constructed thereon shall not be used for a purpose other than a Hotel. Similarly, car parking spaces shall be used only as car parking and for no other purpose.

xv. You shall be permitted to use the permissible percentage of the total covered area for activities/trades, ancillary to the Hotel, as approved by the concerned local authorities.

xvi. You shall not deviate in any manner from the layout plan nor alter the size of the Hotel site for the said purpose either by sub-division, amalgamation, or otherwise falling, which HUDCO in its discretion will be entitled to cancel the sub-lease and forfeit the amount paid by you.

xvii. You may license out the spaces meant for activities/trade up to permissible limits, ancillary to the Hotel only, and for such purposes for which they are meant.

xviii. You shall ensure the licensee of the space carved out of the area meant for activities/trade, ancillary to the Hotel, observes the general condition of the sublease entered into between you and HUDCO and the lease deed entered into between the HUDCO and the Government of India. The license of the space meant for activities/trade, ancillary shall not use or be permitted to be used the space referred to above or any portion thereof for any purpose whatsoever other than the prescribed use.

xix. The allotment will be subject to the outcome of suit No. 1/97 filed before the Additional District Judge Delhi, and any appeals or other proceedings arising therefrom or outcome of the suit No. 275/96 filed before the Honorable High Court of Delhi. MS Shoes East Ltd. Has instituted both the suits, the previous allottee of the Hotel Site. In the event of any order or decree, being passed in the above-mentioned suits, etc. necessitating the refund of the consideration paid by you for the allotment of the hotel site. HUDCO shall refund the consideration as per the orders of the Court, and for which no interest shall be payable by HUDCO.

You are now requested to deposit an amount of Rs. 85,17,72,000/- (Rupees Eighty-Five Crore Seventeen Lacs Seventy-Two thousand only) (US Dollar 23.45 million) after adjusting the amount of Rs. 2.00 crores (Rupees Two crores only) (US Dollar 0.55 million) already deposited by you as earnest money with the offer towards the payment of the first installment of the Hotel site, basement car parking space, and underground linkage space You are requested to execute the above payments and initiate action for obtaining approvals under paragraph 4(iii) above.

The five-star hotel land along with the car park was allotted to Leela Hotels Limited, subject to the outcome of suit no. 1/1997 pending before the Court of Mr. R.S. Arya, Additional District Judge. The property was allotted more than three times than it was allotted to MS Shoes, which means there was a three-fold appreciation of the properties.

Chapter: Twenty-Five

HUDCO Obtained Legal Opinion from Solicitor General of India to Issue Instalments Extension Letter to Ansals without Approval of Government.

Since the interest-free extensions were pending to be approved by the Government, as they were referred to Additional Secretary (Expenditure), Ministry of Finance for their view, HUDCO sympathetically favoring HUDCO promised them in writing of granting the extensions of installment without interest.

In the garb of granting the extensions, HUDCO obtained another legal opinion of Mr. T.R. Andhyarujina, Solicitor General of India, on 9 April 1997.

Opinion of Solicitor General of India, given on 9 April 1997. Ex-parte – HUDCO allotment of Shopping Arcade to Ansals Properties & Industries Ltd.: -

The basic question is, what are the dates on which Ansal is obliged to pay the second and third installments of the premiums under the facts and circumstances of the case.

The important facts to note are the following:

The brochure issued by HUDCO stated HUDCO should provide certain services, the cost of which would be shared on a proportionate basis with the allottee. This included an underground car parking space for 210 cars out of a basement being constructed by HUDCO. The brochure stated that:

"The allottee could take the construction by June 1995, after the allottee obtains the necessary approvals from the concerned authorities." If for any reason the possession of the area was not given to the allottee for construction purposes by June 1995, HUDCO would pay simple interest at 6% to the allottee on the amount till date."

On 1 March 1995, the allotment letter was issued with Ansal. The total consideration was Rs. 157 crores (US Dollar 48.41 million). The payment was to be made in the following manner: -

i. Within 4 weeks from the date of allotment letter (i.e., on or before 6 April 1995)–50%
ii. Within 12 months from the date of allotment letter (i.e., on or before 9 March 1996)–30%
iii. Within 18 months from the date of allotment letter (i.e., on or before 9 September 1996)–20%

On 6 April 1995, Ansal obtained the payment of the first installment of 50%, namely Rs. 82,90,46,000. The second installment in terms of allotment letter was due on or before 9 March 1996. However, the Municipal Corporation's sanction for the construction of the basement by HUDCO was delayed. Though formal possession of the site was given by HUDCO on 10 November 1995, since Ansal had to build the shopping arcade over the underground basement, Ansals could claim it was prevented from taking up its construction until the basement was constructed by HUDCO was sanctioned by the Municipal Corporation of Delhi.

On 21 February 1996, Ansal requested HUDCO for an extension of 8 months from 9 March 1996 for the payment of the second installment, which meant the payment of the second installment on 9 November 1996 (assuming that the expression "by June 1995" meant "on or before 1 June 1995").

In reply to this request, on 1 March 1996, HUDCO agreed to give Ansal an extension of 6 months, i.e., 9 March 1996 to 9 September 1996, for the payment of the second installment.

On 1 March 1996, Ansal noted HUDCO having given the extension of the payment of the second installment for six months, i.e., making it payable on 9 September 1996. Ansals however requested a corresponding extension of the time gap of six months between the payment of the second and third installments. However, Ansal stated, "We had vided our earlier letters asked for a 9 months' extension period, curtailed to 6 months. We would request you to kindly review this and give us the extension of time of 9 months to which we are entitled." This paragraph could mean that Ansal did not accept the extension of the date of the second installment to 9 September 1996. However, as in March 1996, HUDCO's basement was still not sanctioned by the Municipal Corporation of Delhi, Ansal could claim that until HUDCO's basement was sanctioned by the Municipal Corporation of Delhi, it was not in a position to commence construction. June 1995, stipulated in the brochure, would have to be correspondingly extended to a date on which HUDCO had obtained the sanction of the Municipal Corporation of Delhi towards the basement.

HUDCO's plans were regularized by the Municipal Corporation of Delhi only on 8 April 1996. In consequence, HUDCO would have to become an extension of the period of 10 months and 8 days from 1 June 1995, in bringing about a state of affairs in which Ansal could start construction, and the date of the second installment would have to be correspondingly extended from 9 March 1996 by 10 months and 8 days, i.e., 17 January 1997. As Asal is not making any claim for HUDCO not handing over the possession of the site for construction purposes by June 1995 and is not asking HUDCO to pay simple interest at 6% on the amount paid to date by them, in terms of the Brochure, HUDCO also cannot refuse this extension.

On 24 July 1996, Ansal asked for an extension of 13 months, from 1 June 1995 to 11 July 1996, which would constitute the second installment due on 9 April 1997, and a corresponding 6 months gap between the payment of the second installment and the third installment. It appears Ansal is asking for an extension up to 11 July 1996, because its own plans were sanctioned by the Municipal Corporation of Delhi only on 11 July 1996. This would not be correct. The fact that Ansal's own plans were sanctioned on 11 July 1996 is not a relevant consideration. What is relevant is only the date on which Ansal could take up construction? That date, as stated above, is after 8 April 1996, and hence the extension for the second installment can only be for 10 months and 8 days.

On 20 August 1996, HUDCO communicated its rejection of Ansal's proposals for an extension of 13 months. HUDCO's board on 26 November 1996 at its 226th board meeting agreed for a further extension for payment of the second installment for a further period of 4 months and 8 days, i.e., 10 months and 8 days. This was a correct decision, though it may be stated it is not understood on what basis HUDCO resolved that further extension for the third installment would be only for 2 months and 4 days.

HUDCO referred its proposals to the Government of India. It appears the Government has not communicated its views on HUDCO's proposal, and consequently, HUDCO has not intimated the extension of payment of the 2nd installment to 17 January 1997 to Ansal.

In my opinion, it was necessary for HUDCO to communicate the aforesaid extension of 10 months and 8 days to Ansal, so that Ansal was aware of the liability for the payment of the second installment on 17 January 1997. In any case, it is imperative to communicate this extension as early as possible now to Ansal to make it liable to pay the second installment and the third installment on 17 July 1997. If Ansal claims it was not intimated in advance of the due date of the second installment, it is at least liable to make the payment of the second installment immediately on HUDCO's intimation. In that event, HUDCO's claims for interest from 17 January 1997 until payment of the second installment can be reserved for arbitration.

HUDCO is an autonomous company, and in law, it is not obliged to take the approval of the Government of India. However, if the board of directors wants to be on the safe side, it should be pointed out to the Government that its failure to approve HUDCO's proposal will prejudice the recovery of an enormous amount from Ansal, and it is necessary to immediately communicate HUDCO's decision to Ansal.

If, after performing its demand for payment of the second installment as aforesaid, Ansal refuses to pay the 2nd installment, HUDCO would be entitled to terminate the allotment, but HUDCO would have to do that after 17 April 1997, giving Ansal the benefit of the extended period of 3 months with payment of interest at stipulated in the terms of allotment.

Even the Solicitor General of India's opinion, taken by HUDCO to help Ansals, was that unless the car park basement was sanctioned, the construction of the building could not be taken up. In the case of MS Shoes, five-star hotel construction could not be taken up similarly, as even the revised layout plans approval was required to be taken.

In the opinion of the Solicitors General of India, the extension of interest-free installments could be given until the building plans of the car park basement were sanctioned. In the case of MS Shoes to date, HUDCO concealed the entire situation from MS Shoes.

The opinion further stated the car park basement was regularized on 8 April 1996, until then HUDCO was obliged to extend the installments of HUDCO. But in the case of MS Shoes until September 1999, until the revised layout plans were approved, the building plans for the construction of the hotel could not be entertained, which was concealed from Leela Hotels as well. Let us consider what happens to Leela Hotels shortly.

The opinion further strengthened HUDCO is an autonomous company, and in law, it is not obliged to take the approval of the Government of India. In the case of MS Shoes, the scam by HUDCO is still to be watched?

Based on the legal opinion obtained by HUDCO to help Ansals, Chief (disposal), HUDCO, Mr. P.K. Garg to Ansal

Properties & Industries Limited on 11 April 1997 regarding rescheduling of payment of installments.

1. Please refer to your letter dated 22 November 1996. 26 November 1996, 4 December 1996, 23 January 1997, and 28 February 1997 requesting for a further interest-free extension of (i) 4 months, 8 days for the payment of the 2nd installment, and (ii) 4 months and 8 days for the payment of 3rd installment, thereby keeping a gap of 6 months between the payment of 2nd and 3rd installments.
2. Your request was placed before the HUDCO Board of Directors, who kept in view all the facts considered a further extension of 4 months 8 days for payment of 2nd installment without interest, and 2 months 4 days without interest in payment of 3rd final installment, subject to the approval of the Government of India awaited. This decision was subject to your giving an unambiguous disclaimer on stamp paper, as agreed by you, and depositing the payment of the ground rent for two years amounting to Rs.7.85 crores (US Dollar 2.21million).

3. Pending the government approval to the time extension, as you had agreed for the extension of a 2nd installment by further periods of 4 months 8 days, you ought to have compelled the payment of the 2nd installment without interest on or before 17 January 1997, or you may secure payment of the same with interest on or before 17 April 1997, and make arrangements for payment of the 3rd installment on or before 13 May 1997 without interest or 13 August 1997 with interest as you may choose under the letter of allotment.
4. We once again state that the decision of HUDCO to grant the further extension of 4 months 8 days for payment of the 2nd installment, and 2 months 4 days for payment of the 3rd installment (you agreed to which extension during discussions) is subject to approval by the Government of India, and any decision taken by the government of India on the reference made by HUDCO may, if necessary, change the situation, but until any such change if any is communicated to you. You are bound to act following the contents of this letter.
5. The extension as above or which will finally be granted with the approval of the Government will

be binding on you and is not to be deemed as a waiver of time being the essence of the contract, rather reconfirms the same if the 2nd and 3rd installments are not paid on or before the aforesaid dates, the allotment will stand canceled without further reference to you, as no further extension under any circumstances can be granted by HUDCO.

6. Concerning payment of the 2nd installment which fell due on 17 January 1997 (without interest) or can be paid by 17 April 1997 with interest as per clause 6(iii) of the letter of allotment, this extended date has been specifically agreed to by you and has been in your knowledge all along. Please note therefore that no further communication by HUDCO was required for the same, and you are bound now to secure payment of the same by 17 April 1997 with interest, as stated above.
7. You are therefore requested to obtain the payment of the 2nd installment with interest expeditiously, and in any event, not later than 17 April 1997, along with ground rent of Rs.7.85 crores (US Dollar 2.21 million) for two years from the date of possession, i.e., 10 November 1995, failing which the allotment

> will stand terminated. You are also requested to execute a disclaimer in the format enclosed on the requisite stamp terminated. You are also requested to execute a disclaimer in the format enclosed on the requisite stamp paper of Rs.10/-, subject to the execution of which disclaimer HUDCO agreed to the extensions.

HUDCO informed the extensions to Ansals, which were subject to pay off due ground rent of Rs. 7.85 Crores (US Dollar 2.21 million) and an unconditional disclaimer that Ansals will not file/claim any further damages for the delay in the sanction of car park basement building plans. Now let us see whether Ansals would comply with these conditions shortly or any time?

Chapter: Twenty-Six

Mr. V. Suresh, CMD HUDCO Was Anti MS Shoes, Destroyed Mr. Pavan Sachdeva Totally

Chairman-cum-Managing Director, HUDCO, Mr. V. Suresh on 12 April 1997 to Mr. S. Banerjee, Joint Secretary, Ministry of Urban Development:

Kindly refer to the detailed discussion we had today in the Ministry regarding the case of disposal of the Shopping Arcade at HUDCO Place, Andrews Ganj, and an issue related to the extension of time for the payment to obtained by Ansal Properties & Industries Ltd.

While we are anxiously awaiting the decision of the Ministry regarding the proposal sent earlier, and the recent letter seeking permission for asking Ansals to designate the payment as per the decision of the HUDCO board, we had also taken the opinion of the Solicitor General of India (Mr. *Andhyarujina*) on the allotment of HUDCO Place to Ansals. The reply received from the Solicitor General of India is enclosed.

As decided in the meeting with you and Mr. G.C. Bhandari, Joint Secretary (Finance) and Director, HUDCO, we have communicated to Ansal, asking them to designate the payment as per the revised time scheduled by the HUDCO board. I am enclosing a copy of the letter sent to Ansals for your kind information.

We would now seek your early approval of the main proposal for time extension and related issues sent to the Government.

Mr. V. Suresh was anti-MS Shoes, destroyed Mr. Pavan Sachdeva totally by favoring Ansals, giving them interest-free extensions, and giving away the five-star hotel land to Leela Hotels. It also seems Mr. V. Suresh continued to pressure the Government approved Ansals extensions and had been approaching the Government Officers to get the approvals, as he had taken another legal opinion from the Solicitor General of India in respect of Ansals.

The observations of the Ministry of Finance were sent to the Ministry on 15 April 1997:

No previous matters on the subject are available in the PF-II Division.

The case, referred to the Ministry of Finance on the advice of the Prime Minister Office, relates to the extension of time for payment of installments by M/s. Ansal Properties & Industries Ltd. on account of allotment of Shopping Arcade Space (over basement car parking space) by HUDCO under HUDCO place (Community Center), Andrews Ganj Project. HUDCO has taken up the Andrews

Ganj project to augment resources for the construction of general pool government accommodation. This case has also been referred separately to the Ministry of Law & Justice on the advice of the Prime Minister's Office.

A brief history of the case is as under: -

- The space for Shopping Arcade was allotted to Ansals vide allotment letter dated 10 March 1995. As per the allotment letter, the payment of Rs. 168.81 Crores (US Dollar 46.49 million) to HUDCO was to be gained by Ansals in three installments, 50%, 30%, and 20%, by 6 April 1995, 9 March 1996, and 9 September 1996.
- As per the allotment letter, any delay on the part of the Ansals to deposit the installment would attract interest @ 16.48% p.a. or cancellation of allotment.
- Similarly, in case of delay in handing over of sight by HUDCO to Ansals, the party is to be paid 8% on the amount already deposited by them.
- Ansals deposited the first installment of Rs. 64.40 Crores (US Dollar 18.17 million) on 6 April 1995, the due date.
- The possession of the land was to be handed over by June 1995, however, the possession of the

Shopping Arcade space was handed over to Ansals on 10 November 1995. The delay is on the part of HUDCO.

- On 1 July 1995, the building plans were submitted to HUDCO by Ansals for forwarding the same to the Municipal Corporation of Delhi.
- HUDCO forwarded the building plans to the Municipal Corporation of Delhi on 28 August 1995, on the plea it was possible only after signing of the agreement by sub-lease deed, which was executed on 1 August 1995. It may be noted that the delay in execution of the deed and forwarding of the building plans to the Municipal Corporation of Delhi is on the part of HUDCO.
- The Municipal Corporation of Delhi accepted the building plans for examination only on 8 April 1996. Because Municipal Corporation of Delhi linked the sanctioning of the Shopping Arcade plans of Ansals with the regularization/sanctioning of the plans for Car Park Basement (on which the Shopping Arcade was to be constructed) and the Car Parking Basement Plan was regularized by the Municipal Corporation of Delhi on 8 April 1996 only.

As regards the sanction of building plan for the basement, these were submitted to Municipal Corporation of Delhi by HUDCO on 8 November 1995, although the construction of basement was started by HUDCO in the year 1993-94. Hence, the delay up to 8 April 1996, the date on which Municipal Corporation of Delhi accepted the Shopping Arcade building plans for examination, is on the part of HUDCO.

Because of a delay in possession of the site, Ansals requested for deferment of the second installment. The board of directors of HUDCO considered the matter and allowed interest from extension in respect of the 2nd installment from 9 March 1996 to 9 September 1996 and the 3rd installment 9 September 1996 to 8 March 1997. This was done without the prior approval of the administrative Ministry concerned.

Ansals requested a further extension of payment of 2nd & 3rd installments due to delay in sanction of the building plans of the Shopping Arcade due to non-sanctioning of the building plans of the car parking basement being constructed by HUDCO.

Keeping in view the various factors, HUDCO also obtained the legal opinion from Mr. Dipankar K. Gupta, Barrister and Senior Advocate (former Solicitor General of India), who opined this is a case that ought to be negotiated and settled in the public interest (earlier than entering into litigation). Because, if the matter is agitated before the Court, the Ansals may get the benefit of locking up 50% of the amount already paid, escalation in the cost of construction, and other factors including cresson in the reputation of the company due to delay in execution of the project, and accrual of returns, etc.

The matter was discussed with Ansals, who vide their letter dated 22 November 1996 agreed to an interest-free extension of the 2nd installment up to 17 January 1997 and the 3rd installment up to 25 May 1997.

Accordingly, HUDCO, vide their letter dated 28 November 1996 after considering the matter in their board meeting held on 26 November 1996, forwarded the proposal to the Ministry of Urban Affairs & Employment for approval for granting interest-free extension of payment of 2nd installment up to 17 January 1997 and 3rd installment up to 13 May 1997, subject to obtaining a suitable and unambiguous disclaimer on stamp paper from Ansals for any claims and payment of ground rent for two years amounting to Rs. 7.85 Crores by the party.

Considering the decision on HUDCO's recommendations is yet to be conveyed to HUDCO, and the date for obtaining payment of the 2nd installment was fast approaching and the allottee would require a reasonable period to make payment, the following proposal was sent to the Prime Minister Office for approval on 28 February 1997:

i. Extension of time to M/s. Ansals for payment of 2nd installment from 9 September 1996 to 17 December 1996, interest-free and with interest @ 16.48% up to 17 April 1997.
ii. Extension of time to M/s. Ansals for payment of 3rd installment from 9 March 1997 to 17 May 1997, interest-free and with interest @ 16.48% up to 13 August 1997.
iii. The extension of time proposed at (i) and (ii) above will be granted to Ansals, subject to the following conditions: -
    a) Ansals shall furnish a suitable and ambiguous disclaimer on stamp paper for all their claims for damages or otherwise on

account of alleged delay on the part of HUDCO which may have occurred until dated and

b) Ansals shall require payment of ground rent from the date of possession, i.e., 10 November 1995.

The Prime Minister Office, in their note dated 11 March 1997, has observed, although it is basically a matter between HUDCO and Ansals. It has been referred to the Government for orders. It has been stated that orders of Government cannot be decided upon here unless the Ministries of Finance, Law & Justice give their views on the loss to the Government and the legal implications of these decisions.

Given the above, it may be noted the delay on the part of HUDCO has occurred with effect from June 1995, because:

i. The possession of Shopping Arcade space was handed over to Ansals by HUDCO on 10 November 1995 instead of June 1995.
ii. On 1 July 1995, the building plans were submitted to HUDCO by Ansals on 1 July 1995 for forwarding the name of Municipal Corporation of Delhi. However, HUDCO forwarded the building

plans to the Municipal Corporation of Delhi on 28 August 1995, on the plea it was possible only after signing the agreement to sub-lease deed, which was executed on 1 August 1995. It may be noted that the delay in execution of the deed and forwarding of the building plans to the Municipal Corporation of Delhi is on the part of HUDCO.

iii. The Municipal Corporation of Delhi accepted the building plans for examination only on 8 April 1996 due to default on the part of HUDCO, who did not take the approval of the Municipal Corporation of Delhi for the construction of a Car Parking Basement, of which the Shopping Arcade of Ansals was to be constructed.

As regards loss on account of interest to be recovered from Ansals, it will be @ 16.48% on Rs. 50,64,27,960 (US Dollar 14.29 million), the 2nd installment with effect from 9 March 1996 to whatever date is finally decided for interest-free extension of the 2nd installment, and @ 16.48% on Rs. 33,76,18,640/- (US Dollar 9.52 million), the 3rd installment with effect from 9 September 1996 to whatever date is finally decided for interest-free extension of 3rd installment

As regards the first installment of Rs. 84,40,46,600 (US Dollar 23.82 million) received from Ansals, this has been kept in a non-lien account bearing an interest rate of 13%. Against this, HUDCO is liable to pay interest on this amount to Ansals 6% only, as per the allotment letter.

Joint Secretary & Financial Advisor has not examined the case concerned, apparently because he is a member of the HUDCO Board. He has recorded on page 67/N ante that being a member of the HUDCO board of directors. It will not be for him to make any comments.

Submitted please on 11 April 1997 to Joint Secretary (PF-II), who wrote that this is basically the interpretation of terms and conditions of the allotment of shopping arcade space. May therefore be regarded by the Personnel Division.

Signed 15 April 1997

Mr. R.K. Manchanda, Joint Director (Plan Finance. II) On 21 April 1997:

Discussed with Joint Secretary (PF-II)

In the Plan Finance II division, we are primarily concerned with the appraisal of the various projects/schemes.

Normally, we do not come into the picture so far as the matters relating to the actual execution of the implementation of these projects are concerned. This is done at the level of the Ministry/Department or their field-level agencies. This is the reason this file was referred to Joint Secretary (Per) for his advice. As indicated by the pre-page, Joint Secretary (Per) is of the view that Establishment Division is not concerned in this matter since this is a financial/commercial matter about a PSU. Accordingly, whatever information has been provided in the notes of the Ministry of Urban Development on pages 88 to 91 ante, the following observations are made.

It is not clear why the agreement to lease was executed on 1 August 1995, when the necessary approval under the Income Tax was obtained in June 1995 itself. There was a further delay of 3 months and 10 days in handing over space to Ansals, even after executing the lease on 1 August 1995.

It is also not clear why the building plan for the basement, which was started in 1993-94, was submitted to the Municipal Corporation of Delhi only on 8 November 1995. And the Municipal Corporation of Delhi took another 5 months to sanction/regularize the plan. What steps were taken to expedite the approval from the Municipal Corporation of Delhi, keeping in view the fact that non-regularization of the basement had also resulted in a delay in the approval of a building plan for the Shopping Arcade?

It is also not clear why the Municipal Corporation of Delhi accepted the building plans submitted by Ansals only on 8 April 1996, the date when the car parking basement plan was regularized. Why Municipal Corporation of Delhi could not consider the building plan for the Shopping Arcade, along with basement car parking. HUDCO did forward the building plan to the Municipal Corporation of Delhi on 28 August 1995, after signing the sub-lease deed.

An initial extension of six months for the payment of the second and third installment was approved by HUDCO. As per paragraph 6 of notes on pages 89-90. HUDCO board had decided to grant a further extension of 4 months and 8 days for the second installment, and 2 months and 4 days for the third installment. The basis for working out the period of these extensions needs to be spelled out. The maximum delay which could be accepted on the part of HUDCO is for 9 months, from August 1995 (when Ansals submitted the plan) to 8 April 1996 (when HUDCO submitted the plan to the Municipal Corporation of Delhi, and the Municipal Corporation of Delhi accepted the same). Calculation of the period of delay from a date earlier than the date of executing the lease between HUDCO and Ansal may not be justified.

Finally, it is observed the present issue concerning the execution of an agreement is a legal issue, and that is why HUDCO had sought advice from a lawyer. Now, the matter has also been referred to the Ministry of Law and Justice. Any loss to the Government/HUDCO will arise only if it is opined by the Law Ministry that the extension allowed to Ansals was not in order.

The Ministry of Finance finally decided it is not their part of work or decision to be made by the Finance Ministry, the opinion from the Ministry of Law & Justice be taken.

Chapter: Twenty-Seven

Letter Of Allotment 19 March 1996 to HUDCO does not Permit the Site can be Allotted for Hotel to Leela Hotels

As per terms of the allotment of Ansals, the loan could not be obtained from the bank to pay the installments. Ansals obtained a loan from the banks and the payment was forwarded of the 2nd installment by the bank. The allotment terms 6 (vi) states that at the discretion of the HUDCO loan could be raised only for the construction of the building. Ansals raised the loan of Rs. 40 Crores (US Dollar 11.28 million) *towards the payment of the 2nd installment.*

Vice President, Ansal Properties & Industries Limited, Mr. Pradeep Seth to Mr. P.K Garg, Chief (disposal), Crores, Lodhi Estate, New Delhi on 17 April 1997 regarding rescheduling of payment of installments.

Thank you for your letter dated 11 April 1997 communicating the reschedule of payment of installments for the above project as follows.

Second installment without interest up to 17 January 1997 and thereafter with interest till 17 April 1997.

Payment of 3rd installment up to 13 May 1997 without interest or up to 13 August 1997 with interest.

We in our various letters especially dated 23 January 1997 and 28 February 1997 had been requesting you to intimate us about the extension of time sufficiently before the date of expiry of the extended period so that the loan application by our bankers can be processed and the loan sanctioned and released enabling us to make the payments. Your contention that we should have made the payments of the 2nd installment as the decision of the Board of HUDCO was known to us is not tenable. In this connection, please refer to our letters dated 4 December 1996 and dated 28 February 1997 requesting you to communicate the decision of the board regarding rescheduling of payments. In absence of such communication. We could not approach our bakers for processing sanctioning and release of loans However despite the above requests only two banking days viz. 15 April 1997 and 17 April 1997, have been given to us to arrange such large funds.

However, we have been able to make arrangements and are sending payment of Rs. 52,72,92,800/- (Rupees Fifty-Two Crores Seventy-Two Lakhs Ninety-Two Thousand and Eight Hundred only) (US Dollar 14.88 million) being the payment towards 2nd installment with interest whilst the pay orders for payment of the principal amount of the second installment of Rs.50,64,27,690/- (US Dollar 14.29

million) are being sent directly by our bankers i.e., Punjab National Bank. Tolstoy Marg, New Delhi, we are enclosing herewith pay Orders aggregating to Rs.2,08,64,840/- (US Dollar 0.58 million).

As per details given below towards interest for 3 Months thereon.

Pay order No	Date	Amount	Issued By
015623	17.4.1997	1,50,00,000/-	The Bank of Tokyo
015624	17.4.1997	50,00,000/-	Mitsubishi Limited
212505	17.4.1997	8,64,840/-	Punjab National Bank

In principle we are agreeable to give the deed of disclaimer, as mentioned in our earlier correspondence with you we wish you had sent the draft of the disclaimer/release deed at least 15 days earlier for our study. We have sent the draft of the disclaimer to our solicitors for their comments and approval, and on receipt from them, we would execute the deed.

The rescheduling of the 3rd installment is different from what we had requested and we would like to take up the same separately as we still have time for making the payment of the third installment.

Concerning payment of ground rent please refer to our letter dated 9 January 1997 asking you to send us a copy of the perpetual lease deed executed by the president of India in favor of the Corporation and also a draft of the sublease which is to be executed by the president of India and HUDCO in favor of our company. We have not received the above document so far despite our constant follow-up. Notwithstanding the above and without prejudice to our right in this matter we would further like to bring to your notice that the ground rent was supposed to become payable from the date the site is handed over to us and it is possible to commence construction thereon.

Although the site was handed over to us on 10 November 1995, you are well aware that we could not take up the construction of the shopping arcade till the basement work executed by HUDCO was approved by the Municipal Corporation of Delhi. Only thereafter our plans could be entertained by the Municipal Corporation of Delhi Ground rent therefore if payable should become payable from the date, we have approved the plans sanctioned by Municipal Corporation of Delhi, which made it possible to commence construction at the site. The plans were sanctioned in July 1996 and therefore the ground rent if payable should become payable from that date.

The Chief Manager, Punjab National Bank on 17 April 1997 to HUDCO regarding allotment of Shopping Arcade site measuring 14700 sq. mt. to M/s. Ansal Properties & Industries Limited:

Please find enclosed the following pay orders aggregating to Rs. 50,64,27,900 (US Dollar 13.94 million) in your favor, on behalf of Ansal Properties & Industries Ltd. towards payment of installment of cost of the aforesaid plot allotted by you to the said company.

	Name of the Bank	Pay Order No. & Date	Amount (Rs.)
1	Punjab National Bank, Tolstoy House, New Delhi.	757/97 17 April 1997	49,04,27,960 (US Dollar 13.50 million)
2	SBI Commercial & International Bank, Bombay	001597 15 April 1997	1,60,00,000 (US Dollar 0.44 million)
		Total	50,64,27,900 (US Dollar 13.94 million)

We would submit that our bank has advanced a short-term loan of Rs. 40 Crores (US Dollar 11.01 million) to the Company for meeting the cost of date, the 2nd installment payable by the company on the allotted plot and as such we enclose herewith a letter dated 12 April 1997 in original from the company addressed to you. We request you to directly deliver the conveyance/title deed of the said plot to us after the title /conveyance deed is executed in favor of the company and also for marking a lien on the said plot of Shopping Arcade till the execution of the title /conveyance deed.

Please acknowledge receipt of payment of Rs. 50,64,27,960/- (Rupees Fifty Crores Sixty-Four Thousand Twenty-Seven Thousand Nine Hundred Sixty only) and also confirm having created a lien on the said property.

Signed Chief Manager, Punjab National Bank.

MS Shoes application for withdrawal of the suit in respect of 5-star hotel land was allowed on 22 April 1997 Present: Ms. Anuradha Datt, for the MS Shoes, Mr. M. Kumar, for the HUDCO:

I.A. 930/1997 - This application has been moved by MS Shoes for withdrawal of the suit. It was wrongly opposed by counsel for HUDCO. Orally, it was stated that certain averments had been made in the application to which the HUDCO had to controvert. Now the ld. Counsel for the applicant wishes to withdraw the application. Accordingly, this application is dismissed as withdrawn, I.A. stands disposed of.

Suit No. 275/1996 - Counsel for MS Shoes makes a statement that MS Shoes wishes to withdraw the suit unconditionally. Accordingly, the suit is dismissed as withdrawn. Cost of parties.

Signed by A.K. Srivastava, Justice

*A newspaper report reported by Hindustan Times correspondent on 28 April 1997 "**MS Shoes hotel site issue" "Ministry Misled Rajya Sabha on payment details":***

"The ministry of Urban Affairs and Employment appears to have misled Rajya Sabha while replying to a question on extension granted by HUDCO (Housing and Urban Development Corporation Limited) for making the payment of installment by MS shoes Ltd (MSSL) for the five-star hotel site at Andrews Ganj.

The reply concerning giving possession of the land after payment of first installment and completion of legal formalities by MSSL is contrary to the terms of the allotment letter issued by HUDCO says financial institution who had taken a heavy exposure in the project.

According to the Financial Institutions. It was HUDCO that was required to complete all the formalities and execute the sublease agreement.

*The Rajya Sabha members had asked the Minister that whether it is a fact that one of the parties Ansal Builder has been given possession of land and extensions while the other tenderer MS Shoes have neither been given possession of land nor extension for payment of the second installment despite initial payment of Rs.72 crores (*US Dollar 19.82 million) *collected from banks and public.*

In the reply to the question raised in parliament, it is stated that MS shoes did not get the permissions under the income tax Act due to which sublease agreement could not be executed and in the absence of the permissions, no possession could be given.

In contrast, HUDCO in its allotment letter dated 31st October 1994 has stated that it would execute documents that were never executed for obtaining the permissions under the urban land ceiling act and income tax act from these authorities under section 269 UC of the income tax Act.

The Government in its reply to the question of Suryabhan Patil Vahadane and Rajnath Singh Surya had stated that the High Court of Delhi also gave them time over and above the terms of allotment for making part payment of Rs.15 crore (US Dollar 4.13 million) which also did not comply with the MSSL. The non-compliance with the court order and the terms and conditions of the allotment resulted in the termination of the allotment.

However, under para 5 (ix) the allotment letter further mentioned that upon the receipt of the first installment of the premium both the hotel site as well as the car parking space as indicated in Para 5(ii) the agreement to sublease will be made available to you for execution the possession of hotel site will be handed over to you for construction.

According to the reply, Ansal Properties & Industries Ltd. (APIL) has been allotted space for building a shopping arcade over the car Parking basement constructed by HUDCO. As per the terms of the allotment, possession was to be handed over after the payment of the first installment and completion of the legal formalities, and execution of the agreement to sublease. APIL was given possession after complying with all the required formalities.

However, the payment of the second and subsequent installments was held up due to the delay in sanction/ regularization of the plans for the car parking basement of HUDCO as a result of which the plans for a shopping arcade to be built by APIL were not entertained by MCD for processing and consequent approval. Hence extension of time for the second and third installment had to be accorded to APIL. They have also applied for further extensions on the ground which is still under consideration, said the reply. ``

The question raised by parliamentarians to the minister replied by HUDCO also misled on the question of unequal treatment and why the possession was not given on receipt of the first installment by MS Shoes but it seems bureaucracy in India is tricky they can mold whichever way they wish to and V. Suresh was a big impressionist in the ministry besides keeping all officers on the side. No one paid heed to news pacers raising several issues. Normally all Governments around the world are supposed to look into all news and justify their acts but this was a peculiar case as the scam was going in a pre-planned manner against MS Shoes.

Chief (Disposal), HUDCO, Mr. PK Garg on 2 May 1997 to Director (lands) Ministry of Urban Affairs & Employment regarding Shopping Arcade at HUDCO Place, Andrews Ganj, New Delhi–Issue related to the extension of time for payment to be made by Ansals:

Please refer to our discussion on 1 May 1997 in your office regarding the above-mentioned subject. In this connection, I am enclosing herewith a copy of a letter dated 12 April 1997 addressed to Mr. S. Bannerjee, Joint Secretary, (Urban Development). Ansals has paid Rs. 50.64 Crores (US Dollar 13.94 million) and also interest for three months amounting to Rs. 2.08 Crores (US Dollar 0.57 million) on 17 April 1997. This is for your kind information and necessary action, please.

It was recorded by the Land & Development Office that land out of the Community Center at Andrews Ganj is allotted to Leela Hotels for construction of a 5-star hotel but the letter of allotment to HUDCO by the Land & Development Office does not indicate that the site can be allotted for a hotel. The perpetual lease in favor of

HUDCO is yet to be executed by the Land & Development Office.

Mr. Labh Singh Chane, Dy. Land & Development Officer/ noting dated 5 May 1997.

HUDCO has sent us a draft of the agreement of Sublease, which they propose to execute with Leela Venture in respect of the Hotel Site. HUDCO has requested that before the agreement for sub-lease is executed, the Land & Development Officer/Ministry may approve the same. The proposed agreement for Sub-Lease has been examined and the following comments are offered:

In the letter of allotment, the land is allotted for Community Center and all activities. The letter of allotment does not indicate that the site can be allotted for a hotel. However, it appears that HUDCO had earlier allotted this particular site to M/s. MS Shoes. The Ministry before finalizing the agreement for sublease may kindly consider the aspect.

The Perpetual Lease in respect of the site allotted to HUDCO is under finalization in consultation with the Ministry of Law. A clause needs to be incorporated in the agreement for sublease that the terms and conditions of the

Perpetual Lease will be a binding force and any clause in the Agreement for Sublease not in consonance with the Perpetual Lease will have no effect. In other words, the terms and conditions as contained in the Perpetual Lease shall prevail in all circumstances.

We need to clarify in the Agreement of Sub-Lease the status of the present lessee that of a mere license till the sub-lease is executed upon compliance with the terms and conditions of allotment.

As the site was earlier allotted to MS Shoes and it appears that the allotment has been canceled by HUDCO, any decision arising out of the court case will have to be implemented. It is felt that this fact needs to be reflected in the draft agreement for sublease that the same is subject to the outcome of the court case filed by M/s M.S. Shoes.

Subject to the above the agreement for sublease appears to be in order.

Chief Disposal, HUDCO, Mr. P.K. Garg on 5 May 1997 to Ansal Properties & Industries Ltd. Regarding shopping Arcade HUDCO Place Andrews Ganj New Delhi Reschedule of payment of installment:

Please refer to your letter dated 17 April 1997 we acknowledge receipt of the pay orders sent with your letter. The issues missed in your letter are answered in seriatim.

As already intimated, the perpetual lease deed to be executed between the government of India and HUDCO is yet to be finalized. Thereafter the sub-lease deed to be executed between HUDCO and Ansals will be finalized in consultation with the Government of India, therefore it is not possible to apprise you of the copy of the document requested at present.

As regards the payment of the ground rent it may be mentioned that in terms of brochure inviting offers, letter of allotment dated 10 March 1995, and the agreement to sublease dated 1.8.1995 the ground rent is payable from the date of handing over the possession of shopping arcade to Ansals since the possession was handed over to Ansals on 10 November 1995 the ground rent is payable from the date. Given this, HUDCO can't accept your request for charging the ground rent from any subsequent date you are, therefore, requested once again to pay the ground rent immediately failing value consequences following the letter and earlier correspondence on the subject shall follow.

The reschedule of the 3rd and final installment for 2 months 4 days was agreed by your chairman during discussions HUDCO chairman the 2 months 4 days extension as decided for the payment of 3rd installment sand and on this issue there will be no funder consideration however since the matter of extension of this is already under consideration of the government the view taken before the government for extension shall be binding on the Ansals subject to any communication from the government you are advised to make payment of 3rd and final installment within the dates specified in our letter dated 11 April 1997.

You are therefore requested to make payment of the ground rent of Rs. 7.85 (US Dollar 2.21 million) crores and also send a letter of disclaimer in the form already forwarded with our letter dated 11 April 1997.

The ground rent of Rs. 7.85 Crores (US Dollar 2.21 million) *due to Ansals and the extensions of installments granted to Ansals was subject to payment of ground rent and the unconditional disclaimer to be signed by Ansals. HUDCO demanded the same, but let us see whether the same is followed by HUDCO or again waived?*

The Ministry of Finance sent back the proposal after the extensions of Ansals stating why HUDCO had not taken the approval of the car park basement from Municipal Corporation of Delhi? The Ministry of Urban Development should look into the causes of this delay, fix up responsibilities for the delay and resultant loss. But the question is whether the Ministry fixed such responsibilities? No, as the Ministry was part of the entire game.

Joint Director (PF. II) Department of Expenditure Plan Finance II Division, Mr. R.K. Manchanda Letter on 9 May 1997 to Joint Secretary & Financial Advisor, Ministry of Urban Development, New Delhi. Regarding Shopping Arcade Space over Basement car parking space allotted to M/s. Ansal Properties Industries Limited–Extension of time for payments of installments.

The Ministry of Urban Development may please refer to their notes on the pre page.

The issue to be considered is whether HUDCO was legally obliged for the extension proposed/already given. Decisions on this can be taken only after examining the terms and conditions of the NIT and the agreement between

HUDCO and M/s. Ansal Properties Industries Limited. HUDCO did obtain a legal opinion in this case but the legal opinion, as can be made out from the details given in the file, is not based on a legal analysis of the documents but is a compromise formula.

Even if the Ministry of Urban Development agreed with the opinion given by Shri Deepankar Gupta that the matter should be negotiated, the sacrifices should have been from both sides. In the present case, however, it is noticed that the sacrifices are only from one side i.e., HUDCO agreed to an extension of time without payment of interest. At least from the file, it is not clear whether M/s. Ansal Properties Industries Limited has also given any concessions to HUDCO.

Under the circumstances, it is suggested that the case should be examined legally on merits and if it is found that HUDCO does not have a very strong case and mutual settlement by negotiations is called for then further extension of the period for payment of installments as proposed by the Ministry of Urban Development may be given but this extension should only be on payment of interest.

Another point in this connection is that soon after payment of the first installment in May 1995 M/s Ansal Properties Industries Limited took up the matter with HUDCO regarding regularization of the building plans for the basement and car parking. But HUDCO took 6 months to submit the building plans. Had this delay been avoided, it would not have been necessary for HUDCO to agree to the extension of time and the resultant loss of Rs. 6.96 crore due to non-payment of interest by M/s. Ansal Properties Industries Limited could have been saved. The Ministry of Urban Development should look into the causes of this delay, fix up responsibilities for the delay and resultant loss.

This issues with the approval of the Minister of State (Finance)

Sr. Vice President (Marketing), Ansals, Mr. Pradeep Seth on 12 May 1997 to P.K. Garg Housing & Urban Development Corporation Ltd. Regarding Shopping Arcade HUDCO Place Andrews Ganj New Delhi rescheduling of Payment of Installments.

Thank you for your letter dated 5 May 1997 on the above subject

We have noted that the perpetual lease deed to be executed between the government of India and HUDCO for the above-said site is yet to be finalized and that only on its finalization the sublease be executed between HUDCO and our company will be finalized and therefore it is not possible to get a copy of the documents at present.

In this connection, it is requested that we shall feel grateful if these documents are finalized expeditiously as same are required by our prospective space allottees in the shopping arcade.

We are separately sending a representation to you regarding the payment of ground rent for your consideration.

As desired, we are sending the deed of release disclaimer as approved by our solicitors and duly executed for your record.

Without approval of the Government, HUDCO issued the letter to Ansals for extending the 2nd and 3rd installment without interest.

Chapter: Twenty-Eight

Ministry Of Law & Justice Pointed Out that HUDCO Cannot Allot the Land for Hotel

The Ministry of Urban Development informed the Ministry of Law and Justice that the hotel site has been carved out as part of the Community Center, the sub-lease towards Leela Hotels Ltd. may be permitted to be executed. HUDCO will be the lessee. The Ministry of Law & Justice disagreed, stating that the lessee cannot use the land for some other use. The allotment letter towards HUDCO is required to be examined along with the Master Plan and other related documents on whether the land can be used for a hotel.

The Ministry of Law & Justice was required to vet the sublease agreement of Leela Hotels Limited, who submitted their comments to the Ministry of Law & Justice on 15 May 1997:

PUC is for vetting of the sub-lease agreement. The sub-lease agreement is proposed to be executed between the President of India and the HUDCO as an unspecified third party. Apparently, the third party will be Leela Beach Goa, Leela Hotel Venture Ltd.

1. A perusal of the material on record shows that the land has been allotted to the lessee for the purpose of a Community Center. The opinion of the

Department appears the hotel site has been carved out as a part of the Community Center project, and as such components being allowed, the sub-lease deed may be executed. HUDCO will have the status of a lessee. Unless provided otherwise, the Lessee cannot use the land allotted to it for a specified purpose. For some other purpose. To give any opinion about the legality of the proposal to sublease the land for the construction of a hotel, it is necessary to examine the letter of allotment. We will also have to examine the Master Plan and other related documents to find out whether the land can be used for a hotel.

2. The sub-lease is to be granted to the third party by HUDCO. It appears there is a proposal to grant a perpetual lease towards HUDCO. The notes dated 5 May 1997 at page 2/N ante show that the perpetual lease has not yet been finalized and is in the process of finalization. At least on that date, it was with the Ministry of Law for consultation. The lessee can, by a sub-lease, grant only those rights which he possesses. He cannot grant a lease of the rights that are not possessed by him. It will therefore be necessary to peruse the Perpetual Lease if already

> executed. If the perpetual lease has not been executed, the sub-lease can be executed only after the perpetual lease has been executed, and the terms of such perpetual lease are known to the parties. In the circumstances, it will be better if both the proposals are taken together. We have not been able to locate on the file the perpetual lease. We have also requested the office of the Land and Development Office for a meeting with the undersigned. Unfortunately, no positive response has been received. In the circumstances, we cannot give any final opinion on the document. As at present, prima facie, execution of the sub-lease will not be lawful. In case all the relevant documents may be sent to us.

Signed by Mr. V.V. Singh- Legal Adviser, (Conveyancing), Ministry of Law & Justice on 15 May 1997, which was put up to Mr. B.R. Dhiman, Under Secretary on 19 May 1997 marked to Land & Development Minister for further action which was marked to Director (Land) who marked to Joint Secretary (Urban Development) on 21 May 1997 to look into urgently

Mr. B.R. Dhiman, Under Secretary of the Ministry of Urban Development, put up a note on 19 May 1997 after receiving the comments from the Ministry of Finance:

Kindly see the preceding note of the Department of Expenditure, wherein it has been observed that in acceptance of the opinion given by Shri Dipankar Gupta, sacrifices should have been from both the sites and not from one side, i.e., HUDCO agreed to an extension of time without payment of interest. It has been suggested the case should be examined legally on merits, and if it is found HUDCO does not have a strong case and settlement by negotiations is called for, then further extension of time for payment of installments may be given only on payment of interest.

The second point raised is that soon after payment of the first installment in May 1995. M/s. Ansals took up the matter with HUDCO regarding the regularization of the building plan for the basement and car parking. But HUDCO took 6 months to submit the building plans. Had this delay been avoided, there would not have been a resultant loss of Rs. 6.96 crores (US Dollar 1.91 million) due to nonpayment of interest. It has been desired the causes of this delay may be looked into, responsibility fixed up, and necessary action taken against the persons responsible for the delay and resultant loss.

In this context, it may also be submitted the Ministry of Law, to whom the matter was referred for a legal opinion, has also desired to ascertain the observations of the Ministry of Finance before they advise in the matter.

Mr. B.R. Dhiman put up a note to Director (Land) on 19 May 1997. Given this decision, it appears necessary to ascertain the position from the Chairman cum Managing Director, HUDCO, as per the draft placed below for consideration and approval. May kindly be approved. Director (Land), Ministry of Urban Development, further put up for approval with comments for referring to the observations of the Ministry of Finance & Ministry of Law & Justice, which was put to Joint Secretary (Urban Development) on 21 May 1997, further marked to Additional Secretary Mr. Harmender Kumar on 23 May 1997, who sent to the Secretary who approved on 31 May 1997.

Reference above.

1. The issue relating to the auction of Shopping Arcade space allotted to Ansal Properties and

Industries Ltd. and extension of time was referred to the Finance Ministry as well as the Law Ministry.

2. The law Ministry vides their note dated 9 May 1997, desired that the views of the Ministry of Finance should be made available to them to enable the Ministry of Law to examine the matter from a proper perspective. The relevant file is placed below.
3. In this regard, it may be stated the views of the Ministry of Finance are contained in their note on page 92/ante. To examine the matter further, we have since taken up the matter with Chairman-cum-Managing Director, HUDCO, requesting him to examine the causes of the delay, pin-point the delays, fixing up exact responsibility to enable the Ministry to examine the matter further. A communication to this effect was issued on 3 June 1997. Based on the information furnished by the HUDCO, further action will be taken in the matter.

In the meantime, if approved, we may return the file to the Ministry of Law of making available a copy of the note recorded by the Ministry of Finance, as desired by them. Joint Secretary (Finance) may kindly eye. Signed by Under

Secretary Mr. B.R. Dhiman on 3 June 1997. Please issue the endorsement placed below. Also, please retain a copy of the Law Ministry's note:

Signed on 4 June 1997 by the Joint Secretary, Urban Development, and Joint Secretary, Finance.

Under Secretary, Ministry of Urban Affairs & Employment Department of Urban Development, Mr. B.R. Dhiman's letter on 3 June 1997 to Shri V. Suresh, Chairman-cum-Managing Director, HUDCO regarding Shopping Arcade Space (Over Basement Car Parking Space) allotted to M/s. Annual Properties & Industries Ltd. Extension of Time for payment of installments.

I am directed to refer to the correspondence resting with your letter No. HUDCO/AG/SA/96 dated 3 December 1996 on the above-cited subject, and to say that the matter has been considered further, and it is observed while agreeing to the opinion given by Shri Dipankar Gupta, that the matter should be negotiated, the sacrifices should have been from both the sides, whereas HUDCO has agreed for extension of time without payment of interest. It is not clear whether M/s. Ansals has also given any concessions to HUDCO. In the absence of any evidence to this effect, the matter is to be examined legally on merits and further extension of time considered only on payment of interest.

1. Further M/s. Ansals in May 1995 had requested HUDCO for regularization of the building plan for the basement and car parking, but it took 8 months to submit the building plans by HUDCO. Had this delay been avoided, it would not have been necessary for HUDCO to consider an extension of time and the resultant loss of Rs. 6.96 crores (US Dollar 1.91 million) due to non-payment of interest in M/s. Ansals could have been saved.
2. You are therefore requested to take into account the causes of the delay, pinpoint the delays, fix up exact responsibility to enable the Ministry to examine the matter further, and take a view in consultation with Finance and Ministry of Law.

In respect of extensions of installments of Ansals allotment of Shopping Arcade, as asked by the Ministry of Finance, the Ministry asked HUDCO's Chairman-cum-Managing Director to examine the causes of delay in regularizing the Shopping Arcade building plans and to fix up responsibilities of the Officers who were responsible. Mr. V. Suresh, Chairman, who was responsible when he was

Director, Corporate Planning, the entire juggling was done by him in connection with the Officers of the Ministry at the relevant time. What responsibilities of which officer Mr. V. Suresh is going to fix?

Mr. V. Suresh indicated HUDCO has taken all steps to the best of its ability to get necessary statutory approvals in respect of HUDCO Place, Andrews Ganj, and there was no willful negligence by any of the officers. There was a delay in sanction of the building plans of a car park basement constructed by HUDCO, due to extensions being granted to Ansals of the 2nd and 3rd installments on obtaining the legal opinion from Mr. Dipankar P. Gupta, Barrister and Senior Advocate of Supreme Court, who suggested avoiding the litigation as the project is in the public interest which will suffer.

A report appeared in June 1997 at the Business Page of Tribune Newspaper reported by Mr. Punnoose Tharyan ***"HUDCO in no mood to check Ansals Violations":***

"The Housing and Urban Development Corporation (HUDCO) appears to be in no mood to check the Ansals from allegedly violating the terms and conditions laid down

in its allotment letter for a shopping arcade site in the capital.

According to documents available with The Pioneer, the Delhi-based Ansals group has clearly gone scot-free from being penalized by HUDCO for its blatant violations of allotment conditions.

Though these violations call for immediate cancellation of the allotment and forfeiture of the total amount deposited with HUDCO, the latter has time and again been lenient with the building and construction group.

In HUDCO's allotment letter signed by H.K. Dubey to Ansal Properties and Industries. It was clearly mentioned the total amount towards the site worked out to Rs. 168.80 crores (US Dollar 46.49 million), *which was to be paid in three installments.*

The original letter dated 10 March 1995 said that the first installment worth around Rs. 84 crores (US Dollar 23.13 million) *were to be paid within four weeks of the date of the allotment letter, i.e., before 6 April 1995.*

The second installment worth around Rs. 50 crores (US Dollar 13.77 million) were to be paid before 9 March 1996, while the third and last installment for Rs. 33.76 crores (US Dollar 9.29 million) were to be paid before 9 September 1996.

Among the terms and conditions mentioned by HUDCO, it was noted that any delay beyond three months on payment of these two installments (the second and third) would entail cancellation of allotment and forfeiture of the total amount deposited to date.

It was said that in case the construction is not completed within the prescribed period of the extended period, as decided by HUDCO. HUDCO will have the right to take over the land along with the unfinished building with the materials, fixtures, if any, on the site, without payment of any compensation.

More importantly, HUDCO made it clear to Ansals that "you shall not have any authority to sell, transfer, assign or otherwise parting with the extension, whether as fall of in part of the said premises of HUDCO and in no case it would be considered by HUDCO until the full and final payment is made to the HUDCO and construction is completed by you.

Despite all the conclusions. Ansals have neither completed the construction nor paid the full and final payment

(HUDCO has yet again extended the date again to 9 September 1997) and besides, the builders have also been selling the said premises since August last year when the first advertisement for Ansals appeared for selling of a shopping plaza.

Ansal Plaza is presented to you by Ansals, leaders in real estate development in India, and with considerable experience in overseas markets.

The Ansals have appointed vastly experienced international property consultants. Richard Ellis, who will be responsible for property management as well as the marketing of the project, the advertisement read.

The second installment of Rs. 50.64 crore (US Dollar 33.78 million) *was due on 9 March 1996, which was allowed to be extended up to 9 June 1996 with penal interest to be paid. The balance Rs. 33.76 crore* (US Dollar 9.29 million) *was to be paid on 9 June 1996 or 9 December 1996 with penal interest.*

Thus, instead of charging interest on the delayed payments, which crores to approximately Rs. 25 crores (US Dollar 6.88 million). *Ansals were given a waiver of interest in six months on due payments, agreed by all.*

Not only this, it may be recalled that Ansal's due payments have been extended beyond six months, although these six months were allowed under the pretext of completion certificate and possession certificate being submitted late.

Even if these six months were extended for Ansals on the second due installment, they were to pay the amount by 9 December 1996, reportedly still to be paid.

Ansals final installment even after six months extension was legally due on 9 June 1997 with penal interest, including the extension period, which is reportedly set to be paid to date.

It is reliably learned HUDCO has extended until 9 September 1997 the payment toward the last installment."

Why will HUDCO be in the mood to check Ansals violations? They were bent on granting discriminatory treatment to Ansals vis a vis MS Shoes, who continued to struggle in courts, sometimes on technical grounds. Courts have at times held that we should perceive all around and not go into the case on technical grounds. But which court? Strangely, the court is sympathetic to you, as they are not supposed to be. But then HUDCO and Government came with a battery of lawyers, with senior lawyers spending crores of Rupees in the litigation, making the deserving litigant lose the battle he has fought for the last 3 decades.

Chairman & Managing Director, HUDCO, Mr. V. Suresh letter on 4 July 1997 to Mr. N.P. Singh, Secretary (Urban Development), Ministry of Urban Affairs & Employment regarding Shopping Arcade Space (Over Base Car Parking Space) allotted to M/s. Ansals Properties & Industries Ltd.– Extension of time for payment of installments.

This has reference to letter No. J-13014//6/90-LD dated 3 June 1997 on the subject cited above written to HUDCO by Shri B.R. Dhiman, Under Secretary to the Ministry of Urban Affairs & Employment (Land Division)/ In this respect, a detailed note is enclosed with this letter highlighting the relevant issues raised in the above-referred letter. The detailed note will clearly indicate HUDCO has taken all the necessary steps to the best of its ability to obtain the necessary statutory approvals in respect of HUDCO Place at Andrews Ganj, and that there is no willful negligence on the part of any dealing officer of HUDCO.

I hope the detailed note will be helpful to you in resolving the issues.

a) In the urgency of the Afro Asian Games 1991, HUDCO was given the land in July 1990 to start the construction.
b) In the meantime, master plan 2001 was implemented, but the Andrews Ganj was developed as per Master Plan 1962.
c) As per Master Plan 2001, the land use was changed to Convention Center to be developed by Andrews Ganj.
d) 8 September 1992, the land use was restored retrospectively to Master Plan 1962.
e) The building plans were entertained thereafter, but only a conceptual layout plan was approved as per Master Plan 1962.
f) The building plans were submitted, but since the constructions were already carried out, the building plans for the car park basement could not be sanctioned, which was later compounded.
g) The allotment made to HUDCO was initially for 32 years, which was amended to 99 years on 19 March 1996, and Municipal Corporation of Delhi demand was off the title towards HUDCO.
h) In response to various requests by HUDCO, the lease deed was not executed.

Consequently, there was a delay in sanctioning the plans of the Shopping Arcade of Ansals due to non-regularization/sanction of the building plans of the car parking basement constructed by HUDCO.

Therefore, an initial extension of 6 months (without interest) was granted to Ansals for the payment of the second installment and third installment by the board of directors of HUDCO on 1 March 1996 and 23 August 1996, respectively. Accordingly, the payment date for the second installment was due on 9 September 1996, and the third installment was due on 9 March 1997. The interest in this period as per terms of the allotment letter works out to Rs. 6.96 Crores approximately.

Ansals requested HUDCO for a further extension on similar grounds. In this connection, HUDCO obtained the opinion of Mr. Dipankar P. Gupta, Barrister and Senior Advocate of Supreme Court, who opined that if litigation results at this stage, either by way of cancellation of the agreement or claim of damages or otherwise, the project which is in the public interest, will suffer. He, therefore, recommended this is a case that ought to be negotiated and settled at this stage itself. It was accordingly advised that extension may be considered by negotiations on the conditions that Ansals would drop all their claims for damages or otherwise on account of alleged delays on the part of HUDCO which may have occurred to date.

The matter for further extension of time was considered by the board of directors of HUDCO in their board meeting held on 26 November 1996, keeping in view the legal opinion and applying commercial prudence, it was recommended that further extension of a second installment by 4 months 8 days without interest (i.e., payment date of 9 September 1996 to 17 January 1997) and 2 months and 4 days for the third installment without interest (i.e. 9 March 1997 to 13 May 1997) to be accorded with the approval of the Government. The party could thus obtain payment with interest within 3 months from the date up to which the extension was to be accorded. The loss of interest due to proposed further extensions recommended by a board of directors of HUDCO works out to Rs. 3.95 Crores (US Dollar 1.08 million) as per the terms of allotment letter dated 10 March 1995.

The extension already granted by HUDCO and the proposed extension resulted in a grant of extension for payment of the second installment by 10 months 8 days and 8 months 4 days for the third installment, as the building plans for Shopping Arcade by Ansals were taken up for consideration by the Municipal Corporation of Delhi on 8 April 1996.

The proposal of the HUDCO for extension of time was examined by the Ministry, and given the all-relevant factors, it was recommended Ansals may be given an extension of time for payment of the second installment by 3 months 8 days instead of 4 months 8 days, as recommended by HUDCO without interest, and 2 months 4 days for the third installment.

This was suggested subject to a suitable and unambiguous disclaimer on stamp paper by Ansals for all their claims for damages or otherwise on account of alleged defaults on the part of HUDCO and payment of ground rent from the date of actual possession, i.e., 10 November 1995.

Consequently, it would reveal that HUDCO has pursued the matter from time to time with the concerned agencies at all levels. The time taken in the process at various stages is also indicated in the note. HUDCO has intimated each activity takes a certain time on account of Government procedure, and there has not been any lapse on the part of HUDCO in pursuing the approvals with the principal of the efforts possible. Further, the whole process was delayed due to circumstances beyond the control of HUDCO, including land use requirement, location of ownership document.

As regards fixing of responsibility for the delay in submission of plans and sanction thereof in respect of the car parking area, the matter could either be referred to Executive Director (Vigilance) for examination, or the explanation furnished by the HUDCO could be accepted, i.e., the delay being procedural and the matter of delay being procedural, and the matter has been pursued at all levels by HUDCO. No further action on this account is called from the Ministries of Finance and Law informed accordingly.

Mr. V. Suresh, HUDCO's Chairman Cum-Managing Director, further clarified the extensions have been granted subject to unambiguous disclaimer by Ansals of not claiming any damages and on payment of ground rent from the date of possession. There has been no lapse by HUDCO in pursuing the approvals of the building plans, which were delayed due to circumstances beyond the control of HUDCO, including land use, title, and other documents.

He suggested that the fixation of responsibility may be marked to HUDCO's Executive Director, Vigilance, or the explanation be accepted. It was obvious that the explanation was reckoned to be accepted by HUDCO's Chairman-cum-Managing Director. The question lies here is if the building plans of the car park basement were not sanctioned, which also included the building plans of guest house blocks were not approved. Ansals were extended interest-free installments, whether MS Shoes installments were extended interest-free?

Chapter: Twenty-Nine

False Statement in Lease Executed on 4 July 1997 by Government with HUDCO Stating Land Given for Development as Per Master Plan 2001 Contrary to Notification 8 September 1992 Restoring to Use Under Master Plan 1962

To cover-up the allotment of the hotel to Leela Hotels Limited, the advice of the Ministry of Law & Justice was not followed, instead, the lease deed was executed by the Land & Development Office in favor of HUDCO on 4 July 1997, with a false statement in the lease that the Government wishes to develop the Community Center as per Master Plan 2001. Here the Scam again takes place. The Government itself had notified the Andrews Ganj land restoring to Master Plan 1962 retrospectively, as per Zonal Development Plans F-3 Zone, which did not permit using land for the hotel.

Not only this, even the allotment letter dated 19 March 1996, changing the lease from 32 years to 99 years, finally amended on 15 October 1996, did not specify the land can be used for the hotel, a false condition was stipulated illegally in the lease.

The certain relevant conditions of Perpetual Lease Deed - (For 17.6 Acres Land for Community Center)

THIS INDENTURE made the 4 days of July 1997 BETWEEN THE PRESIDENT OF INDIA (hereinafter called "the Lessor") of the one part and the Housing and Urban Development Corporation Limited, having its registered office at "HUDCO BHAWAN" India Habitat Centre, Lodhi Road, New Delhi–110003 (hereinafter called "the Lessee") of the second part.

Whereas the lessor owns land measuring 17.6 acres comprising Khasra No. Of village Pinjrapole, Delhi, now known as Andrews Ganj, which plot of land measuring 17.6 acres situated in Pinjrapole, Andrews Ganj, for community center complex, is more particularly described as Schedule hereunder written, and with boundaries thereof for greater clearances have been delineated on the plan annexed to these presents and thereon colored red (hereinafter referred to as the "plot").

And Whereas the Lessor wishes to develop, the said land as a community center, as described in the Master Plan - 2001 as an integrated urban design complex.

And while the Lessee, being one of the premier Public Sector Organizations engaged in urban development, has offered to develop the plot according to the directions of the Lessor.

Area of 17.6 acres or thereabouts situated at Pinjrapole (Andrews Ganj), New Delhi. Together with all rights, easement, and appurtenances whatsoever to the said plot of land to be used for construction of a community center at Pinjrapole, (Andrews Ganj), New Delhi, belonging or appertaining to hold the premises hereby demised the Lessee for 99 years from the first day of November one thousand nine hundred and ninety yielding and paying therefor yearly rent payable in advance of Rs. 1/- per acre (Rupee One per acre only) or such other sum as may hereafter be assessed under the convents conditions hereinafter contained clear of all deductions by yearly payments on or before the 15 day of January in each year at the Reserve Bank of India, New Delhi or at such other place as may be notified by the Lessor or such officer as may be authorized by him on his behalf (hereinafter referred to as the said "officer" for this purpose from time to time the first of such payment was made on 29 day of March 1996.

After the completion of the construction and development of the community center, but not later than ten years from the date of this perpetual Lease Deed, the Lessor will have the authority to review the arrangement with the Lessee and enter into a fresh arrangement with any other government agency or public sector undertaking for lease/maintenance and administration of the properties. The rights and liabilities of the Sub-Lessee under the sub-lease entered into by the Lessee with sub-lease in respect of the properties developed in the community center complex shall, however, continue in the same manner by the designated agency.

The Lessee on the said plot of land hereby demised shall undertake the construction of the Community Center as detailed hereinabove, after obtaining the requisite sanction of the building plans from the proper municipal or other authority at its own expense.

The Lessee hereby agrees the net resources generated, if any, from the development and disposal of the properties erected on the said demised plot of land leased out shall be utilized by it for the construction of a maximum permissible number of houses, flats on 25 acres of residential land allotted and placed in possession of the Lessees separately. However, in case the land falls short of the money available, the general pool accommodation will be constructed elsewhere, and if so, the land is available for constructing general pool residential accommodation (beyond 25 acres), the surplus may be credited with the Government or used with the permission of the Ministry of Urban Affairs & Employment to build general pool residential accommodation elsewhere in the country.

The Lessee or any of the Sub-Lessees shall not, without sanction or permission, be writing of the proper municipal or other authority concerned to erect any buildings or make any alterations or additions to such buildings constructed on the said plot of land.

The said plot of land and building constructed thereon or any part thereof shall not be used for a purpose other than as specified herein.

- Signed and registered on 4 July 1997
- Signed by Mr. B.L. Nimesh, Land & Development Officer
- Witness: Mr. Labh Singh Chane. Deputy Land & Development Officer and Mr. Ld. Ganhotra, Land & Development Officer.
- Signed by Mr. S.K. Sinha, Chief (Law) HUDCO
- The authorized representative of HUDCO Witness: Mr. P.K. Garg, Chief Disposal, Mr. Charanjit Kumar, Executive Director Planning

HUDCO executed on the same day, Agreement to Sublease with Leela hotels, of which certain relevant conditions:

President of India has allotted a piece of land, measuring 17.6 acres or thereabouts at Pinjrapole Andrews Ganj, for the development of Community Center, including the construction of a hotel out of total land allotted of 17.6 acres at Pinjrapole Andrews Ganj, New Delhi. The President has permitted the Corporation to dispose of part of land measuring 11,480 sq. meters with a buildable space of 25000 sq. meters.

The time for payment of premium as stated shall be the essence of the contract, irrespective of whether the intended sub-lessee has been able to start the construction on the demised premises or not deemed to any reason whatsoever.

Signed and registered on 4 July 1997.

- Signed Mr. S.K. Sinha, Chief (Law) Authorized representative of HUDCO
- Witness: Mr. P.K. Garg, chief (Disposal), Mr. P.K. Aggarwal, Deputy Chief (Finance)
- Signed by Mr. Vivek Nair, Director, Leela Hotels Ltd.
- The authorized representative of Leela Hotels Ltd. Witness: Mrs. Vanita Saxena, Mr. S. Rajaraman.

The Ministry of Law & Justice specifically advised that the hotel is a specific land use, and unless mentioned in the lease towards HUDCO, the same cannot be sub-leased for the hotel. To circumvent using the hotel which is not permitted, HUDCO and the Government cleverly placed the word Master Plan 2001 in their lease and mentioned in the agreement with Leela Hotels that the Government has given the land at Community Center, including using the hotel.

Thereafter, on 7 July 1997, Leela Hotels was given possession by executing a Certificate of Provisional Entry on License Basis upon the Hotel Site in the Urban Design Complex at HUDCO Place, Andrews Ganj, New Delhi:

Certified that M/s. Leela Hotels Ltd. have on 7 July 1997 at 4.45 pm been put in possession as a licensee of the premises described in the Second Schedule (as shown red on the plan annexed) to the Agreement to Sublease dated 4 July 1997 executed between the HUDCO and Leela Hotels Ltd., and in terms of the said agreement and the letter of allotment no. HUDCO/AG/Hotel/97 dated 31 March 1997, for the sole and exclusive purpose of constructing and erecting thereon Hotel building, and for executing the related and permitted works in the manner and for the period mentioned in the said agreement for use and the extent as stipulated thereon, without prejudice to the rights of the parties in the following witnesses.

The Licensee shall not upon the entry upon the said premises be deemed to have acquired any right, title, or interest in the same, except to the extent mentioned in the agreement. The possession herein given is subject to the terms and conditions of the Agreement to sublease dated 4 July 1997.

M/s. Leela Hotels Ltd. put in use of the premises shown in red on the

Plan annexed provisionally.

- Signed Mr. S.K. Sinha, Chief (Law) Authorized representative of HUDCO
- Witness: Mr. P.K. Garg, chief (Disposal), Mrs. Arti Tyagi
- Entered upon the premises shown in red on the plan annexed and
- Provisionally occupied the name by Mr. Vivek Nair, Director
- The authorized representative of Leela Hotels Ltd. Witness: Mrs. Vanita Saxena, Mr. S. Rajaraman.
- Chief (Disposal) HUDCO, Mr. P.K. Garg letter on 11 July 1997 to The Director (LANDS) Department of Urban Development Land Division Ministry of

Urban Affairs & Employment, New Delhi. Regarding Allotment of the Hotel Site at HUDCO Place, Andrews Ganj New Delhi.

- Enclosed please find herewith a photocopy of the following documents.
- Agreement to Sublease (Hotel Site) dated 4 July 1997, executed between HUDCO and M/s. Leela Hotels Ltd.
- Certificate of Provisional Entry on License Basis upon the Hotel Site at HUDCO Place, Andrews Ganj, New Delhi.
- The sublease agreement is as per the format approved by the Government on 4 June 1997.

This is for your kind information and necessary action, please.

HUDCO entered the agreement to sublease with Leela Hotels on receipt of the 1st installment, but they never did so with MS Shoes after receipt of the 1st installment. HUDCO handed over the possession to Leela Hotels for construction of the building, but they never gave possession to MS Shoes after receipt of the 1st installment.

Chapter: Thirty

Another Interest Free Extension of Instalments Subject to Payment of Ground Rent of Rs. 7.85 Crores (US Dollar 2.21 million)

Chief (Disposal), HUDCO on 15 July 1997 to M/s. Ansal Properties & Industries Limited New Delhi regarding Shopping Arcade HUDCO place, Andrews Ganj, New Delhi Payment of 3rd installment and ground rent:

Please refer to our letters dated 11 April 1997 and 4 June 1997 regarding the payment of the third installment. It has already been informed to you that the same was/will be due on or before 13 May 1997 without interest or 13 August 1997 with interest subject to the Government's approval. Since 13 May 1997 has already expired, and you have not made the payment, you are again advised to secure the payment as early as possible, but no later than 13 August 1997 with interest.

It may also be mentioned that as per communication throughout letters dated 11 April 1997 and 4 June 1997, it was made clear to you that the extension granted by the HUDCO Board of Directors was subject to the payment of Ground Rent as well. However, we are yet to receive the amount of Rs. 7.85 crores (US Dollar 2.21 million) payable as Ground Rent as of date.

You are therefore advised to obtain the payment of Ground Rent amounting to Rs.7.85 crores (US Dollar 2.21 million) without further delay, ensure payment of the third installment within the stipulated date mentioned above with interest, failing which the allotment will stand terminated. Please also expedite to submit the deed of Release/Disclaimer as per the revised draft sent to you vide letter dated 4 June 1997.

*The Correspondent of Nav Bharat Times Hindi Edition reported on 15 July 1997 "**Whether Ansals has violated in respect of the land taken from HUDCO**":*

The news being in Hindi could not be translated properly by me due to the detailed news I am not producing herewith. The conclusion of the news is Ansals did violate the entire conditions of allotment, and HUDCO accepted all the violations further, granting interest-free extensions to Ansals.

*In Times of India report by the Business Times Bureau on 15 July 1997, "**HUDCO turns blind eye to Ansals Violation".***

"The sale of the shopping arcade at Andrews Ganj by Ansal Properties & Industries Limited (APIL) managed by Sushil Ansal violates the conditions spelled out in the allotment letters issued by Housing and Urban (HUDCO) dated

March 10, 1995. HUDCO has not taken any action against the builder, who has already sold countless shops and offices in the complex so far.

According to the allotment letter, APIL has no authority to sell transfer assign or otherwise part with the possession, whether in full or in part of the premises at Andrews Ganj, without the prior permission of HUDCO, and in no case will HUDCO consider it before the full and final payment is made to HUDCO. The construction at the site has been completed by the Ansals.

But APIL has not made the full payment so far, which was according to the conditions of the allotment letter to be produced before September 9, 1996. APIL secured the allotment of the land in April 1995 for consideration of Rs.168.80 crores (US Dollar 46.49 million).

Though it paid the first installment of Rs. 84.40 crores (US Dollar 23.13 million), it failed to meet the commitment of obtaining the payment of the second installment of Rs. 50.64 crores (US Dollar 13.78 million) before March 9, 1996.

HUDCO has given APIL an extension of six months for paying the second installment without any interest, saying that according to the agreement, the structure on which the arcade was to be built was not completed by them, and hence the extension.

However, no such clause was mentioned in the allotment letter. According to the letter, an extension of three months is permitted. But for this interest at the rate of 19 percent per annum inclusive of a penal interest of 3 percent per annum should have been charged.

The letter further said any delay beyond three months on payment of these two installments would entail cancellation of allotment and forfeiture of the total amount deposited to date, but HUDCO not only turned a blind eye to the sale of the shopping arcade before the full payment had been made, but also gave another interest-free extension of six months until March 9, 1997, to pay the second installment. In a similar case against MS Shoes East Limited, HUDCO had canceled the allotment letter.

Though APIL paid the second installment in June 1997, it has not paid the third installment, which was due on September 9, 1996, so far.

Another condition violated by the developer selling shops and offices in the arcade of the floor area of less than 110 square meters, which according to the allotment letter is the minimum partible portion."

From what I can see, there was nothing of the type that there were some terms and conditions of allotment to be followed in the case of Ansals. All such terms and conditions were meant for MS Shoes only. This talk of a greater scam, which required a probe by not the department of company affairs, but by the CBI.

In Pioneer, Mr. Punnoose Tharyan, the reporter of the business page of the newspaper, reported on 15 July 1997
"Ansals flouts lease agree for shopping arcade"
"HUDCO turns blind eye to alleged violation of sale clause"

"CLOSE ON the heels of the Uphaar fire tragedy and subsequent controversy surrounding the Ansals group, the Delhi-based builders are finding themselves involved in another controversy with the Housing and Urban Development Corporation Ltd. (HUDCO). The controversy involves the alleged flouting of a lease agreement by Ansals which it had signed for a shopping arcade with HUDCO. If rules are strictly adhered to. HUDCO will have to give up its entire deal it signed up with Ansals for the alleged

violations of the conditions by the letter. However, since no such action is being contemplated by HUDCO. It is clear the latter has turned a blind eye to the house. All efforts to contact HUDCO Chairman V. Suresh proved futile.

Officials in Ansals land told the Pioneer they were not clear whether any sale had been transacted for the building space coming up at their site. Though booking amounts may have been collected from prospective buyers. But it can be pointed out that collecting a token booking amount also tantamount to a sale transaction.

Ansals were allotted a shopping arcade site to HUDCO in March 1995, and as per one of the conditions of the allotment letter, Ansals have no right to sell transfer, assign, or otherwise part with the possession, whether in full or in part of the said premises, without the prior permission of HUDCO.

Moreover, the clause in the lease also said that in no way would HUDCO consider the above case before the full and final payment was made to HUDCO and the construction was completed by Ansals.

Neither has the full payment been made in HUDCO nor has Ansals completed the construction.

Highly placed sources told The Pioneer that despite the said conditions laid down in the agreement with HUDCO, Ansals began advertising in August last year seeking bookings from prospective buyers.

Ansal Plaza is presented to you by Ansals, leaders in real estate development in India, and with considerable experience in overseas markets. The Ansals have appointed vastly experienced international property consultants. Richard Ellis, who will be responsible for property management as well as the marketing of the project, the advertisement read.

HUDCO's lenient approach towards Ansals can also be gauged from the fact it allowed the company to go-slow on the installments towards the full payment of the shopping arcade site. After it was allotted the site by HUDCO in March 1995, Ansals were required to pay 50 percent (Rs. 84.40 Crores) (US Dollar 23.13 million) *of the bid amount (Rs. 168.80 Crores)* (US Dollar 46.49 million) *in four weeks, i.e., by 6 April 1995, which was duly paid by Ansals.*

The next installment of 30 percent, i.e., Rs. 50.64 Crores (US Dollar 13.78 million)*, was due on 9 March 1996, which was allowed to be extended up to 9 June 1996 with penal interest* *to be paid. The balance of 20 percent (Rs. 33.76 Crores)* (US Dollar 9.29 million) *was to be paid on 9 June 1996 or 9 December 1996 with penal interest.*

Thus, instead of charging interest on the delayed payments, which comes to approximately Rs. 25 crores (US Dollar 6.88 million), *Ansals was given a waiver of interest in six months on due payments agreed by all. Not only this, it may be recalled Ansal's due payments have been extended beyond six months, although these six months were allowed under the pretext of completion certificate and possession certificate being submitted late. Even if these six months were extended for Ansals on the second due installment, they were to pay the amount by 9 December 1996, reportedly still to be paid.*

Ansals' final installment even after six months extension was legally due on 9 June 1997 with penal interest, including the extension period, reportedly set to be paid to date.

What is surprising is the entire sequence of events all violations by Ansals. HUDCO has been losing footing on taking any action since such violations committed invite cancellation of allotment of the property."

After reading the news about the Ansals case on Uphar Cinema tragedy, I got inquisitive to find out more about it. There was too much information on search engines, but I decided of restricting myself to Wikipedia, which comes here as follows:

*The **Uphaar Cinema fire** was one of the worst fire tragedies.[1] The fire started on Friday, 13 June 1997 at Uphaar Cinema in Green Park, Delhi during the three o'clock screening of the movie Border. Fifty-nine people were trapped inside and died of asphyxiation, while 103 were seriously injured in the resulting stampede **(suffocation).***

The victims and the families of the deceased later formed The Association of Victims of Uphaar Fire Tragedy (AVUT), which filed the landmark civil compensation case. It won ₹25 crores (equivalent to ₹51 crores or US$7.1 million in 2019) in compensation for the families of the victims. The case is now considered a breakthrough in civil compensation law in India. However, on 13 October 2011, the Supreme Court nearly halved the sum of compensation awarded to victims by the [Delhi high court] and slashed punitive damages to be paid by cinema owners, the Ansal brothers, from ₹2.5 *crores (equivalent to ₹4.1 crores or US$580,000 in 2019) to ₹25 lakh (equivalent to ₹41 lakh or US$58,000 in 2019).*

In its final order on August 25, 2015, the Supreme Court modified its earlier order and sentenced the Ansal brothers to a two-year jail term if they failed to pay the families of the victims Rs.30 crore each within three months. The Supreme Court reviewed this order again on February 9, 2017, and sentenced Gopal Ansal to a year in jail for the case. The other accused, Sushil Ansal, did not have to serve a sentence due to his old age.

On June 13, 1997, at about 6.55 a.m., the bigger of the two transformers installed and maintained by DVB on the ground floor of the Uphaar Cinema building caught fire. At around 7 a.m., the security guard heard an explosion, Sudhir Kumar, who then discovered smoke in the transformer room. The fire brigade and the Delhi Vidyut Board (DVB) were informed, and the fire was brought under control by 7.25 a.m. Inspection of the transformer by the Superintendent of the DVB and his team revealed that three of the low-tension cable leads of the transformer had been partially burnt. At around 10.30 a.m., inspectors from DVB and Senior Fitter conducted repairs on the transformer by replacing two aluminum sockets on the B-Phase of the low-tension cable leads. The repairs, it appears, were carried out with the help of a die and hammer, and without a crimping machine. DVB completed its repairs between 10:30 a.m. and 11 a.m. The transformer was recharged for the resumption of electric supply by 11.30 a.m. on June 13, 1997.

It is alleged that repairs conducted on the transformer in the earlier part of the day were unsatisfactory and resulted in loose connections that caused sparking on the B-Phase of the transformers. This resulted in the loosening of one of the cables of the transformer, which eventually came off and started dangling loose along with the radiator, and burned a hole in the radiator fin. Through this hole, the transformer oil started leaking out, which, on account of the heat generated by the loose cable touching against the radiator, ignited the oil at about 4.55 p.m. on 13 June 1997. Since the transformer did not have an oil soak pit, as required under the regulations and the standard practice, the oil that spread out of the enclosure continued leaking and spreading the fire to the adjacent parking lot where cars were parked at a distance of no more than a meter from the door of the transformer. The result was that all the cars parked in the parking area on the ground floor of the cinema hall were ablaze. Smoke started billowing in the northern and southward directions in the parking lot of the cinema complex. The northern bound smoke encountered a gate, which was adjacent to a staircase leading to the cinema auditorium on the first floor. Due to the chimney effect, the smoke gushed into the stairwell and eventually entered the cinema auditorium through a door and the air conditioning ducts. The southward bound smoke similarly traveled aerially through another staircase and into the lower portion of the balcony of the auditorium from the left side. All this happened while many people were seated in the auditorium using the matinee show of 'BORDER', a popular Hindi movie with a patriotic theme.

Because of smoke and carbon monoxide released by the burning oil and other combustible material, the people in the auditorium started suffocating. The Shift In-charge of the Green Park Complaint Centre of DVB received a telephonic message at the relevant point of time, regarding the fire. It was only then that the AIIMS grid to which the transformer in question was connected was switched off and the flow of energy to the cinema complex stopped. According to the prosecution, the supply of the 11 KV outgoing Green Park Feeder tripped off at 5.05 p.m., thereby discontinuing the supply of energy to the cinema. Inside the auditorium and balcony, there was complete pandemonium. The people in the balcony are said to have rushed towards the exits in pitch darkness, as there were neither emergency lights nor any cinema staff to help or guide them. No public announcement regarding the fire was produced to those inside the auditorium or the balcony, nor were any fire alarms set off, no matter the management and the employees of the Uphaar Cinema were aware of the fact that a fire had broken out. Even the Projector Operator was not given instructions to stop the film while the fire was raging, nor was any patron informed about the situation outside. On the contrary, doors to the middle entrance of the balcony were found to be bolted by the gatekeeper, who had left his duty without handing over charge to his reliever. More importantly, the addition of a private 8-seater box had completely closed off the exit on the right side of the balcony, while the addition of a total of 52 extra seats over the years had completely blocked the gangway on the right side of the balcony. Similarly, the gangway on the right of the middle entrance was significantly narrower than required under the regulations. All these obstructions, deviations, violations, and deficiencies had resulted in the victims getting trapped in the balcony for at least 10–15 minutes, exposing them to lethal carbon monoxide, to which as many as 59 persons eventually succumbed.

An off-duty Capt. Manjinder Singh Bhinder of the 61st Cavalry of the Indian Army, and a talented horse-rider, out celebrating his success at recent national games with his family, and a junior officer at the movie hall, gave his and his family's lives up saving over 150 people, on his initiative. Rushing out along with his family at first, realizing the gravity of the unfolding tragedy, he and his people went back inside and tried to set order and guide people out to safety. Fire services were delayed due to the heavy evening traffic and the location of the cinema hall, situated in one of the busiest areas of Delhi. At *least 48 fire tenders were pressed into service at 5.20 p.m., and it took them over an hour to put out the fire. Later, the dead and the injured were rushed to the nearby All India Institute of Medical Sciences (AIIMS) and Safdarjung Hospital, where scenes of chaos and pandemonium followed, as relatives and family members of the victims scurried around to look for known faces.*

In the beginning, a magisterial probe ***(judicial review)*** *took place, which submitted its report on 3 July 1997, wherein it held cinema management, Delhi Vidyut Board, city fire service, the Delhi police's licensing branch, and municipal corporation responsible for the incident, saying "it contributed to the mishap through their acts of omission and commission". It also blamed the cinema management for losing precious time in alerting the fire services, and for not maintaining proper distance between the transformer room* *and the car park. It also said "when the fire broke out at 1645 hours, the movie was not stopped nor any announcement made to evacuate the audience. Exit signs were not battery-operated and once the lights went out, panic-struck people had to grope in the dark for exits, many of which were blocked by seats". Subsequently, the courts issued non-bailable warrants against Sushil Ansal, his brother Gopal, a Delhi Vidyut Board inspector, and two fire service officials. After evading arrest for many days, Sushil and his son Pranav Ansal, the owners of Ansals Theatres and Club Hotels Limited, which owned the Uphaar cinema, were finally arrested in Mumbai on 27 July 1997, and sent to judicial custody, though were later released on bail. Also, among those arrested was the company's director, V K Aggarwal.*

Following the inquiry, the Union Home Ministry transferred the probe to the Central Bureau of Investigation (CBI) amidst charges by victims' families of cover-up, which on 15 November 1997 filed a charge sheet against 16 accused, including theater owners Sushil and Gopal Ansal, for causing death by negligence, endangering life, and relevant provisions of the Cinematograph Act, 1952. By 2000, the prosecution had completed the recording of evidence with the testimony of its 115 witnesses. The court case continued for over a decade, and the court had over 344 hearings during the first seven years. Four of the accused died, and eight witnesses, mostly relatives of Ansals, turned hostile witnesses, despite the High Court responding to AVUT's plea and asking the trial court in 2002 to expedite the case. Meanwhile, as the criminal trial dragged on, in 2003, a presiding judge commented upon the repeated requests (for adjournment) as being intended to delay the case.

Almost nine years after the tragedy, a trial court judge visited the Uphaar cinema hall in August 2006, accompanied by CBI officials who investigated the case to get a first-hand look at the seating and fire safety arrangements, blamed for the tragedy. The site had been preserved as "material evidence" since the tragedy. The visit followed a High Court order in which the trial court was asked to examine all available evidence in the matter, as the court's proceeding was coming to an end. In its report, the court observed that on the second-floor balcony of the theater, where victims were asphyxiated, "the space provided for exhaust fans on the walls was found blocked with the help of a cardboard".

In 2003, the public prosecutor in the case reported that several important documents filed along with the charge sheet were missing from the court record of the case, or had been tampered with or mutilated. The court ordered an inquiry and dismissed the court clerk. In 2006, the Economic Offences Wing (EOW) of the Delhi Police registered the case on a Delhi High Court direction on a petition by 'Association of the Victims of Uphaar Tragedy (AVUT) convener Neelam Krishnamurthy.

In February 2008, after the charge-sheet filed by the Economic Offences Wing of the Delhi Police for allegedly removing, tampering, and mutilating important documents of the Uphaar fire tragedy case in conspiracy with a clerk in a trial court there in 2003, the Delhi court summoned Uphaar cinema hall owners Sushil Ansal and Gopal Ansal and four others in the evidence tampering case, under Sections 120-B (criminal conspiracy), 201 (causing disappearance of evidence or giving false information to screen offenders) and 409 (criminal breach of trust) of the Indian Penal Code.

In short, in 2003, the public prosecutor found the important documents along with the charge sheet missing. An inquiry took place and the court officer was dismissed. In 2006, the case was registered on the directions of the Delhi High Court by EOW of the Delhi Police. In February 2008, based on a charge sheet filed by the Economic Offence Wing of Delhi Police for illegally removing the important documents and charge sheet of the UPHAAR fire case in the conspiracy of a court officer in a trial court in 2003, the Delhi court called the hall owners SUSHIL ANSAL and GOPAL ANSAL and four others in spoiling of evidence, under Sections 120-B,201,409 of the INDIAN PENAL CODE.

The final verdict came four years later on 20 November 2007, and the quantum of sentences is given out on 23 November, in which 12 people, including the two Ansal brothers, were found guilty, and later convicted of various charges including causing death by a negligent act, and were given the maximum punishment of two years' rigorous imprisonment. They were also fined Rs.1,000 each for violating Section 14 of the Cinematograph Act. The court also directed the CBI to investigate the role of other officials who had been giving temporary licenses to the Uphaar cinema hall for 17 years.

The other seven accused, three former Uphaar cinema managers, the cinema's gatekeeper, and three DVB officials, were all given seven years' rigorous imprisonment, under Section 304-A (culpable homicide not amounting to murder) of the Indian Penal Code (IPC), and housed at the Jail. The *court also fined all the 12 accused Rs.5,000 each, and sentenced all of them to two years' rigorous imprisonment, as they were found guilty of endangering the personal safety of others. Both the sentences however were to run concurrently. Sources' News But in the court session, only the staff and the head were punished, and not the DVB superintendent and the DVB laborers.*

One year after the verdict, one of the managers, who had allegedly fled from the hall soon after the fire broke out and the fire safety measures were not followed, died at a Delhi hospital on 6 December 2008. In December 2008, the High Court, while upholding the trial court order convicting the Ansal brothers, had reduced their sentences of imprisonment from two years to one year. On 30 January 2009, an Apex bench of the Supreme Court granted bail to Sushil Ansal and Gopal Ansal. On 5 March 2014, the Supreme Court upheld the conviction of the Ansal brothers. The apex court further stated Ansals were more concerned about making money than ensuring the safety of cinema-goers. The issue on the quantum of punishment referred to a three-judge bench, given the difference in opinion between the two judges who delivered the verdict.

On 26 March 2014, Sushil Ansal left India without seeking permission from the Apex Court. The Supreme Court has expressed displeasure over real estate baron Sushil Ansal, convicted in the Uphaar fire case, leaving the country without its permission. The apex court however allowed Ansal to stay abroad for medical treatment after he gave an assurance that he would return on 11 April.

On 19 August 2015, the Supreme Court of India imposed a fine on the Ansal brothers for ₹ 30 crores each, and held that their jail terms will be reduced to the term already undergone by them if they pay the fine, considering their old age. The court ruled that the lack of a trauma center at the nearby AIIMS hospital had contributed to the high death toll in the incident. However, the victims' families have criticized this decision. The fire exposed the poor safety standards at public places in the country's capital. This was not the first instance of such a fire. On 6 July 1989, a fire had broken out at Uphaar cinema due to a fault in the substation. After an earlier transformer caused a fire at Gopal Towers, a high-rise in Rajendra Place, New Delhi in 1983, the licenses of 12 cinemas, including Uphaar, had been canceled. The Deputy Commissioner of Police (Licensing), who inspected Uphaar, had listed ten serious violations, however, all remained uncorrected until the fire 14 years later.

What I observed here was Ansals were too arrogant in front of a small fry MS Shoes, who was an entrepreneur of the year to grow bigger and join the league of richer people and prominent industrialists and had dreamt, so at the time he was 16 years in his school. But the country's system did not allow him to do so and wanted his failure by the business competitors, but I must say he is heroic and a hero who still fought the system. Did not run away from difficulties, nor did he keep any penny of any one of his creditors, banks, or financial institutions all were paid back by him.

But what I realize is this man is still struggling to get justice, but bureaucracy and government do not let it happen, to rely on the final court to decide. What I realize is he has been scammed by Congress Government and HUDCO being hand in gloves, someone behind him to destroy him totally, but he still stands as one alone fighter for MS Shoes for his 51000 shareholders. My dear readers, if you have a different opinion after reading these ten books of HUDCO Andrews Ganj Land scam, please do respond in public openly.

To this date, HUDCO had been placing their submissions before the court that MS Shoes is not equally placed, and that the court gave time to pay to MS Shoes. All were lies, as the court gave the time of 15 days to pay that also with 24 % interest, which orders HUDCO did not accept and had filed an appeal against this order. MS Shoes had deposited Rs. 35 crores (US Dollar 9.63 million) *in court and tendered a draft of Rs. 90 crores* (US Dollar 24.78 million), *but HUDCO declined to accept as the value of properties had trebled. But still, HUDCO had one option, they could have returned the money received from MS Shoes, which was received in any case on the decent practiced by HUDCO. No, HUDCO did not want to return the money, as they wanted to earn interest in lending to corporate @18 % compounded quarterly.*

HUDCO was aware the laws of the country are so flimsy it will take MS Shoes to reach the final court another 50 years, and yes, 25 years had passed, and no light of understanding any monies. The government was a hypocrite, instituting litigation policies for an eyewash, which was never followed practically.

*Economic Times New Delhi Bureau reported on 17 July 1997 "**Ansals flouts HUDCO deal, sell space in Arcade**"*

"Ansal properties and industries Limited is selling the commercial space of Ansal Plaza in violation of its agreement with Housing and Urban Development Corporation Limited. (HUDCO)

HUCO also appears to have turned a blind eye to Ansal's activities. The shopping arcade site, situated at Andrews Ganj in South Delhi, was allotted to Ansals in March 1995.

According to conditions number five of the allotment letter issued by HUDCO. Ansals have no right to sell, transfer, assign, or otherwise part with the possession either in full or in part of this property without prior permission of HUDCO.

Moreover, the granting of permission to sell the property cannot be considered by HUDCO before full and final payment is made and construction is completed by Ansals.

This clause has also been included in the agreement of sub-lease, signed by HUDCO and Ansals officials.

Despite this, HUDCO has been allowing Ansals to sell the property since August 1995, when the first advertisement for selling the space of Ansals Plaza appeared.

As Ansals neither completed the construction nor have obtained a full and final payment. It is a clear violation of the terms and conditions of the allotment letter.

As per the tender conditions, Ansals was supposed to pay 50 percent of the bid amount of Rs. 168.80 crores (US Dollar 46.49 million) in three installments.

The first installment of Rs. 84.40 crores (US Dollar 23.24 million) were to be paid before 6 April 1995, which was paid by Ansals in time.

The second installment of Rs. 50.64 crores (US Dollar 13.78 million) were due on 9 March 1996, which was extended up to 9 June 1996, and the balance of Rs. 33.76 crores (US Dollar 9.29 million) were to be paid before 9 June 1996, which was again extended until 9 December 1996, to be paid with penal interests."

It seems terms of allotment letters were only meant for MS Shoes and not Ansals, whose terms of allotment letters were exactly similar and identical. My dear readers, is it not a scam, is it not a shame to an organization owned by the President of India? It was Deed of Release/Disclaimer *only HUDCO, it was Congress Government, ministers involved as well. This scam is to be exposed to the public at large, and all over the world it must be exposed to open the eyes of the administration and courts.*

Executive President Ansal Properties & Industries Limited, Mr. Pradeep Seth, letter on 24 July 1997 to Mr. P.K. Garg Chief (Disposal) Housing and Urban Development Corporation Limited regarding Payment of 3rd & last installment for Shopping Arcade HUDCO Place Andrews Ganj New Delhi. Kindly refer to your letter dated 15 July 1997, on the above subject.

We are thankful to HUDCO for granting us an extension/reschedule amount of time for payment of 2nd and 3rd installments. In this connection however, we may point out that the reschedule Ent is not in conformity with the letter and spirit, as was contained in the brochure inviting tender, allotment letter and agreement to sublease. As per the payment terms stipulated in the above-mentioned documents, 50% of the purchase price was to be paid within 4 weeks of the allotment, and 30% within 12 months thereafter, and 205 within 18 months thereafter, i.e., to say there was always a time gap of 6 months between the payment of 2nd installment and 3rd installment. The delay in handing over meaningful possession of the site to us has been entirely due to the fault of HUDCO, whereby your plans for the basements could not be sanctioned until 28 May 1996, resulting in non-sanction of plans for the superstructure of the Shopping Arcade to be built thereon, and on account of which you have agreed to reschedule the payment, representing the second installment due on 17 January 1977 without interest and 17 April 19977 with interest. However, you have not maintained the gap of six months between the payment of the 2nd installment and the 3rd installment, and have asked us to obtain the payment of the 3rd installment on 13 May

1997 without interest and by 13 August 1997 with interest. In this manner, the gap between the payment of the 2nd and 3rd installment has been reduced to 3 months and 27 days.

As pressed and insisted upon by you, we have even executed a release/disclaimer deed releasing you from the liability of damages for delay in handing over possession to us. This was done primarily on the premise that you would reschedule the payment of 2nd and 3rd installments by the period for which we could not have the meaningful possession of a site for the purpose of carrying out construction. Although the basement building plans were sanctioned in July 1996 on your insistence, we had agreed to an extension of 10 months and 8 days for the reschedule Ent of 2nd installment, although there was a delay of 13 months between the stipulated date of handing over possession of the site, i.e., from 1 June 1995, till the date of sanction of our building plans, i.e., from 11 July 1996, because we had invested more than 150 crores, and we could not afford to jeopardize the project. You are requested to kindly refrain from writing us threatening letters for cancellation of our allotment, and to kindly allow us the requested time for taking the third and last installment to which we are entitled. We have already given you the payment of a 2nd installment on 17 April 1997, with up-to-date interest. You are requested to kindly maintain the time gap of 6 months between the 2nd installment and 3rd installment by 16 October 1997, with interest in the period of 3 months, i.e., from 17 July 1997 to 16 October 1977.

We also understand you still have not received the completion certificate in respect of basements, and the same is held up because you have not complied with various conditions stipulated by Municipal Corporation of Delhi, which includes the stipulation regarding fire clearance as well as structural stability certificate. We further wish to mention here that cracks have developed in the basement roof slab (the site for construction of our shopping arcade). This matter was brought to your kind notice as back as on 25 January 1997. Thereafter, we have been regularly pursuing the matter with you, and you had informed us that you had appointed an outside agency, i.e., Structural Engineering Research Center of Madras, to carry out various tests, including load tests etc, to check the stability of structure and to ascertain why the cracks had appeared, but so far you have not been able to give us any satisfactory reply to this development. Due to this reason, we have not been able to carry out the construction of a work at site as planned, and this is further delaying the construction of the shopping arcade. Needless to mention, HUDCO shall be responsible for this delay, which is being caused. Further, we are also worried about the safety of the construction, as well as of our staff working at the site if the structure given by HUDCO is found unsafe. You are requested to take immediate remedial measures on this account.

You are requested to kindly look into all the above matters at the earliest, so that we can construct a beautiful masterpiece, as has been conceived jointly by us.

Executive President (Marketing), Ansal Properties & Industries Limited, Mr. Pradeep Seth on 26 July 1997 to Mr. P.K. Garg Chief (Disposal) Housing and Urban Development Corporation Limited regarding Shopping Arcade–HUDCO Place:

Please refer to your letter dated 4 June 1997 on the above subject. Our para wise comments are as under.

Deed of Release/Disclaimer – The Deed of Release/Disclaimer has been executed by our Managing Director, who is duly authorized to execute by us at your instance, and on your insistence that Ansals and in respect of sanctioning of building plans. The changes advised by you for the release deed are unacceptable to us. Moreover, the changes are an afterthought and were not there in the original draft sent by you. We had initially agreed to execute a Release/Disclaimer, provided HUDCO agreed to the reschedule of the 2nd & 3rd installment for the period for which we could not have a meaningful possession of the site for the purpose of carrying out construction. The basement building plans were sanctioned on 28 May 1996, and our buildings plans for construction were sanctioned in July 1996. On your instances, we had agreed to an extension of 10 months and 8 days for the reschedule of the 2nd installment, although there was a delay of 13 months between the stipulated date of handing over possession of the site and the date of sanction of our building plans, which was entirely due to the fault of HUDCO. Despite the above, we have executed the Release/Disclaimer deed in your favor, because we did not wish to jeopardize the project in which hundreds of crores had been invested.

Payments of 3rd Installment – Regarding this matter, kindly refer to our letter dated 24 July 1997.

Ground Rent – In respect of ground rent, we wish to make the following submissions.

We had requested you a wide letter dated 9 January 1997 to send us a copy of the lease deed executed by the President of India towards HUDCO, as well as a draft of the Sub Lease deed which is to be executed by the President of India and HUDCO towards our company. The agreement of sublease contemplates a lease being executed by the President of India for HUDCO, and thereafter a sublease being executed for Ansals. Since no lease has yet been executed, there is no title with HUDCO to execute the sub lease.

HUDCO is in no position to demand Ground Rent because it has not yet become the lessee of the land. Land in these circumstances continues to be Nazul rules. All Nazul land is held subject to statutory rules, and Ground Rent is a subject governed by statutory rules which have the force of law. The position of HUDCO as on date is of licensee, and of Ansals as a Sub Licensee and Ground Rent must be charged as per Nazul rules. In Nazul rules, ground rent for the first five years can only be charged on a nominal basis, i.e., Rs.1 per annum, and it is only after five years it can be charged at the rate of 21/2% per annum.

HUDCO had been allotted the land by the Government of India under Allotment letter No J-13014/6/90 dated 15

March 1993. In terms of this Allotment letter, HUDCO must pay ground rent @Rs.1.00 per acre per annum. As the liability of HUDCO is limited to Rs. 1/per acre per annum on this account, HUDCO can at best raise the demand on us on the basis. The quantum of ground rent cannot be different from what HUDCO would be paying to the Government.

Without prejudice to what has been stated above, we also wish to submit that although the site was handed over to us on 10 November 1995, you are well aware that we could not raise any construction thereon until the basement work executed by HUDCO was approved by the Municipal Corporation of Delhi, as such there was no meaningful possession of the site with Ansals until that date. Only thereafter, our plans could be entertained by the Municipal Corporation of Delhi, and were passed in July 1996. Ground Rent is related to handing over of the site for the purposes of conversion, and construction was possible only after our building plans were sanctioned. As such, the deemed date of possession should be taken as 11 July 1996.

We wish to request you to kindly consider this matter from the proper perspective, as HUDCO cannot legally charge us ground rent for a property of which HUDCO itself is not a lessee as on date.

Ansals, after receipt of the extension of their installments, refused to pay any ground rent as demanded by HUDCO. They granted extensions subject to payment of Rs. 7.85 Crores (US Dollar 2.21 million) of ground rent due. Ansals also took a plea that the Government has executed no lease with HUDCO, which means HUDCO has no title until date. Ansals were unaware that at the instance of Leela Hotels, the Government executed the lease with HUDCO in hurry.

Ansals took a plea that since HDCO is paying ground rent of Re. 1/- per annum to the Government, the same is payable by them. It was my view to let us understand whether Ansals execute an unambiguous disclaimer and whether they pay the ground of Rs. 7.85 Crores (US Dollar 2.21 million)? Here is the result, but Government Officers and HUDCO Officers were bent upon helping Ansals and discharging MS Shoes, which they succeeded jointly.

Chief Disposal, HUDCO, Mr. P.K. Garg on 5 August 1997 to Ansals Properties and Industries ltd. Regarding payment of 3rd installment for shopping arcade at HUDCO Place, Andrews Ganj:

Please refer to your letters dated 24 July 1997 and 26 July 1997 on the above subject. The issues raised in the above two letters are responded as follows:

Payment of 3rd installment – As regards you for granting extension/reschedule Ent of time for payment of 3rd and final installment. The position was made abundantly clear to you in our letters No. HUDCO/AG/SA/97 dated 11 April 1997 and No. HUDCO/AG/SA/97 dated 5 May 1997 No. HUDCO/AG/SA/97 dated 4 June 1997. No. HUDCO/AG/SA/97 dated 15 July 1997. It surprises us that your chairman, having agreed with us on the extension of the third installment by 2 months, 4 days, is going back on its agreement and is raising frivolous and unconnected issues to intentionally avoid payment of the third and last installment. HUDCO's decision for further extension of time both for the second and third installments communicated to you vide our letter of 11 April 1997 was a package based on unconditional acceptance of both the second and third installments, and it is not open for you to act upon a part of the package advantageous to you and challenge the other part of the package. You are therefore advised to pay the third installment with interest on or before 13 August 1997, failing which the allotment will stand automatically terminated, as categorically started in our letter of 11 April 1997 (para 5) We do hope, however, that you will reconsider your payment connotation and not force HUDCO to resort to necessary remedies available to sub-lease.

Deed of Release/Disclaimer – Our letter dated 11 April 1997 contained a package which also forwarded to you with our letter. HUDCO would have accepted the deed of release/disclaimer if it was furnished in the form provided by us, but the Ansals has forced HUDCO to suggest some modifications, at least two over the requirements of the package to which you are now objecting. Since you are not willing to sign the release/disclaimer letter in the revised form furnished vide, our letter dated 4 June 1997 or revised format sent with our 4 June 1997 letter, as you may decide. But the requirement of submission of disclaimer is the part of the package and needs to be complied with by your expeditiously.

Ground Rent – Your attentions drawn to the terms of the brochure invited the bids for shopping arcade site, as well as the clause of xv of the agreement to sub-lease dated 1

August 1995, pursuant to which ground rent @ 2.5% from the date of handing over of the passions is to be paid. The procedure adopted by the Delhi Development Authority referred to in your letter under reference concerning ground rent is irrelevant in our case. As the ground rent is payable by you pursuant to the terms of allotment letter as well as agreement to sublease, and therefore, you have no legal basis to deny the payment of the ground rent incidentally, it may be pointed out that HUDCO land imposed a similar condition on 1st other allottees of vacant land, and they have also paid the ground rent in accordance with the allotment letter.

Although, HUDCO is under no obligation to furnish you the perpetual lease deed between the president of India and HUDCO. However, a copy of the same executed between the President of India and HUDCO is enclosed, which clearly indicates immediately on the allotment of the spaces. The sub-leases and space bursars are required to pay 2.5% of the premium paid as ground rent, as HUDCO is required to pay the same to the government of India. Thus, in accordance with your own contention, as stated in your letter 26 July 1997, you would be bound to pay ground rent from the date of allotment. However, as per our earlier demand, you are once again called upon to obtain the payment of ground rent of Rs. 7.85 Crores (US Dollar 2.21 million) along with a third installment, i.e., ground rent due from the date of handing over possession, without prejudice to HUDCO's right to claim ground rent from the date of allotment.

We would like to make it clear that in terms of the brochure inviting bids and the letter of allotment, ground rent is payable from the date of handing over possession and is in no way connected with construction on site.

In the end, we hope you will not delay the payment of the third installment within the specified period, as well as the ground rent, and jeopardize your project yourself.

HUDCO continued to demand ground rent of Rs. 7.85 Crores (US Dollar 2.21 million) *and the required disclaimer, but however continued to extend the interest free installments favoring HUDCO, resulting in discrimination vis-à-vis MS Shoes.*

*A correspondent of Hindustan Times Newspaper reported on 5 August 1997 "**Ansals failed to pay third installment to HUDCO**":*

"Despite repeated extensions granted by HUDCO, the Ansals have defaulted on payment of a third installment of about Rs. 33.76 crores (US Dollar 9.29 million) *against the purchase of the site allocated for a shopping arcade at Andrews Ganj in the Capital.*

The Prime Minister has failed to secure payment of its installment worth Rs. 33.76 crores (US Dollar 9.29 million), *even after HUDCO extended the deadline to 8 March this year. The third installment in the Rs. 168.80 crores* (US Dollar 46.49 million) *deal was originally scheduled for payment on 9 September 1996.*

Interestingly, HUDCO has granted the extension to Ansals properties for the payment of the second and third installment "purely as goodwill and gesture".

As per the letter given by Mr. P.K. Garg, Chief (Disposal) to Ansals. HUDCO has made it clear that there cannot be any linkage between the payment of the second installment and the payment of the third installment.

However, purely in view of the difficulties expressed by you, we agree to grant you (Ansals) a final extension of time for payment of the third installment up to 8 March 1997, states the letter.

The letter further reveals Ansal, itself, had delayed in accepting the possession of the site on various grounds. The various reasons given by Ansals are neither tenable nor justified in any way, said HUDCO.

Replying to the Ansals letter dated duly 24 and 27 August requesting for re-extension for third installment due on 8 September 1997 and an extension for third installment due, the letters state the payment of second installment and third installment were unrelated to any stage of development or construction, but were to be fixed time payments.

We do not accept your contention that we had granted the said extension of time for reasons stated in your said letter. We repeat the said extension for the second installment was granted by us at your request only for the consideration stated above.

The letter further repeats that there cannot be any linkage between the installments to be paid at the times fixed and stipulated, and the extension of time.

We do not agree with your contention that you have delayed completion because the said installment has been delayed due to non-completion of the construction work by the earlier contractor.

HUDCO made it categorically clear to the Ansals that there was no delay in handing over possession of the site to Ansals, as alleged by them. (Ansals).

According to the letter, HUDCO deliberately avoided joining issues with Ansals on these matters, as the same in views do not affect the contract or the contractual stipulation. "It is singularly unfair that the accommodation granted by us (HUDCO) to you (Ansals) has not been properly acknowledged," it states.

Interestingly, as per the allotment letter dated 10 March 1995, Ansals did not have the authority to sell, transfer, assign or otherwise part with possession in full or the part of the said premises "without the prior permission of HUDCO, and in no case it would be granted by HUDCO before the full and final payment is made to HUDCO and construction is completed by you. (Ansals)

This is to ensure the development of property in an integrated manner, as per the urban design approved, and within the stipulated time frame."

One side HUDCO in writing states while granting interest free extensions, they do not agree with Ansals that there had been any lapse of HUDCO; did not delay in giving over the possession. HUDCO is admitting that they have been accommodating Ansals, and they should acknowledge their accommodation being given by granting interest free extensions which as per contractual terms could have not been granted. My dear readers do this not amount to discrimination vis a viz Ansals. This is scandalous of HUDCO.

*Another news appeared on 6 August 1997, reported by Mr. P.N. Andley, "***Ansals goes scot-free despite violations":**

"The Delhi based Ansals group has been going scot-free from being severally penalized by the Housing and Urban Development Corporation (HUDCO). In its blatant violations of allotment conditions for a shopping arcade site in the capital. The latter has failed to back the group from allegedly violating the terms and conditions of land given by HUDCO by it in its allotment letter.

Though these violations call for an immediate cancellation of the allotment and forfeiture of the total amount deposited with Hidcote, the latter has failed to pay, and HUDCO has been lenient with the construction group. The Prime Minister has failed to secure payment of its installment worth Rs. 50 cores (US Dollar 13.77 million), *even after*

HUDCO extended the deadline to March of this year. This third installment in the Rs. 168.80 crores (US Dollar 46.49 million) *of total deal were originally scheduled for payment in September last year.*

Interestingly, HUDCO has granted extension to Ansals Properties for the payment of the second and third installment "purely as a goodwill gesture". As per the letter given by Mr. P.K. Garg, Chief (Disposal) to Ansals. HUDCO has made it clear there cannot be any linkage between the payment of the second installment and the payment of the third installment.

However, purely in view of the difficulties expressed by you, we agree to grant you (Ansals) a final extension of time for payment of the third installment up to March 8, 1997, the letter from HUDCO states.

The original letter dated 10 March 1995 said that the first installment worth around Rs. 84 crores (US Dollar 23.13 million) were to be paid within four weeks of the date of the allotment letter, i.e., before 7 April 1995. The second installment worth around Rs. 50 crores (US Dollar 13.77 million) were to be paid before 9 March 1996, while the third and last installment for Rs. 33.76 crores (US Dollar 9.29 million) were to be paid before 9 September 1996.

Among the terms and conditions mentioned by HUDCO, it was noted that any delay beyond three months on payment of these two installments (the second and third) would entail cancellation of allotment and forfeiture of the total amount deposited till date.

It was said that in case the construction is not completed within the prescribed period of the extended period, as decided by HUDCO. HUDCO will have the integrity to take over the land along with the untinned building with the materials, fixtures, if any, on the site, without payment of any compensation.

More importantly, HUDCO made it clear to Ansals that "you shall not have any authority to sell, transfer, assign or otherwise parting with the extension, whether as fall of in part of the said premises of HUDCO, and in no case it would be considered by HUDCO before the full and final payment is made to HUDCO and construction is completed by you.

Despite all the conditions, Ansals have neither completed the construction nor paid the full and final payment. The date has been extended yet again by HUDCO to 9 September

1997, and besides, the builders have also been selling the said premises since August last year, when the first advertisement for Ansals appeared for selling of a shopping plaza."

It was all deliberate to destroy MS Shoes, corruptions involved behind extensions, for keeping eyes and ears closed for Ansals on the same allotment conditions of land in the same community Centre but hanging MS Shoes until death, living the final decision of courts. It is interesting that the interesting the law says you get interest on your principal amount and simple interest, but HUDCO continues to earn compounded interest, getting unjustly enriched. It is a scam by HUDCO and needs to be looked into by the present Government of the scam committed by the Congress Government but who has time to ratify it?

Chapter: Thirty-One

Fire Department Did Not Clear Car Park Basement and Guest House Blocks till August 1997–Allotments of MS Shoes Cancelled in January 1996 and May 1996

*A Newspaper report reported by Mr. Shroff D. Rangnarkar and Mr. Shubham Mukerjee in Economic Times on 11 August 1997 "**Ansal Plaza Shaky as banks review loan**":*

"A Consortium of banks, including the Punjab National Bank (PNB), has decided to reconsider its Rs. 40 Crores (US Dollar 11.01 million) loan to Ansals Properties & Industries Ltd.

This puts in doubt Ansal's ability to pay the final installment for the HUDCO shopping arcade.

Ansals had sought the loan to pay the final installment for a shopping arcade in HUDCO Place – Ansal Plaza.

According to PNB sources, while the Rs. 40 crores (US Dollar 11.01 million) loan has been sanctioned; banks are uncertain of disbursing the amount since certain Ansals directors are in judicial custody.

Moreover, the signatory to the sub-lease of the property. Mr. Gopal Ansal is not traceable.

Clearing of such a loan, banking sources say, would be against ethics and Reserve Bank of India guidelines.

For Ansals, it is imperative that the money is disbursed, as its possession of the shopping arcade depends on the payment of this amount.

Ansal is to pay up about Rs. 43 crores to HUDCO as the last installment. This includes the interest of about Rs. 10 crores.

The loan, according to PNB sources, was to be disbursed on August 13, the same day Ansals had to pay the final HUDCO installment.

When contacted, a spokesman of Ansals told the Economic Times that the construction company is still hoping for the loan to come through, and that company officials are still in talks with the banks.

The spokesperson pointed out that one of the company directors, Mr. Pranav Ansal, had been given bail on Monday.

However, Mr. Sushil Ansal, another director, has not been granted bail yet, and efforts to procure it are to be added."

From what I see here, the directors of Ansals were either absconding or granted bail. Banks were susceptible to release a loan to pay to HUDCO for installments towards Ansals shopping arcade, but it seems they were infix, as they had already given Rs 40 crores towards the second installment. Now HUDCO threatened to cancel the allotment, and the bank was forced to pay to save Rs. 40 crores already paid.

Mr. P.N. Andley from another newspaper Tribune reported on 12 August 1997 ***"Need to Scrutinize PNB, HUDCO role":***

"Are the banks flouting banking rules, regulations, and guidelines of the Reserve Bank of India by granting loans to Ansals to pay towards the installment due to HUDCO, even while Mr. Gopal Ansal's Director of Ansals and signatory of an agreement to sublease is still absconding?

A few banks, including the Punjab National Bank, find themselves on a sticky wicket concerning the disbursal of loans worth around Rs. 40 crores (US Dollar 11.01 million) *to the Ansal group for a shopping complex site in the Capital.*

Ansals close sources reported that although the banks had given the loans to Ansals, the extension of judicial custody of the two directors – Mr. Sushil Ansal and Mr. Pranav Ansal – until August 21 has put the banks in a dock. Since banking rules and regulations do not allow banks to release loans to a company at a time when its directors are either absconding or are in custody, the banks are now finding themselves in some type of blind in the Ansal case.

According to these sources, Punjab National Bank alone has sanctioned around Rs. 20 crores towards the final payment of the HUDCO site. However, Ansals had been given time until tomorrow (August 13) by HUDCO to pay up its third and last installment towards the shopping arcade. If it fails, then HUDCO would have to immediately cancel its agreement with Ansals and will have the authority to forfeit the amount paid by Ansals.

Amid all the controversy surrounding the land allotment, the role of both HUDCO and Punjab National Bank needs to be further scrutinized. PNB had released around Rs. 40 crores (US Dollar 11.01 million) *in April this year to Ansals for payment of a second installment towards the shopping arcade. This was even though Clause (vi) of the allotment letter dated 10 March 1995 and agreement to sublease dated 1 August 1995 stipulated that Ansals, at the discretion of HUDCO, could only be permitted to raise a loan only for the construction of a building.*

Thus, the grant of an unsecured loan in the form of a short-term loan was given by PNB, ignoring the terms of the agreement to sell between HUDCO and Ansals. Moreover, though HUDCO had refused to even mark lien on the property towards PNB, the latter went out of its way and released the loan.

Now, despite these controversies and all the extensions granted by HUDCO, the last installment is due tomorrow, as per HUDCO letters sent to Ansals. The said installment due is Rs. 33.76 crores (US Dollar 9.29 million) plus interest which comes to Rs. 2.24 crores (US Dollar 0.61 million) and Rs. 7.85 crores (US Dollar 2.21 million) on account of ground rent, thus making a total of Rs. 43.85 crores (US Dollar 12.07 million).

While on the one hand, Ansals are facing CBI prosecutions and investigations and are under arrest, the banks continue to be inclined towards the company in granting such loans, while conversely, the first loan already sanctioned is on a sticky wicket, although HUDCO had fully refused the lien.

However, it remains to be seen whether HUDCO follows the agreement drawn up with Ansals, clause by clause, as it did in the case of MS Shoes East for a site in the same area for a five-star hotel complex."

Doesn't it seem they were well-informed to the Government about what was happening? The Congress Government stayed deaf and kept the eyes closed only to help Ansals and Dupe MS Shoes, and yes, why not? They were using monies of MS Shoes to drag them to several years of litigation maintaining the Andrews Ganj Land Scam. Ansals were allowed to raise a loan towards payment of the second and third installment, which was not allowed, and the commitment in writing was delivered to banks to create the mortgage.

Now we will see in subsequent books, how Leela Hotels was scammed by HUDCO and duped for several years to get their money of the same five-star hotel land allotted to MS Shoes. They were not allowed to mortgage the land, as the property was subject to the outcome of MS Shoes. But poor Leela Hotels also suffer, which will be read in the next two books as they could not get the building plans sanctioned for the hotel despite keeping possession of the land for two years. There was a land-use problem, and after approval of layout plans, building plans could be sanctioned, which finally happens in the next book on 7th September 1999.

It becomes obvious that had MS Shoes paid the entire amount, then until 1999, his building plans could not be entertained. Is it not a scam and being scandalous? For me, the story is becoming interesting as I go ahead to read the documents leading to the Andrews Ganj scam by the Congress Government, who earlier wanted to usurp the Andrews Ganj Land, and they failed as the Supreme Court had ratified the scam twice. That time also took several years to free the Andrews Ganj Land, and this time to 25 years has passed land lying unutilized all these years and buildings deteriorated.

*Business Times Bureau of Times of India reported on 12 August 1997 "**Ansals misled PNB in Andrews Ganj plot case":***

"Ansal Properties & Industries Ltd. has allegedly misled Punjab National Bank (PNB) to get a loan of Rs. 20 crores sanctioned to pay the third installment of HUDCO for the land plot at Andrews Ganj to build a shopping arcade. In the light of this latest development, the bank was considering holding back the loan, a senior bank manager said.

The Delhi based property developer, it is learned had informed the bank that one of its senior directors, Gopal Ansal, who was the signatory of the agreement to the sublease of Andrews Ganj land piece, was abroad, and therefore could not come to sign the loan agreement which was finalized on 7 August 1997.

But the fact is Mr. Gopal Ansals is absconding as a non-bailable warrant has been issued on 21 July 1997 against him in the Uphaar Cinema fire tragedy case, where 59 people had died.

The Central Bureau of Investigation (CBI) has also sounded the international police agency, Interpol, for securing his arrest.

Sources said that the bank was considering stopping the disbursal of the amount on 13 August 1997, which is the last date to pay the third installment.

Moreover, by raising debt against creating a lien on the plot towards PNB, Ansals have violated clause 6 of the allotment letter, wherein the promoters are not allowed to raise funds except to construct the building. Surprisingly, even HUDCO did not inform the PNB that such arrangements were impossible. Ansals has already raised Rs. 40 crores (US

Dollar 11.01 million) from PNB to pay the second installment. The loan was disbursed on 17 April 1997.

In the covering letter, issued along with the pay order on 17 April 1997, PNB had said they were advancing Rs. 40 crores (US Dollar 11.01 million) *to the company for meeting the cost of the land allotted to the company. The bank in the letter said that as per the instructions given by Ansals to HUDCO, the title deed of the plot should be already delivered to them after it was executed towards the company. The lien on the plot should be marked in the bank's favor*

However, the sources in PNB said they had advanced loans to the company against the other properties. He said that Rs. 40 crores (US Dollar 11.01 million) *were disbursed against a property worth Rs. 87 crores* (US Dollar 23.96 million). *They sanctioned Rs. 20 crores* (US Dollar 5.05 million) *against another property of Rs. 27 crores* (US Dollar 7.43 million). *He also said the bank sought to mark the lien of the Andrews Ganj land in their favor to bolster their securities further. However, banking sources said HUDCO should have informed the PNB in time that no such lien could be created in their favor.*

HUDCO has been siding with Ansals in this project since it was allotted on 10 March 1995. The second and third installment was due on 9 March 1996 and 9 September 1996. HUDCO gave two interest-free extensions each to pay the second and third installments respectively so far."

HUDCO's favoritism in a commercial transaction is obviously proved by taking legal opinions stating the project to be in the public interest. All classes are relaxed to Ansals and MS Shoes be contested in courts. What a beautiful carved-out scam still hiding in various files of Andrews Ganj.

Till August 1997, there was no clearance from the Fire Department regarding the car park basement or the guest house blocks. Had MS Shoes paid another Rs? 100 Crores (US Dollar 27.54 million), *he would have been totally ruined with the burden of interest on Rs. 170 Crores* (US Dollar 46.81 million) *approximately until the approvals of the Fire Department and revised layout plans were obtained by HUDCO, which means four years interest burden.*

The Chief Fire Officer, Delhi Fire Service letter on 13 August 1997 to Mr. N. Charamrajan, Chief (Project), HUDCO regarding the no-objection certificate for firefighting system in Car Parking at HUDCO Place Project, Andrews Ganj, New Delhi.

In response to a telephonic message from Municipal Corporation of Delhi and your good self, and fax dated 9 June 1997. The re-inspection of Block of Cluster A & B and shortcoming pointed out vide this office letter NO. F6/DFS/MS/97/356 dated 1 June 1997.

The re-inspection of the HUDCO complex and car parking was carried out on 31 July 1997 and 5 August 1997 by Sh. NK Batura Dy. Chief Financial Officer and Sh. Radhey Shyam along with a team of officers from HUDCO headed by V. Suresh Chairman-cum-Managing Director.

During the inspection, it was observed that all the shortcoming has been rectified, as given below: -

Ringman: - Ringman in the entire complex was found completely charged, and two, three hydrants on different locations were operated, and adequate pressure was available.

1. Riser: - Rise in a block in cluster A&B were tested and found in functional condition.

2. First Hose Reel: - First Hose reels were treated and found in working condition.
3. Electrically operated manual call point: - Found functional.
4. Fire Extinguishers: - Fire extinguishers have been provided on all the floors bearing the 151-satisfaction mark and found operative.
5. Fireman Switch: - Lifts, Fireman switches have been installed on the lifts located in the block in clusters A & B.
6. Draw of connection: - is being erected and work is in progress. However, Chief (Project) HUDCO has However furnished undertaking.
7. D.G. Sets: - DG Sets installed and found functional, but the synchronizing with AFM penal will only be possible, after the sanctioned power load. However, the undertaking is also given.
8. The ventilation system in the car parking on points 2 & 3 has been rectified.
9. The Ringman is completely charged, but the work of the pits of the hydrants valve is being widened.
10. Exit signs have been provided in the car parking as well as in the block in clusters A & B.

Given the above, this department has no objection to the occupancy of a block in cluster A&B and car parking, wherein all the fire protection/fire safety arrangements have been provided as recommended by this department, such as an automatic sprinkler system in the car parking area, wet riser system, Hose reel Yard Hydrant (Ringman) Automatic heat & smoke detected system, underground water storage tank of three lacks liters, fire pumps house, Automatic Co2 flooding system in the electrical panel and electrical substation, technical ventilation, fire as a switch, PA equipment, Compartmentations. Portable fire extinguisher, etc. All the systems were operated and found functional.

Given the above, this department has no objection to the occupancy of underground car parking and blocks in clusters A & B only, from fire safety and means of escape. However, the following fire safety condition must be adhered to: -

1. All the firefighting and fire detection systems shall be maintained. All the time in perfect functional working conditions of combat, any fire incident takes place as soon as the inspection. Any lapse rendering the firefighting and fire detection system. Un-functional will be at the risk and responsibility

of the management, and liable for action under rule (Fire Safety and Fire Prevention Act, 1986).

2. Means of escape shall always be kept free of any obstruction for quick and safe evacuation in case of fires.
3. A qualified fire officer and staff shall be appointed.

*Mr. Punnoose Tharyan in Business Pioneer reported on the first page on the top on 13 August 1997, "**HUDCO ignores the Ministry directive on Ansals Loan**":*

"The Housing and Urban Development Corporation (HUDCO) has paid no heed to its nodal Ministry's directive to insist on a disclaimer, as well as charge around rent from Ansal for allowing its extension of time to pay up for the shopping arcade site in the Capital.

A four-page extensive note was prepared by the Department of Urban Development (Land Division), under the Ministry of Urban Affairs & Employment as early as 23 March 1997, on the modalities of payment to be made by Ansals for a shopping arcade space allotted by HUDCO.

In paragraph 8 of the note, the Ministry recommended Ansals be allowed to extend their time for paying up the second installment for the site up to 17 May 1997.

The extension recommended by the Ministry in para 8 above is subject to a suitable and unambiguous disclaimer on stamp duty by Ansals for all their claims for damages or otherwise on account of alleged defaults on the part of HUDCO which may have occurred till date, and that the party shall make payment of the ground rent from the date of actual possession, i.e., 10 November 1995. It was stated.

Even though the Ministry made it mandatory for Ansals to pay ground rent, as well as execute a disclaimer. It is reliably learned that both were not furnished on time.

Yet HUDCO went out of its way to extend the time for Ansals to pay its second installment.

In April 1997, HUDCO sent a letter to Ansals requesting them to obtain the payment of the second installment Rs. 50.64 crores (US Dollar 13.78 million) with interest expeditiously and in any event not later than 17 April, along with ground rent of Rs. 7.85 crores (US Dollar 2.21 million) for two years from the date of possession, i.e., 10 November 1995 failing which the allotment will stand terminated. You are also requested to execute a disclaimer in the format enclosed on a requisite stamp paper of Rs. 10, subjects to the execution of which disclaimer, HUDCO agreed to the extensions.

Surprisingly, a letter as late as 16 July 1997, written by HUDCO to Ansals, which is in the possession of the Pioneer, stated "It may also be mentioned that as per communications through our letter dated 11 April 1997 and 4 June 1997, it was made clear to you that the extensions granted by HUDCO board of directors were subject to the payment of ground rent as well. However, we are yet to receive the amount of Rs. 7.85 crores (US Dollar 2.21 million) *payable as ground rent as on date."*

The letter went on to say that you are therefore advised to make payment of ground rent amounting to Rs. 7.85 crores (US Dollar 2.21 million) *without further delay, ensure payment of the third installment with the stipulated date mentioned above with interest, failing which the allotment will stand terminated.*

Please also expedite to submit the deed of release/disclaimer as per the revised draft sent to you vide letter dated 4 June 1997.

These facts prove beyond doubt HUDCO paid no heed to the advice of the Ministry while extending the dates for Ansals to win its second installment towards the shopping arcade site in the Capital's Andrews Ganj area.

Now, it has been noticed HUDCO has repeatedly threatened to cancel its allotment to Ansals for the shopping arcade site but appears to have changed its mind at the last moment.

Meanwhile, the Ministry also said in note Ansals insisted HUDCO for a further extension on similar grounds. In this content, HUDCO obtained the opinion of Mr. Dipankar Gupta, Barrister and Senior Advocate of the Supreme Court. Mr. Gupta opined that if litigation results at this stage either by the cancellation of the agreement or claim of damages or otherwise, the project which is in the public interest will suffer.

It may be pointed out that the project is purely a commercial asset."

The Government approved an interest-free extension of Ansals, subject to the unambiguous disclaimer on stamp duty, by Ansals for all their claims for damages or otherwise on account of alleged defaults on the part of HUDCO, which may have occurred till date, and that the ground rent from the date of actual possession, i.e., 10 November 1995 of RS.7.85 crores. But HUDCO only sent a letter to Ansals, but never could obtain an unambiguous disclaimer nor pay the ground rent as demanded from 10 November 1995. It will be ushered in the next book, Ansals claimed damages too, and interest on their installment too, besides not paying ground rent. What would you call it? A scam, a bigger scam, but unexposed by the Government of today's date as well.

*A Hindi newspaper reported "**Banks broke the rules to give loans to Ansals**":*

The same problem with Hindi news, I could not produce word to word. But what I understood was that banks could have not granted loans to Ansals to pay towards the installments of land, and HUDCO could not have given the lien letter to the bank on asking by Ansals or banks.

Chapter: Thirty-Two

HUDCO And Government Never Paid Heed to the Newspapers Reports

HUDCO and the Government of India never paid heed to the newspaper's reports and continued to favor Ansals.

Vice President, Ansal Properties & Industries Limited, Mr. Pradeep Seth to Mr. P. K Garg, Chief (disposal), HUDCO, Lodhi Estate, New Delhi on 17 August 1997 regarding Shopping Arcade HUDCO Place.

This has reference to your letter dated 5 August rejecting our request for rescheduling Ent of the 3rd installment, although the reschedule Ent is due to us, as you are forcing us to make this payment, we are endeavoring to organize the funds through the banks to obtain the payment of the third installment as desired by 13 August 1997. We have approached our Bank - Punjab National Bank for grant of the loans of Rs.20. Crores (US Dollar 5.05 million) to enable us to obtain the payment of the third installment, and in this respect, the bank has desired a letter from HUDCO stating that HUDCO has no Objection in Ansals, storing this property towards the bank after full and final payment of HUDCO has been made and after the Sublease deed executed with Ansals; you are also requested to kindly do the needful at your end for allowing mortgage towards Punjab National Bank. A copy of the letter as desired by Punjab National Bank is enclosed here. You are requested to kindly give this letter immediately to enable us to raise the funds from the bank. We hope HUDCO will have no objection in issuing such a letter, as by pressing the third and final installment, HUDCO's entire consideration towards the Ansal Plaza site would have been satisfied,

Chairman & Managing Director, HUDCO, Mr. V. Suresh on 19 August 1997 to Mr. N.P. Singh Secretary (UD) Ministry of Urban Affairs & Employment New Delhi. Regarding Shopping Arcade Space over Base Car Parking Space allotted to M/s. Ansal Properties and Industries Ltd. Extension of Time for Payment of installment.

This is in continuation of my earlier letter, 4 July 1997, and subsequent discussions by our officers with Shri Dhiman, Under Secretary (L). Shri Dhiman had requested a note highlighting the sequence of actions taken by HUDCO in seeking approval from the local bodies exclusively in respect of the car parking block component. A detailed note has accordingly been prepared and is enclosed herewith. It can be seen from the note HUDCO had been taking all necessary steps consistently to obtain the necessary statutory approvals.

I hope this additional note will be helpful to you in resolving the issues.

Housing & Urban Development Corporation Ltd., Mr. R.K. Safaya letter on 3 September 1997 to Mr. Anil Prakash Superintendent Engineer Municipal Corporation of Delhi Regarding Completion Certificate for Guest Houses, Car Parking Block and Type Vi Housing at Andrews Ganj

Please refer to the minutes of the meeting held under the chairmanship of the Secretary (UD) on 9 July 1997, wherein the Ministry inquired about the status of the completion certificate on the building components of the HUDCO place project mentioned above. Engineer-in-Chief, Municipal Corporation of Delhi, had indicated that HUDCO should immediately procure no objection certificate from Chief Financial Officer, without which it is becoming difficult for Municipal Corporation of Delhi to process the case for completion certificate. We have obtained the no-objection certificate from Chief Financial Officer, and the same along with the requisite drawings have been submitted to your true self on 22 August 1997. We would now request you to kindly issue us the completion certificate concerning the above three building components at the earliest. We have also requested an Engineer-Chief separately for the same.

*A newspaper in Hindi reported "**HUDCO in respect of Andrews Ganj land granted favors to Ansals":***

Again, Hindi problem translation is not possible, but what I understood was that HUDCO granted undue favors to Ansals, which were not considered for MS Shoes.

On considering the request of Ansals regarding the ground rent payable by Ansals, HUDCO submitted to the Ministry by Chief Disposal, HUDCO letter on 15 September 1997 to Secretary, Ministry of Urban Development, Ministry of Urban Affairs & Employment regarding Shopping Arcade Site–HUDCO Place, Andrews Ganj, New Delhi allotted to M/s. Ansals Properties & Industries Ltd. (Ansals)– regarding Ground Rent.

The Shopping Arcade Site at HUDCO Place, Andrews Ganj, New Delhi allotted to M/s. Ansals Properties & Industries Ltd. (Ansals) vide allotment letter dated 10 March 1995. Agreement to Sublease, to which the President of India is also signatory, was signed on 1 August 1995, and physical possession of the site was handed over on 10 November 1995. As per the terms of the brochure inviting the bid for the Shopping Arcade site, allotment letter dated 10 March 1995 and Agreement to Sublease dated Its August 1995, the Ground Rent @ 2.5% of the premium is payable to Ansals from the date of handing over of the physical possession of the site.

As per the Perpetual Lease Deed dated 4 July 1997 executed between the President of India and HUDCO, executed much after the date of execution of the Agreement to Sublease dated 1 August 1995, the allottee of the built spaces are required to pay 2.5% of the premium paid at Ground Rent, and HUDCO is required to pay the same to the Government of India from the date of allotment. Thus, following the provisions in the Perpetual Lease Deed. Ansals is to pay Ground Rent from the date of allotment, i.e., from 10 March 1995. However, HUDCO, as per the terms of the Agreement to Sublease and Allotment letter, is demanding payment of the ground rent from Ansals w.e.f. the date of possession, i.e., 10 November 1995 after execution of the Perpetual Lease Deed. HUDCO vide its letter dated 5 August 1997 (Agreement-1) to Ansals, while demanding the Ground Rent from the date of possession, also reserved its light to claim the Ground Rent from the date of allotment.

Ansals letter dated 13 August 1997 claims the Ground Rent is a matter governed by the Statute, and hence the same is not. The Ground Rent payment be linked with rescheduling Ent of payment realizing that meaningful possession was not made available to Ansals until 11 July 1996. The letter further states that although the Ground Rent demand is incorrect. Ansals is compelling the payment of Rs. 3.935 crores (US Dollar 1.08 million) towards Ground Rent for one year from 11 July 1996 to 10 July 1997.

This matter was considered in the 237th Board Meeting of HUDCO held on 22 August 1997. The Board noted the viewpoint of Ansals for payment of Ground Rent not from the date of actual handing over the possession of Site but only from the date of construction work could have been started based on the approval to the building plan made available by Municipal Corporation of Delhi and felt that this has merit for consideration. However, keeping in view the benchmark of 8 April 1996 as the date of deemed possession, and which has been date kept in view for giving further time extension for 2nd and 3rd installments by HUDCO subject to Government approval, keeping in view the above, the Board decided the final decision regarding Ground Rent may be given by the Government Board Agenda No. 237.2.19, and its Minutes along with enclosure are enclosed. It is requested that the decision of the Government may kindly be requested that the decision of the Government may kindly be communicated at an early date. However, Ansals has already been requested to make the payment of Ground Rent, w.e.f. 10 November 1995, vide our letter dated 15 September 1997.

*Mr. Punnoose Tharyan reported on Pioneer's business page "**Banks in a bind over Rs. 40 Crores (US Dollar 11.01 million) loan to Ansals**":*

"Banks had against shopping site at Andrews Ganj disbursed loans around its 40 crores to the Ansal group for a shopping complex site in the capital.

Through, the banks have reportedly cleared the loans to the Delhi based builder. The extension of judicial custody of the company's two directors, Sushil and Pranav Ansal, until 21 August, has put a spokeswoman in the group, had the plan to pay up for the prestigious shopping complex site allotted by the HUDCO.

Since banking rules and regulations do not allow banks to release loans to a company at a time when its directors are absconding or are in custody. The banks are now finding themselves in some kind of hold in the Ansals case.

While both Sushil and Pranav Ansal are in judicial custody, another director, Gopal Ansal, is absconding.

The latter was the signatory of the agreement to sublease signed between HUDCO and Ansals.

Sources confirmed that PNB alone has sanctioned around Rs. 20 crores towards the final payment of the HUDCO site. The disbursal will now have to wait in light of the new development.

Ansals had been given time until 13 August by HUDCO to pay up its third and last installment towards the shopping arcade site in South Delhi.

If it fails, then HUDCO would have to immediately cancel its agreement with Ansals and will have the authority to forfeit the amount paid by Ansals.

However, it must be considered whether HUDCO follows the agreement drawn up with Ansals, clause by clause, as it did in the case of MS Shoes East for a sail in the same area for a five-star hotel complex.

According to the allotment letter signed by HUDCO's Assistant Chief H.K. Dubey dated 10 March 1995. Ansals had to pay up Rs. 168.80 crores (US Dollar 46.49 million) in three installments, as per its schedule given in the letter. The business group had to pay up Rs. 84.40 crores (US Dollar 23.24 million) before 6 April 1995, Rs. 50.64 crores (US Dollar 13.78 million) before 9 March 1996, and Rs. 33.76 crores (US Dollar 9.29 million) by 9 September 1996.

The second installment of Rs. 30.64 crores (US Dollar 8.44 million) were due on 9 March 1996, which was allowed to be extended up to 9 June 1996 with penal interest to be paid. The balance is Rs. 33.76 crores (US Dollar 9.29 million) were to be paid on 9 June 1996 or 9 December 1996 with penal interest.

HUDCO had written to Ansals in June 1996, in which it mentioned "It has already been informed to you that the same third installment will be due on 13 March 1997 without interest or 13 August 1997 with interest subject to the Government approval". Since 13 May 1997, it has already expired, and the payment has not been made by you. You are again advised to obtain the payment as early as possible, but not later than 13 August 1997 with interest.

The letter concluded by saying that the company would have to pay an additional Rs. 7.85 crore towards ground rent, as well as the third installment by 13 August 1997, failing which the allotment will stand terminated.

Amid all the controversy surrounding the land allotment, the role of both HUDCO and the Punjab National Bank needs to be further scrutinized. PNB had released around Rs. 40 crores (US Dollar 11.01 million) on 17 April 1997 to Ansals for payment of the second installment towards the shopping arcade site.

This was although clause (vi) of the allotment letter dated 19 March 1995 and agreement to sublease dated 1 August 1995 very clearly stipulated that Ansals at the discretion of HUDCO could only be permitted to raise a loan only for the construction of the building. Thus, the grant of an unsecured loan in the shape of the short term was given by PNB, ignoring the terms of the agreement to sell because of HUDCO and Ansals.

Moreover, though HUDCO had refused to even mark lien on the property towards PNB, the latter went out of its way and released the loan.

As early as 17 April 1995. HUDCO had pointed out in a letter to Ansals that the request contained in your banker's letter dated 6 April is a new dimension to which HUDCO never agreed to our stand in this regard, was clarified in our letter dated 31 March 1995. However, as a goodwill gesture, and as already communicated in a vide letter dated 31 March 1995. We are enclosing the undertaking addressed to your bankers on the lines forwarded with your letter dated 21 March 1995."

*Another report in the newspaper The Pioneer came reporting "***Loose ends remain in HUDCO land deal":**

"Though the Ansals have finally stuck to the 13 August deadline for final payment to the ***HUDCO*** *towards the installment of land for a shopping arcade in the Capital, several loose ends remain.*

The cancellation threat, which was so frequently produced by HUDCO, was not strictly implemented despite Ansals not strictly adhering to the condition laid down by HUDCO as well as the Ministry concerned.

Though the third installment has been paid with the Punjab National Bank clearing an Rs. 20 crores (US Dollar 5.05 million) loan, Ansals chief Sushil Ansals is cooling his heels in judicial custody. HUDCO has failed to collect Rs. 7.85 crores (US Dollar 2.21 million) as ground rent, as well as the disclaimer deed simultaneously.

Ansals paid Rs. 39.07 crores (US Dollar 10.76 million), of which Rs. 33.76 crores (US Dollar 9.29 million) were towards the third installment. Rs. 1.39 cores (US Dollar 0.38 million) were for interest, and Rs. 3.92 crores (US Dollar 1.10 million) were part of ground rent for one year. The balance amount due from Ansals is towards interest against the third installment for three months, as per the Ministry's order, and the confidentiality of ground rent of Rs. 6.16 crores (US Dollar 1.82 million).

You are therefore advised to obtain the payment of ground rent accounting to Rs. 7.85 crores (US Dollar 2.21 million) without further delay, ensure payment of the third installment within the stipulated date mentioned above with interest, failing which the allotment will stand terminated. Please also expedite to submit the deed of released /disclaimer as per the revised draft sent to you, the HUDCO letter dated 15 July 1997 to Ansals had said.

It may also be pointed out that HUDCO has been demanding Rs. 7.85 crores as ground rent from the Ansals for the Andrews Ganj site on the premium of land and not on the premium of car parking allotment.

In an allotment letter for a different company at the same site, HUDCO had mentioned you shall pay ground rent at the rate of 2.5 percent on the premium for land and the proportionate cost of land underneath the car parking space from the date of handing over of possession of the site and the car parking space.

HUDCO had also laid down other conditions which stated the ground rent and maintenance charges shall be payable in advance for each year. The first installment of these charges will be a proportionate period up to 31 March of the year following the allotment, and thereafter the payment shall be made on 1 April each year.

One wonders why HUDCO did not make this point clearly in its deal with the Ansals.

Even all the time of the payment for the second installment, the Government had insisted on HUDCO procuring both disclaimer bond and ground rent for the site from the date of possession of the same, i.e., 10 November 1995.

However, as a goodwill gesture, Ansals words asked to pay ground rent from 1 March 1996.

Unless these were procured, HUDCO should not have accepted the second installment, rather than should have gone ahead and canceled the allotment. Since the second installment was paid three months after the due date of 17 January 1997. Interest in the principal amount of Rs. 50.64 crores (US Dollar 13.78 million) worked out to Rs. 2.02 crores (US Dollar 0.55 million).

Besides, the ground rent from 10 November 1995 till 31 March 1998 worked out to Rs. 10.08 crores (US Dollar 2.77 million). Contrary to the Ministry's directive and the HUDCO board's decision, both the ground rent and interest for three months have yet to be paid by Ansals. Yet again the cancellation threat was made, but was not seriously put into effect."

Interestingly, HUDCO itself admits granting favors to Ansals as goodwill and gesture to them when all brothers were absconding or behind jail. But MS Shoes was not equally placed, as its public issue had failed.

The interest-free extensions of installments granted to Ansals subject to payment of ground rent Rs. 7.85 Crores (US Dollar 2.21 million) was relaxed by HUDCO besides more than Rs. 10 Crores (US Dollar 2.75 million) interest waived by placing in its board meeting, recommending to the Government for approval waiver of ground rent of Rs. 7.85 Crores (US Dollar 2.21 million). The unambiguous disclaimer was denied by Ansals, which was one of the conditions for the extension of interest-free installments.

The condition of raising the loan to pay the 2nd and 3rd installment was allowed to Ansals, besides not being allowed under the terms of the allotment letter. The same was allowed as goodwill and gesture towards Ansals. It also involved government officers, as the board of directors comprised two Joint Secretaries from the Ministry of Urban Development. Ansals were also permitted to sell the proposed constructed property and collect the money from the purchaser, while the allotment terms never permitted so.

We also will see or read what will happen to the land allotted to Leela Hotels for the construction of the hotel, the land use of a hotel in the Community Center, and whether the land was developed as per Master Plan 1962, since the land use was restored retrospectively to Master Plan 1962, uses as per Zone F-3. The lease was executed on 4 July 1997 that the Government has given land to be developed as per Master Plan 2001. They did this to cover the land use for a hotel, as otherwise under Master Plan 1962, the hotel could not be constructed, nor the allotment letters to HUDCO permitted so.

One of the reporters, Mr. Sameer, called Mr. Pavan Sachdeva in August 1997, and said he owns all the correspondence between Ansals and HUDCO. We mutually fixed an appointment to meet the next day. Mr. Sameer handed over all the correspondence he had in possession, from where it revealed the Car Park basement and Guest Houses all constructions were illegal at the time of forfeiture of the money received from MS Shoes.

MS Shoes immediately filed these papers in case no. 2/1997 regarding guest house blocks before the court of Mr. R.S. Arya to consider the pending application of the stay in respect of Guest House Blocks. These documents have been dealt with later by the Court in the order dated 23 February 1998, which will be exposed in the next book. In suit No. 1/1997 regarding 5-star hotel land HUDCO had denied producing these documents stating that MS Shoes were not equally placed to Ansals otherwise the application of MS Shoes would have been allowed and the application of HUDCO would have been dismissed.

What does this conclude? Corruption? Scam? Scandal? Discriminatory Treatment? Cheating? My answer is all. I am sure the reader will also have the same opinion.

Chapter: Thirty-Three

What Does It Conclude to? Corruption? Scam? Scandal? Discriminatory Treatment? Cheating? Misuse Of MS Shoes Money Rs. 68.68 Crores (US Dollar 21.89.44 million) for 25 Years Obtained Fraudulently by HUDCO/Congress Government.

Now let me go through the various search engines to find what is happening around us, similarly in respect of the above title of the present chapter, to make the topic more interesting as HUDCO, HUDCO, HUDCO, HUDCO, HUDCO, HUDCO has gone fatiguing. The major hero and the villain are the blue-eyed officers of the Government. I leave it to be guessed by the readers.

I could locate there have been scientific frauds in the past 50 years? There have been, unfortunately, several. See Jan Hendrik Schon. But the present fraud by HUDCO is extraordinary, exceptional, astounding to be exposed to the public at large that in the garb of the legal opinions, the Government Officers can grant any extraordinary favor to the private parties. Another sector is the Ministry of Law & Justice, whose opinion if taken helps the Government officers to relax any exceptional conditions in any business affair.

In the case of MS Shoes, the plea was that the matter was sub-justice and the courts would decide. But we have to realize HUDCO or the Government obeyed Unfortunately, the biggest impact was the potential damage decisions of the court. Appeal after appeal, several courts passed by, several applications, whether frivolous or otherwise, filed to delay the decisions so that HUDCO could continue to earn the money obtained fraudulently from MS Shoes. In courts, several technical issues also get involved, but still, the courts in India are superb and the only rightest alternative, although delayed justice to all suffering.

Let me come to Schon fraud. In the late nineties and early 00s, Schön was the wunderkind of condensed matter physics and nanotechnology. After receiving his Ph.D. in 1997, he went to work for the prestigious Bell Labs, working on new types of semiconductors. His work revolved around replacing conventional semiconducting materials, like silicon, and replacing them with crystalline organic materials. Now, this is a well-known concept, it is present in field-effect transistors, especially (obviously) organic field-effect transistors, and these have gained significant interest in the past decade or so. As they are beginning to compete with inorganic silicon-based Mosfets and similar technology.

However, what Schön was claiming was.... Revolutionary. Now, "revolutionary" is a term thrown around a lot, it is a buzzword. But what Schön's papers were showing was literally revolutionary. The on/off numbers were in the superconducting range, they could work as lasers, as different types of gates. The only issue was that the results coming out of Bell Labs were hard to replicate.

Then, in 2001, Nature published a paper by Schön, where he introduced a molecular transistor, composed of organic materials. He used organic dye materials that self-assembled into a transistor. No photolithography, no nothing. It's how they "worked". This was during a blitz of papers; he was publishing papers once every eight days. If a reader is unfamiliar with the pace of scientific research, Schön was pretty much being a physicist version of Usain Bolt. This is a breakneck pace for publication. One of the papers was the Nature article mentioned above.

It could have changed everything. I mean literally, I could have meant the end of silicon's dominance in the field of electrical engineering, and a move towards organic substrates. It could have allowed Moore's law to be extended far beyond its projected limits (we are encountering this right now). It could have changed so much. Our world would not be the same place.

There was only one issue, due to visa issues. Schön was in Germany at the lab facilities of the University of Konstanz, and there was no specific special equipment there, yet physicists elsewhere struggled to replicate the aluminum-oxide insulating layers that allowed the transistors to function. The sputtering machine Schön used was at the University of Konstanz, and again, there was nothing special about it. But no one else could replicate the insulating layers. They couldn't get the process to work.

And so, the suspicions began. But in the MS Shoes case, where will the suspicion begin since Government and Government-owned companies can spend crores of rupees in frivolous litigations, as they cannot correct the wrongs done by any previous officers or the Governments.

In the case of Schon, the figures were off, other physicists at Bell Labs and those outside of it started to bring attention to the figures. Several graphs were suspiciously similar. Almost... identical. Same with the numbers, they were too close, too similar. Then it was noticed the data was too precise, some of it even contradicted the laws of physics, or at least how physics was then understood.

Then Dr. Lydia Sohn, then at Princeton University and now at the University of California, Berkeley, when reading the papers, noticed that two experiments carried out at two drastically different temperatures produced the same results. The same figures. Here, the noise was not merely similar, but identical. When asked, Schön said he mistakenly submitted the same graph twice. This can (rarely) happen, so it was accepted at first. Then, Dr. Paul McEuen at Cornell noticed the same thing; the graphs of transistor noise were identical at three different temperatures. Not possible.

Doctors Sohn and McEuen began to collaborate, and they discovered "the smoking gun" as the linked article from The Independent phrased it. 90 papers published, and several using the same graphs, the same data. Exactly identical. When asked, Schön said he didn't have the original data, that he didn't keep it. Bell Labs placed Dr. Malcolm Beasley in charge of the commission that would investigate the claims that the inconsistencies in his papers were the result of fraud and not of Schön being sloppy.

Dr. Beasley's commission found 16 verified cases of scientific misconduct. They were detailed in a 127-page report released in 2002, in response to Jan Hendrik Schön made the following statement:

"I have to admit I made various mistakes in my scientific work, which I deeply regret. However, I would like to state

that all the scientific publications that I prepared were through experimental observations."

Bell Labs was not convinced and promptly fired Jan Hendrik Schön.

This was the first known case of fraud in the history of Bell Labs, and over 15 papers were retracted through the misconduct. In 2004, the University of Konstanz revoked Schön's Ph.D., citing "dishonorable conduct", and the department of physics spokesperson Wolfgang Dietrich called the entire scandal "the biggest fraud in physics of the last 50 years." And went on to say that "the credibility of science has been brought into dispute." The departmental statement said: "he has strongly damaged the credibility of science to the public."

Schön lost the appeal, challenging the stripping of his doctorate, and has since faded from view. His current status is unknown today.

This was significant due to the hopes it raised, then dashed. It was significant because it caused a remarkable waste of money in labs around the world that sought to replicate his results.

Unfortunately, the biggest impact was the potential damage done to the way the public perceives science. When the public understands this type of institutional fraud, fraud that took a couple of years to catch and act against, it brings organized proactive science to question significant people.

And this type of thinking continues today, as we observe an increasing anti-science bias among many people. Legitimate results are questioned, and vaccine nonsense by Wakefield is taken as gospel. How hundreds of scientists can dispute the world of people like Wakefield, and that work is dismissed because "well, there has been another fraud before".

Science is, at the end of the day, a pursuit of truth. Whether those truths are uncomfortable, it seeks to know more about the world we live in. As such, facts must dictate it and repeatable experimentation. People like Schön weaken the entire system, the faith in the process.

And they deliver us jaded. We look upon any development with substantial skepticism. This isn't a bad thing, but it can create inertia to fight against.

There is a positive side to his fraud, though; that the scientific community much more aggressively vet data, much more aggressively conducts peer review, and slashes those who don't pass the standard when it comes to data transparency. Schön made us more careful researchers, but perhaps that made us better.

Sometimes the hardest lessons are the best.

What is the darkest truth about ace investors like Rakesh Jhunjhunwala in India?

Rakesh Jhunjhunwala did not start with Rs 5,000. The media twisted what he told. He always says that:

a) *He had no money. All he had was Rs 5,000 saved from his article ship days.*
b) *His father wouldn't give him money, and his father forbade him from asking his father's friends for money.*
c) *His brother was a practicing CA and had a wealthy client who lent him Rs 12.5 Lakhs at 18% p.a. Whatever shares he purchased from her money; he gave it to her as collateral.*
d) *Another rich "Christian Gentleman" gave him a few lakhs at 18% to 21% p.a.*

He invested the entire amount in Tata Power, and the dividend he got covered the interest payments. The stock price of Tata Power skyrocketed.

He invested in Tata Tea at Rs 43 and sold off those shares at Rs 143.

For 4 years, he did not do any trading. "Badla" as something called futures, then was a popular financing option, and he first used it for Sesa Goa shares only.

He bet his entire net worth (Rs 2.5 Crores) on the 1989 Madhu Dandavate's budget, and was worth Rs 50 Crores in a month after the budget.

This is no mean feat. Imagine a 25-year-old today borrowing ~ Rs 2.5 Crores at 18% p.a. and investing it in stocks. What is the probability of betting your entire net worth on a single budget and creating 25x returns in a month? Most of the traders and investors in such cases would go bankrupt. What Rakesh Jhunjhunwala did is no mean feat. I doubt if anyone else can even repeat it!

Hedge fund managers manage other people's money. They do not bear the losses. Rakesh Jhunjhunwala borrowed money to trade and invest! He is the greatest risk manager in the world, and then the greatest trader too. The principal trader is not one who generates the highest return, but one who uses leverage wisely.

Even today, Rakesh Jhunjhunwala borrows money against his long-term investments and uses this leverage to trade. He pays interest on it too.

So, the darkest truth is he is what every trader/investor wants to be, but none will match his feat. Even Jesse Livermore touted as the greatest trader ever, went bust many times. Leverage is a two-sided sword, most of us cannot handle it.

What's disappointing to note is the pattern of the poor losing money and these fraudsters who duped them into getting away with extremely short jail sentences. The Modi Government has decided that notorious builders will go to jail. The Uttar Pradesh Government noticed homebuyers have been failing to get possession of their flats despite years of delay, as many builders have collected money from homebuyers, but allegedly diverted the same to other businesses.

Chief Minister Yogi Adityanath, Chief Minister of Uttar Pradesh, instructed to collect details of all builders and stated "notorious ones will soon be behind bars". I have directed it to form a committee to collect details of projects, funds collected from whom buyers, funds spent on construction, and irregularities to take action against the builders.

But the Government is blindfolded towards the Andrews Ganj project, wherein HUDCO has received the monies from MS Shoes fraudulently under the eyes of the Congress Government in 1994-95, but refusing to return the money, although the decision of the Government on the private builders is strict to give them punishment. Even the courts have held against the builders who have cheated the buyers. But what about the Government and a public sector wholly owned by the Government cheating the buyer? MS Shoes and the courts have not taken it seriously, being the case of MS Shoes against HUDCO, a government-owned company.

Rakesh Jhunjhunwala borrowed money and became a billionaire. Warren Buffett managed other people's money and became a billionaire. You cannot become a billionaire managing your own money of Rs 5–10 Lakhs of capital that you have.

I must say Rakesh Jhunjhunwala is a safe and convenient player in his work, appreciated as all cannot do so. I would not call it a scam. But HUDCO's fraudulent game along with Government Officers have played well, but fraudulently obtained MS Shoes believe they had the lease in their favor. They would get Income Tax and Urban Land Ceiling Act Authorities approvals after receipt of its installment, which was not granted for want of title or in case guest house blocks were not even submitted. HUDCO openly committed fraud on MS Shoes by concealing material facts regarding statutory approvals of the constructed buildings allotted, and cleverly permitted interest-free extensions of all the installments to Ansals, besides relaxing various other conditions of the allotment but keeping the ill-gotten money of MS Shoes.

In December 1996, Emanuel Pinez, the CEO of Centennial Technologies, and his management recorded the company performed $2 million in revenue from PC memory cards. However, the company was shipping fruit baskets to customers. The employees then created fake documents as evidence they were recording sales. Centennial's stock rose 451% to $55.50 per share on the New York Stock Exchange.

According to the Securities and Exchange Commission (SEC), between April 1994 and December 1996, Centennial overstated its earnings by about $40 million. Amazingly, the company reported profits of $12 million when it had lost approximately $28 million. The stock plunged to less than $3. Over 20,000 investors lost almost all their investment in a company once considered a Wall Street darling.

Similarly, in the case of Bre-X Minerals (1997), a Canadian company was involved in one of the largest stock swindles in history. Its Indonesian gold property, which was reported to contain over 200 million ounces, was said to be the richest gold mine ever. The stock price for Bre-X skyrocketed to a high of $280 (split-adjusted), making millionaires out of ordinary people overnight. At its peak, Bre-X had a market capitalization of $4.4 billion.

The party ended on March 19, 1997, when the gold mine proved fraudulent, and the stock tumbled to pennies shortly after. The major losers were the Quebec public sector pension fund, which lost $70 million, the Ontario Teachers' Pension Plan Board, which lost $100 million, and the Ontario Municipal Employees' Retirement Board, which lost $45 million.

The Bottom Line of these scams is fraud has taken place. Why scam of Andrews Ganj land cannot be compared with them, which is a larger issue of fraud committed by HUDCO. The land price at present is more than Rs. 5000 Crores, HUDCO has become a company of more than Rs. 9000 Crores at the cost of MS Shoes money obtained fraudulently in 1994-1995 by HUDCO using the same till date, earning 18% interest compounded quarterly on Rs. 68.68 Crores.

The worst thing about financial stock exchange scams is that these scams blindsided the investors. Those convicted of fraud might serve several years in prison, which costs investors/taxpayers even more money. The SEC works to prevent such scams. However, with thousands of public companies in North America, it is nearly impossible to ensure that disaster will not strike again.

In the present story of MS Shoes, Pavan Sachdeva has been determined blindsided, to make him believe the buildings constructed by HUDCO are legal and have all approvals as the project is of Government, who could not be believed to conceal the material facts required to be disclosed to MS Shoes as an investor in the projects.

After going through several records, if the project of Ansals under the same allotment conditions and the same Community Center at Andrews Ganj could be in the public interest, then why not the projects of MS Shoes in the same Community Center at Andrews Ganj are in the public interest?

It is a scam required to be ratified one day and must be ratified by the Supreme Court as even the present Government is not willing to open the Scam committed by Congress Government along with HUDCO owned by the President of India

Author Bio

A one-man army or private complaint no one pursues, as in the present case of Andrews Ganj land Scam.

Exposed! No, not yet. The progress of this magician, Mr. V. Suresh, would be shown in the later books of this series to come. The unfortunate situation is that the villain of this film was nowhere, as no one was watching the entire story of what to say of the lens. Till now, there has been no one who could rip off the dubious activities of HUDCO and the then Government of India. Even now, such scams do not bother the present Government committed by HUDCO and the then Congress Government.

In the Hudco Land Scam Series, by Alborz Azar reveals the widespread corruption behind the precious Andrews Ganj land in the heart of New Delhi. A media condemned man whose innocence remained unknown struggles with the unfounded accusations which caused public opinion to falter, leading to a guilty sentence before any trial could be scheduled.

The victim behind the scam in this situation was MS Shoes; founder Pavan Sachdeva. Behind the lies and deception, a brilliant entrepreneur took the fall for the underhanded dealings of the Hudco Land Scam.

The same man accused of underhanded dealings fulfilled his debts due to these deceptive lies, with no compensation for the legally awarded settlement. Alborz proves how Pavan's commitment not only caused financial stress on his family, but mental anxiety dealing with this issue for over two decades.

Yet, rulings go unanswered, Hudco ignores legal court findings to repay the ill-gotten monies from MS Shoes. The only response is more excuses as to why the court decisions have not been met by Hudco.

As the culprits hide in the shadows, Pavan struggled through court case after court case, proving his innocence. Official Supreme Court rulings were seen as frivolous orders to corrupt officers and business executives. Alborz brings light on the scam to reveal the truth that has deprived innocent victims of due justice for decades.

alborzaza.net
info@alborzazar.net

HUDCO SCAM SERIES

- **Book One:** Delhi Andrews Ganj Land Scam
- **Book Two:** Government HUDCO Andrews **Ganj Scam**
- **Book Three**: HUDCO Place **Andrews Ganj Land Scam**
- **Book Four:** Andrews Ganj Land Scam Continues
- **Book Five:** Bureaucrats Disputed Bjp Government Ratification of Andrews Ganj Land Scam
- **Book Six:** HUDCO Scammed Leela Hotels as Well - Refunded Entire Amount with Contractual Compounded Interest
- **Book Seven:** HUDCO Place Scam Led Andrews Ganj Project Account to Negative
- **Book Eight:** Courts Concluded HUDCO Scam Defrauded Discriminated Cheated MS Shoes

- **Book Nine:** Government Had No Time to Consider Bureaucrats Ratification of Andrews Ganj Land Scam
- **Book Ten:** Most Awaited Ratification by The Supreme Court of India of Andrews Ganj Land Scam by HUDCO

MS SHOES EAST LIMITED LTD. - PAVAN SACHDEVA STRUGGLING

- **BOOK ONE:** PAVAN SACHDEVA SCAM 1995: K MADHAVAN CBI FORMER JOINT DIRECTOR GAPL SOLICITOR ROLE
- **BOOK TWO:** PAVAN SACHDEVA SCAM 1995: UNDERWRITING PUBLIC ISSUE A FARCE
- **BOOK THREE:** PAVAN SACHDEVA SCAM 1995: A FALSE CASE BY CBI
- **BOOK FOUR:** PAVAN SACHDEVA SCAM 1995: MS SHOES HUDCO GOVERNMENT ANDREWS GANJ LAND
- **BOOK FOUR:** PAVAN SACHDEVA SCAM 1995: 1995 PUBLIC ISSUE AWARDS

- **BOOK FOUR:** PAVAN SACHDEVA SCAM 1995: PAVAN SACHDEVA STRUGGLING

Made in the USA
Monee, IL
05 November 2026

67807948R00292